Macromedia® Dreamweaver® 8

ILLUSTRATED

INTRODUCTORY

Bishop

THOMSON
COURSE TECHNOLOGY™

Australia • Canada • Mexico • Singapore • Spain • United Kingdom • United States

THOMSON
™
COURSE TECHNOLOGY

Macromedia® Dreamweaver® 8—Illustrated Introductory
by Sherry Bishop

Managing Editor:
Marjorie Hunt

Product Manager:
Jane Hosie-Bounar

Associate Product Manager
Shana Rosenthal

Editorial Assistant:
Janine Tangney

Production Editor:
Marissa Falco

Developmental Editor:
Barbara Clemens

Marketing Manager:
Joy Stark

Composition House:
GEX Publishing Services

QA Manuscript Reviewers:
Ashlee Welz, Chris Carvalho

Text Designer:
Betsy Young

Cover Designer:
Illustrated Team

Author's Vision

There are few fields of study more creative or stimulating than multimedia and Web design. It has been a joy to write a textbook about Macromedia Dreamweaver 8, the Web designer's dream program. If this is your first experience with Dreamweaver, you are in for an exciting learning experience. If you have used previous versions of Dreamweaver, you will be very happy with the improved features introduced with Dreamweaver 8. My goals for writing this book were similar to my goals as a classroom teacher. I hoped to create a book that:

- Stimulates the senses and stretches the mind
- Conveys my excitement for the Dreamweaver 8 program
- Incorporates basic design principles
- Makes learning fun
- Creates a desire to experiment and learn more

Acknowledgments

There is not enough space to thank the many individuals who have guided and encouraged me. The Illustrated Team is a group of creative and dedicated professionals. It is a delight to work with each of them. Special thanks go to Marjorie Hunt, the Managing Editor, a very talented individual with clear vision. I owe a debt of gratitude to both Marjorie and Nicole Pinard, Executive Director, Learning Solutions, who gave me my first opportunity to work with Course Technology.

Jane Hosie-Bounar, the Product Manager, skillfully guided the project along and made sure things worked smoothly. She led the way with a gentle hand and a strong spirit and was always available and ready to help. I will miss my talks and emails with my gifted and sweet-natured editor, Barbara Clemens. Barbara brings such fresh and creative suggestions to the table. She never forgets the tiniest detail! I am totally indebted to her. Ashlee Welz and Chris Carvalho patiently tested each file and offered insightful suggestions for improvement. The dedicated validation team, headed by Jeff Schwartz, is what sets us apart from other textbook publishers. Ashlee also captured our Mac screen shots and wrote the Mac steps for us. Thank you, Ashlee! Marissa Falco, our Production Editor, guided the pages throughout the production process, keeping us all on track. Deborah VanRooyen, Andrew Huff, and Nancy Goulet helped us with some of the Web site banners. My heartfelt thanks go to each of you and to everyone behind the scenes that I did not have the pleasure of "meeting."

The Beach Club (www.beachclubal.com) in Gulf Shores, Alabama, generously allowed us to use several photographs of their beautiful property for the Striped Umbrella Web site. Florence Pruitt, the club director, was extremely helpful and gracious.

Dreamweaver is such an outstanding Web development tool. It plays easily with both the professional Web developer and the beginning student. We are all indebted to the inspired team at Macromedia.

Lastly, I want to thank my family and friends, all of whom have encouraged me along the way. I regret that I always neglect them terribly when I am working on a book project. Special thanks go to my husband, Don, who has cheerfully sacrificed much over the last few months. Our travels together with our children and grandchildren provide happy memories for me and content for the Web sites. You will see pictures of my precious grandchildren, Jacob, Emma, Thomas, and Caroline, peeking out from some of the pages.

Sherry Bishop

Preface

Welcome to *Macromedia Dreamweaver 8—Illustrated Introductory*. This highly visual book offers users a hands-on introduction to Macromedia Dreamweaver 8 and also serves as an excellent reference for future use.

Organization and Coverage

This text is organized into eight units. In these units students learn how to plan and create a Web site; plan Web page layout and set page properties; format text; create and apply cascading style sheets; use and manage graphics; create and manage Web site links and navigation bars; work with tables and layers; and work with HTML forms. The text also includes two appendixes, one on updating, maintaining, and publishing your Web site, and one on file management.

About This Approach

What makes the Illustrated approach so effective at teaching software skills? It's quite simple. Each skill is presented on two facing pages, with the step-by-step instructions on the left page and large screen illustrations on the right. Students can focus on a single skill without having to turn the page. This unique design makes information extremely accessible and easy to absorb and provides a great reference after the course is over. This hands-on approach also makes it ideal for both self-paced or instructor-led classes.

Additional Features

The two-page lesson format featured in this book provides the new user with a powerful learning experience. Additionally, this book contains the following features:

Each two-page spread focuses on a single skill.

Clear step-by-step directions explain how to complete the specific task, with what students are to type or select in green. When students follow the numbered steps, they quickly learn how each procedure is performed and what the result will be.

Concise text that introduces the basic principles discussed in the lesson and integrates the brief case study (indicated by the icon).

UNIT
G

Dreamweaver 8

Creating a Table

Before you begin creating a table in any mode, it is imperative that you plan in advance where you want to place the table and how you want it to look. If you plan to insert images into a table, you should know exactly where you want them to appear on the page. Having an overall plan before you begin saves you a lot of time. You should also consider whether you want the table borders and the cell walls to appear in the browser window. You can make a table "invisible" by setting the border value to zero. Then the viewer will not be aware that you used a table to arrange the text or images on the page. You can also create a table inside a cell of another table. This is called a **nested table**. After consulting with the restaurant manager, you sketch your ideas for the new cafe page in The Striped Umbrella Web site, as shown in Figure G-4. You then insert a table using Standard mode.

STEPS

1. **Open The Striped Umbrella Web site, then double-click** cafe.html **in the Files panel to open the cafe page in Design View**
   The cafe page needs a descriptive title.

2. **Type** The Sand Crab Cafe **in the Title text box on the Document toolbar, replacing Untitled Document, then press** [Enter] (Win) or [Return] (Mac)

TROUBLE
You cannot use the Table button in Layout mode.

3. **Click the** Standard mode button `Standard` **in the Layout group on the Insert bar if necessary, then click the** Table button 🔲
   The Table dialog box opens.

4. **If necessary, type** 7 **in the Rows text box,** 3 **in the Columns text box, and** 750 **in the Table width text box, click the** Width list arrow, **click** pixels **if necessary, type** 0 **in the Border thickness text box, type** This table is used for page layout **in the Summary text box, as shown in Figure G-5, then click** OK
   You can leave the cell padding and cell spacing blank or with a value of 0 to not include padding or spacing. A value of 0 will make the table a little tighter. A table with three rows and three columns appears on the page. Because the table is selected, the Property inspector displays the table settings that you entered in the Insert Table dialog box. You can modify the table by changing its values on the Property inspector.

TROUBLE
To select a table, move the pointer slowly to the top or bottom edge of the table until you see the pointer change to ┗╦, then click the table border.

5. **With the table still selected, expand the Property inspector if necessary, click the** Align list arrow **on the Property inspector, then click** Center **to center-align the table on the page**
   Because you chose to measure table width using pixels rather than percent and because the table has been center aligned, it will appear in the same position and size in all browser window sizes. This will look nice with an 800 × 600 resolution. With larger sized windows, the table will remain the same size and appear centered in the window. Viewers using a 640 × 480 resolution will be forced to scroll to view the table, but they would have to anyway due to the width of the banner.

QUICK TIP
If the Getting Started in Layout Mode window opens, click OK to close it.

6. **Click the** Layout mode button **on the Insert bar**
   The table appears in Layout Mode, as shown in Figure G-6. The Property inspector now displays the properties for tables shown in Layout Mode.

7. **Click the** Standard mode button **on the Insert bar, then save your work**
   The table again appears in Standard Mode. As you place content into the table cells, the table will lengthen.

Clues to Use

Selecting a table

There are several ways to select a table in Dreamweaver. First, you can click the insertion point in the table, click Modify on the menu bar, point to Table, then click Select Table. Second, you can select a table by double-clicking the table border when the pointer changes to ┗╦. Finally, you can click the table tag icon **<table>** on the tag selector on the Status Bar.

162 DREAMWEAVER 8 WORKING WITH TABLES AND LAYERS

Hints as well as troubleshooting advice, right where you need it—next to the step itself.

Clues to Use provides additional information for using the program effectively.

Every lesson features large full-color representations of what the student's screen should look like after completing the numbered steps.

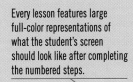

FIGURE G-4: Sketch for the table on the cafe page

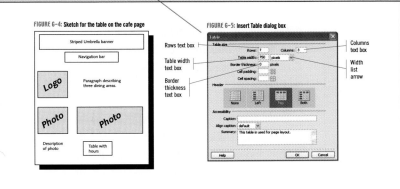

FIGURE G-5: Insert Table dialog box

FIGURE G-6: Table in Layout Mode

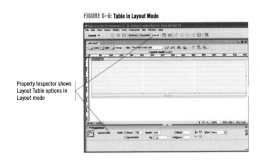

Property Inspector shows Layout Table options in Layout mode

Rows text box
Table width text box
Border thickness text box

Columns text box
Width list arrow

Design Matters

Setting table and cell widths for page layout

If you use a table to position text and graphics on an entire Web page, it is wise to set the width of the table in pixels. This way, the table does not resize itself proportionally if the browser window size is changed. If you set the width of a table using pixels, the table remains one size, regardless of the browser window size. Most designers today design to a setting of 800 x 600. By using a table width of slightly under 800, the table will cover the width of the window. Those viewers using a higher resolution, such as 1024 x 768, then can view the table without having it spread out across the screen and altering your intended formatting, as would happen if the width were set using a percent. You can also set each cell width as either a percent of the table or as pixels. If you expect your users to print the page, consider making the table narrower so it will fit on a printed page.

WORKING WITH TABLES AND LAYERS **DREAMWEAVER 8 163**

Dreamweaver 8

Sidebars called Design Matters help students apply smart design principles to their Web sites. Each sidebar deals with design considerations for Web pages or Web sites, such as ease of use, navigation, and appeal.

Dual Platform
The text in this book can be completed on either a Macintosh or Windows operating system. (Mac) and (Win) notations are included next to any step where differences occur, and Mac and Win icons also split lessons when more explanation is needed for both platforms.

Real-World Case
The case study used throughout the textbook, a fictitious resort called The Striped Umbrella, is designed to be "real-world" in nature and introduces the kinds of activities that students will encounter when working with Dreamweaver. With a real-world case, the process of solving problems will be more meaningful to students.

End-of-Unit Material
Each unit concludes with a Concepts Review that tests students' understanding of what they learned in the unit. The Concepts Review is followed by a Skills Review, which provides students with additional hands-on practice of the skills. The Skills Review is followed by Independent Challenges, which pose case problems for students to solve. At least one Independent Challenge in each unit, the E-Quest, asks students to use the World Wide Web to find information to complete a project or to research topics related to the unit. A Design Quest is the fourth Independent Challenge in the unit. It directs students to Web sites and asks them to evaluate effective design elements from each site. Your Site, the fifth Independent Challenge, is based on personal Web sites that the students will build from unit to unit using their own files. No Data Files are supplied. This gives the students the opportunity to apply the skills they learn on a higher cognitive level than by following specific step-by-step instructions. It also introduces the opportunity to develop critical thinking skills and encourages creativity. The Visual Workshop follows the Independent Challenges and helps students further develop critical thinking skills. Students are shown completed Web pages or screens and are asked to recreate them.

Instructor Resources

The Instructor Resources CD-ROM is Thomson Course Technology's way of putting the resources and information needed to teach and learn effectively into your hands. With an integrated array of teaching and learning tools that offers you and your students a broad range of technology-based instructional options, we believe this CD-ROM represents the highest quality and most cutting-edge resources available to instructors today. Many of these resources are available at *www.course.com*. The resources available with this book are:

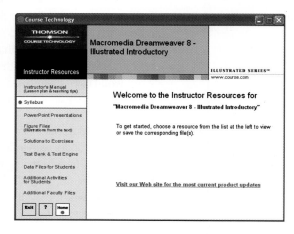

- **Instructor's Manual**—Available as an electronic file, the Instructor's Manual is quality-assurance tested and includes unit overviews, file listings, and detailed lecture topics with teaching tips for each unit. The Instructor's Manual is available on the Instructor Resources CD-ROM, or you can download it from *www.course.com*.

- Syllabus—Prepare and customize your course easily using this sample course outline (available on the Instructor Resources CD-ROM).

- **PowerPoint Presentations**—Each unit has a corresponding PowerPoint presentation that you can use in lecture, distribute to your students, or customize to suit your course.

- Figure Files—The figures in the text are provided on the Instructor Resources CD-ROM to help you illustrate key topics or concepts. You can create traditional overhead transparencies by printing the figure files. Or you can create electronic slide shows by using the figures in a presentation program such as PowerPoint.

- **Course Faculty Online Companion**—You can browse this textbook's password-protected site to obtain the Instructor's Manual, Solution Files, Data Files, and any updates to the text. Contact your Customer Service Representative for the site address and password.

- Data Files for Students—Data Files contain all of the data that students will use to complete the lessons and end-of-unit material. A Readme file includes instructions for using the files. Adopters of this text are granted the right to install the Data Files on any standalone computer or network. The Data Files are available on the Instructor Resources CD-ROM and in Review Pack, and can also be downloaded from *www.course.com*.

- Solutions to Exercises—Solutions Files contain every file students are asked to create or modify in the lessons and end of-unit material. A Help file on the Instructor Resources CD-ROM includes information for using the Solution Files.

- ExamView Test Bank and Test Engine—This textbook is accompanied by ExamView, a powerful testing software package that allows instructors to create and administer printed, computer (LAN-based), and Internet exams. ExamView includes hundreds of questions that correspond to the topics covered in this text, enabling students to generate detailed study guides that include page references for further review. The computer-based and Internet testing components allow students to take exams at their computers, and also save the instructor time by grading each exam automatically.

Brief Contents

Contents

UNIT E   Using and Managing Images   105

Read This Before You Begin

Data Files

To complete the lessons and end-of-unit material in this book, you must obtain the necessary Data Files. Please refer to the directions on the inside back cover of the book for various methods to obtain these files. Once obtained, select where to store the files, such as the hard drive, a network server, a USB storage device, or a Zip drive. The instructions in the lessons will refer to "the drive and folder where your Data Files are stored" when referring to the Data Files for the book.

Dreamweaver for Windows and Macintosh

This book is written for the Windows version and the Macintosh version of Macromedia Dreamweaver 8. Both versions of the software are virtually the same, but there are a few platform differences. When there are differences between the two versions of the software, steps written specifically for the Windows version end with the notation (Win) and steps for the Macintosh version end with the notation (Mac). In instances when the lessons are split between the two operating systems, a line divides the page and is accompanied by Mac and Win icons.

If you are starting Dreamweaver for the first time after installing it, you will see the Workspace Setup dialog box, which asks you to choose between two workspace layouts. This book uses the Designer workspace layout throughout. Also, in this book, Macintosh commands instruct users to press the [return] key to enter information. On some newer Macintosh keyboards, this key may be named [enter] or the keyboard may include both [return] and [enter].

Creating Web sites that have not been built through previous consecutive units (Windows)

If you begin an assignment that requires a Web site that you did not create or maintain earlier in the text, you must perform the following steps:

1. Copy the Solution Files folder from the preceding unit for the Web site you wish to create onto the hard drive, Zip drive, or USB storage device. For example, if you are working on Unit E, you need the Solution Files folder from Unit D. Your instructor will furnish this folder to you.
2. Start Dreamweaver.
3. Click Site on the menu bar, then click Manage Sites.
4. Click New, then click Site.
5. Type the name you want to use for your Web site in the Site Name text box. Spaces and uppercase letters are allowed in the Site name.
6. Click the Advanced tab, then click the Browse for File icon (folder) next to the Local root folder text box.
7. Click the drive and folder of your newly copied folder to set the local root folder. The local root folder contains the name of the Web site you are working on. For example, the local root folder for The Striped Umbrella Web site is called striped_umbrella.
8. Double-click the local root folder, then click Select,
9. Click the Browse for File icon (folder) next to the Default images folder text box. A message appears stating that the site cache is being updated. This scans the files in your site and starts tracking links as you change them.
10. Double-click the assets folder in your Web site, then click Select.
11. Verify that the Links relative to: Document option is checked.
12. Click OK to close the Site Definition dialog box.
13. Click Done to close the Manage Sites dialog box.
14. Expand the site folder if necessary, then click index.html in the Local View list in the Files panel to select it.
15. Click the Files panel option button, point to Site, then click Set as Home Page.

Creating Web sites that have not been built through previous consecutive units (Macintosh)

If you begin an assignment that requires a Web site that you did not create or maintain before this unit, you must perform the following steps:

1. Copy the Solution Files folder from the preceding unit for the Web site you wish to create onto the hard drive, Zip drive, or USB storage device. For example, if you are working on Unit E, you need the Solution Files folder from Unit D. Your instructor will furnish this folder to you.
2. Start Dreamweaver, click Site on the menu bar, then click Manage Sites.
3. In the Manage Sites dialog box, click New, then click Site. This opens the Site Definition dialog box.
4. Type the name you want to use for your Web site in the Site name text box. Spaces and uppercase letters are allowed in the Site name.
5. Click the Browse for File icon (folder) next to the Local root folder text box.
6. Click the drive and folder where your Solution Files folder is placed to locate the local root folder. The local root folder contains the name of the Web site you are working on. For example, the local root folder for the TripSmart Web site is called tripsmart.
7. Click the local root folder, click Choose, then click OK to close the Site Definition dialog box.
8. Click Done to close the Manage Sites dialog box.
9. Click index.htm in the Local view list in the Files Panel to select it.
10. Click the option button (at the upper-right of the Files Panel header), point to Site, then click Set as Home Page.

Using Dreamweaver on multiple computers

If you are using Dreamweaver on multiple computers, such as one in the classroom and one at home or in a lab, you must define each Web site on each computer before you can access your Web site files on each computer. You only have to do this once for each Web site, but the root folder must be accessible from both machines. For instance, if you are storing your Web sites on a USB storage device and using it on a computer in a lab and your computer at home, you must define the Web site on each machine. Once you tell Dreamweaver where to find the files (the USB device), it will find them automatically from that point forward.

Browsers

We recommend using Microsoft Internet Explorer 5.5 or later or Netscape Navigator 6.2 or later for browser output.

The Internet as a learning tool

This book uses the Internet to provide real-life examples in the lessons and end-of-unit exercises. Because the Internet is constantly changing to display current information, some of the links used and described in the book may be deleted or modified before the book is even published. If this happens, searching the referenced Web sites will usually locate similar information in a slightly modified form. In some cases, entire Web sites may move. Technical problems with Web servers may also prevent access to Web sites or Web pages temporarily. Patience, critical thinking skills, and creativity are necessary whenever the Internet is being used in the classroom.

UNIT A
Dreamweaver 8

Getting Started with Macromedia Dreamweaver 8

OBJECTIVES

Define Web design software
Start Macromedia Dreamweaver 8
View the Dreamweaver workspace
Work with views and panels
Open a Web page
View Web page elements
Get Help
View a Web page in a browser window
Close a Web page and exit Dreamweaver

Macromedia Dreamweaver 8 is a Web design program for creating multimedia-rich Web pages and Web sites. Its easy-to-use tools let you incorporate sophisticated features, such as animations and interactive forms. In this unit, you learn to start Dreamweaver and examine the workspace. Next, you open a Web page and learn how to use the Help feature. Finally, you close the Web page and exit the program. You have recently been hired as a manager at The Striped Umbrella, a beach resort in Florida. You have been asked to develop the resort's Web site using Dreamweaver. You begin by familiarizing yourself with the Dreamweaver program.

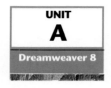

Defining Web Design Software

Macromedia Dreamweaver 8 is a powerful **Web design program** that lets you create interactive Web pages containing text, images, animation, sounds, and video. You can create Web page objects in Dreamweaver, or you can import objects created in other programs. Dreamweaver creates files that have the .html extension. **HTML** is the acronym for **Hypertext Markup Language**, the language Web developers use to create Web pages. Your first day you learn some basic Dreamweaver features.

DETAILS

Using Dreamweaver you can:

- **Create Web pages or Web sites**

  Dreamweaver lets you create individual Web pages or entire Web sites, depending on your project needs. **Web pages** are collections of text in HTML format combined with images in special image formats. **Web sites** are collections of related Web pages. Web pages and Web sites are stored on **servers**, computers connected to the Internet. Users can view Web pages and sites using a **Web browser**, software used to display pages in a Web site, such as Internet Explorer, Mozilla Firefox, or Netscape Navigator. You can also import Web pages created in other programs, then edit them in Dreamweaver or incorporate them into an existing Web site. The program provides predefined page layouts called **templates** that you can apply to existing pages or use as a basis for designing new ones.

- **Add text, images, tables, multimedia files, and JavaScript code**

  You can add text, images, tables, and multimedia files to a Dreamweaver Web page by using the Insert bar. The **Insert bar** contains buttons for creating or inserting objects, such as tables, images, forms, frames, and layers. Using the Insert bar, you can also insert objects made with other Macromedia software programs, including Fireworks, Flash, and Shockwave. Table A-1 describes Insert bar categories and their corresponding buttons.

- **Display Web pages as they will appear to users**

  Pages you edit in Dreamweaver appear as **WYSIWYG**, which stands for "What You See Is What You Get." As you design a Web page in Dreamweaver, you see the page exactly as it will appear in a browser window.

- **Use the Property inspector to view and edit page elements**

  The **Property inspector** is a panel that displays the characteristics of a page's currently selected object. Figure A-1 shows a Web page open in Dreamweaver. The properties of the highlighted text appear on the Property inspector. The Property inspector changes as different types of page objects are selected. For example, when an image is selected, the Property inspector displays image properties. When text is selected, the Property inspector displays text properties.

- **Use Roundtrip HTML**

  Because Dreamweaver utilizes **Roundtrip HTML**, HTML files created in other programs can be opened with no additional coding. Conversely, you can open and edit a file created in Dreamweaver in other software programs, such as Microsoft FrontPage. Your HTML code can "travel" between programs without coding problems.

- **Manage Web sites**

  Dreamweaver lets you manage Web site pages to ensure that all the **links**, or connections among the pages, work properly. As new pages are added to a Web site, this feature's importance increases. One important management tool is the **site map**, a graphical representation of your Web pages that shows how the pages relate to each other. Dreamweaver also has special tools that help you manage a site when you are working with others on a site development team.

FIGURE A-1: Web page open in Dreamweaver

Insert bar ├──

Web page ├──

Property inspector
showing
properties
for selected text

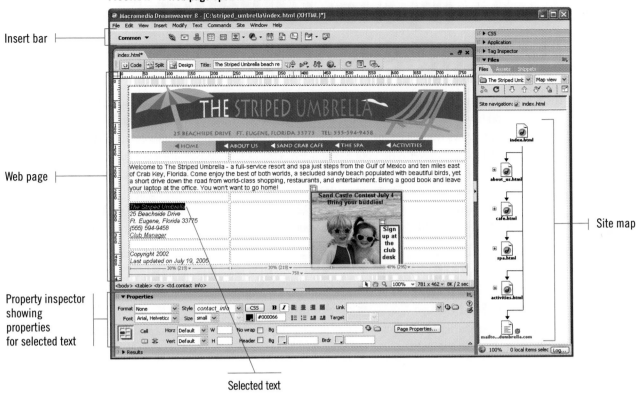

Site map

Selected text

TABLE A-1: Insert bar categories and corresponding buttons

category	buttons
Common	Commonly used buttons, such as graphics, tables, and hyperlinks
Layout	Buttons for inserting layers, tables, and frames
Forms	Buttons for inserting form objects
Text	Buttons for formatting text; for example, strong, headings, and lists
HTML	Buttons for inserting HTML tags, such as head tags and scripts
Application	Buttons for inserting dynamic content
Flash elements	Buttons for inserting Macromedia Flash elements
Favorites	Buttons you can add to, from among those you use most frequently

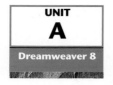

Starting Macromedia Dreamweaver 8

There are many ways to start Dreamweaver, depending on the type of computer you are using and the type of installation you have. Although the steps below start the program using the Start menu (Win) or the hard drive icon (Mac), and always work, the fastest way to start Dreamweaver is to place a shortcut (Win) or an alias (Mac) for Macromedia Dreamweaver 8 on your desktop. **Shortcuts** and **aliases** are icons that represent a software program stored elsewhere on your computer system. When you double-click a shortcut (Win) or an alias (Mac), you do not need to use the Start menu (Win) or open submenus (Mac) to find your program. When Dreamweaver is open, the Start page appears. The Start page provides shortcuts you can click to open files or create new files or Web sites. ▗▚▞ You are given your first assignment and begin by starting Dreamweaver.

STEPS

WIN

QUICK TIP
Your Start button may look different, depending on your version of Windows or your Windows settings.

1. **Click the** Start button [⊞ start] **on the taskbar**
   The Start button lets you open the Programs menu, which displays the names of the software programs installed on your computer.

TROUBLE
Your Start menu may list different programs than those shown in Figure A-2.

2. **Point to** All Programs, **point to** Macromedia, **then click** Macromedia Dreamweaver 8, **as shown in Figure A-2**
   Dreamweaver opens, and the Start page appears.

3. **Under Create New, click** HTML
   A new blank HTML document opens.

MAC

1. **Double-click the** hard drive icon, **as shown in Figure A-2**
   The hard drive icon is in the upper-right corner of the desktop.

TROUBLE
Your Macromedia Dreamweaver folder may be in another folder called Applications. See your instructor or technical support person if you have trouble locating Dreamweaver.

2. **Double-click the** Macromedia Dreamweaver 8 folder
   The Macromedia Dreamweaver folder contains the Macromedia Dreamweaver 8 program icon.

3. **Double-click the** Dreamweaver 8 program icon
   Dreamweaver opens, and the Start page appears.

4. **Click** HTML **on the Start page**
   A blank document named Untitled-1 appears on the screen.

FIGURE A-2: Starting Dreamweaver (Windows and Macintosh)

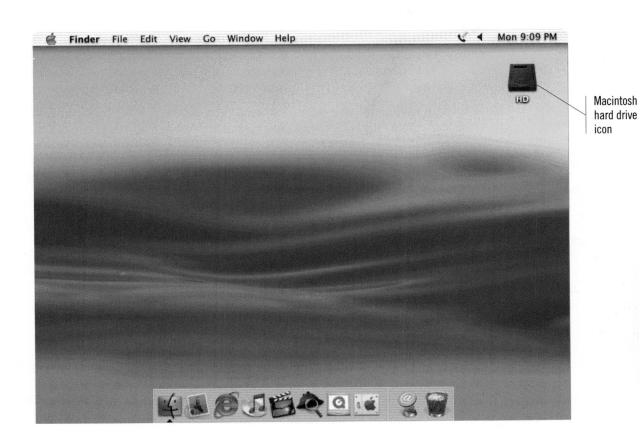

Macintosh hard drive icon

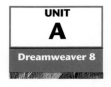

Viewing the Dreamweaver Workspace

The **workspace**, shown in Figure A-3, consists of the document window, the menu bar, toolbars, inspectors, and panels. If you are starting Dreamweaver for the first time after installing it (Win), you are asked to choose between the **Designer** and the **Coder** layout. Both layouts are built with an integrated workspace using the **Multiple Document Interface (MDI)**. This means that all document windows and panels are positioned within one large application window. In the Designer workspace layout, the panels are docked on the right side of the screen, and Design view is the default view. In the Coder layout, the panels are docked on the left side of the screen, and Code view is the default view. **Panel Groups** are sets of related panels that are grouped together. **Inspectors** are panels that display the properties of the currently selected object. Inspectors allow you to make formatting changes quickly and easily, without having to open menus. ▓▓▓▓ You spend some time familiarizing yourself with the Dreamweaver workspace. Use Figure A-3 to find the elements detailed below.

DETAILS

- The **title bar** displays the name of the program (Dreamweaver), the name of the file, and the title of the open page enclosed in parentheses. If the Document window is not maximized, the filename and page title appear in the Document window title bar. The title bar also includes buttons for minimizing, resizing, and closing the window in the upper-left or upper-right corner, depending on which type of computer you are using. (On a Macintosh computer, the program title bar and the menu bar are combined.)

- The **menu bar**, located under the title bar, lists the names of the **menus**, which contain Dreamweaver commands. You can also issue commands by using shortcut keys or by clicking corresponding buttons on the various panels.

TROUBLE

If you don't see the Insert bar, click Window on the menu bar, then click Insert.

- The **Insert bar** contains buttons that allow you to insert objects, such as images, tables, and horizontal rules. The buttons on the Insert bar change depending on what category appears in the drop-down menu. Each category contains buttons relating to a specific task. When you insert an object using one of the buttons, a dialog box opens, letting you choose the object's characteristics. The last button selected becomes the default button for that group until you choose another one.

TROUBLE

If you do not see one of the toolbars, click View on the menu bar, point to Toolbars, then click the toolbar name. The Standard and the Style Rendering toolbars do not appear by default.

- The **Document toolbar** contains buttons for changing the current Web page view, previewing and debugging Web pages, and managing files. The toolbar buttons are listed in Table A-2.

- The **Standard toolbar** contains buttons for some frequently used commands on the File and Edit menus.

- The **Style Rendering toolbar** contains buttons that can be used to render different media types.

- The **Coding toolbar** is used when you are working with the HTML code and can only be accessed in Code view.

- The **Document window** is the large white area under the Document toolbar. Open Web pages appear in this area.

- The **Property inspector** displays the characteristics of the selected Web page object. You can change an object's properties using the text boxes, shortcut menus, and buttons on the Property inspector. The contents of the Property inspector vary according to the object currently selected.

- The **Status bar** appears at the bottom of the Dreamweaver window. The left end of the status bar displays the **tag selector**, which shows the HTML tags being used at the insertion point location. The right side displays the window size and estimated download time for the current page.

- **Panels** are small windows containing program controls. Related panels appear together in **panel groups**, such as the Design, Code, Application, and Files. Display a panel by choosing its name from the Window menu. You can dock panel groups on the right side of the screen, or undock them by dragging the gripper ⸬ on the upper-left corner of the panel. When two or more panels are docked together, you can access the panel you want by clicking its name tab. As you click each tab, the panel contents appear. To collapse or expand a panel, click the expander arrow ▶ on the left side of the panel group or the panel group name.

FIGURE A-3: The Dreamweaver 8 workspace

Title bar
Menu bar
Insert bar
Document toolbar
Macintosh users will not see a title bar
Document window
Status Bar
Property inspector

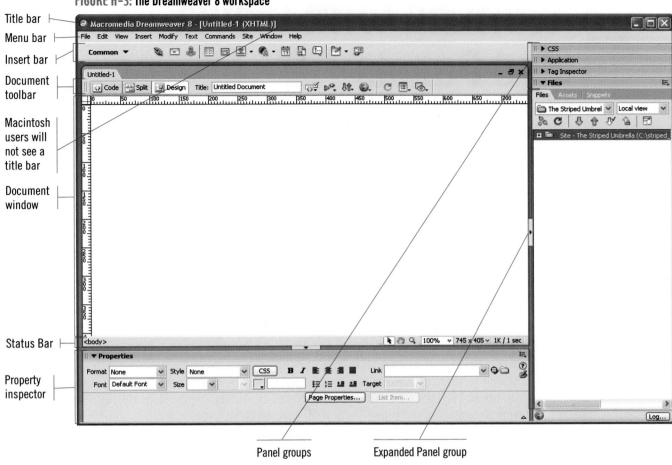

Panel groups

Expanded Panel group

TABLE A-2: Document toolbar buttons

button	name	function
Code	**Show Code View**	Displays only the Code View in the Document window
Split	**Show Code and Design Views**	Displays both the Code and Design Views in the Document window
Design	**Show Design View**	Displays only the Design View in the Document window
	No Browser Check Errors	Displays information about potential problems in browsers
	Validate Markup	Used to validate the active document or a selected tag
	File Management	Displays file management options
	Preview/Debug in Browser	Activates the browser for viewing or debugging the page
	Refresh Design View	Forces Dreamweaver to reread the page to view changes made in Code View
	View Options	Activates the View Options menu
	Visual Aids	Choices of visual aids to use as you design your pages

Working with Views and Panels

Dreamweaver has three ways you can view your Web pages. **Design View** shows a full-screen layout and is primarily used when designing and creating a Web page. **Code View** shows a full screen with the HTML code for the page; use this view to read or directly edit the code. **Code and Design Views** is a combination of Code View and Design View in separate windows within the Document window. This view is the best for debugging or correcting errors because you can see both views simultaneously. Panels and Panel groups appear on the right side of the screen, although you can move them and use them as as "floating panels." **Panels** are individual windows that display information on a particular topic, such as Answers or History. **Panel groups** are sets of related panels that are grouped together. The panels are listed by groups under the Window menu and are separated by horizontal lines (Win) or with space (Mac). You spend some time experimenting with opening and closing panels.

STEPS

1. **Click the** Show Code View button **⟨ᐱ⟩ Code on the Document toolbar**

    The HTML code for the untitled, blank document appears, as shown in Figure A-4. Even though the page has no content, basic HTML code for a blank, untitled page appears. Notice that the title bar shows that this is an XHTML file, although the file extension is .html. **XHTML** is the most recent standard for HTML files and has slightly different tags and rules. Although XHTML files are more updated versions of HTML files, they still use the same file extension, and you still refer to the code as "HTML code."

2. **Click the** Show Code and Design Views button **⟨⟩ Split on the Document toolbar**

    A split screen appears. The top half displays the HTML code, and the bottom half displays the page. The page is blank because there is no page content.

3. **Click the** Show Design View button **⟨⟩ Design on the Document toolbar**

    The blank page appears.

4. **Click the** expander arrow ▶ **on the CSS panel group or the panel group name**

    The CSS panel group expands and displays two panel tabs. The expander arrow changes to ▼, indicating that the panel group is expanded.

5. **Click each** panel tab **to expand it and display the contents of each panel**

    As you click each panel tab, the panel tab lightens, and the panel contents appear. See Figure A-5.

6. **Click the** ▼ **or the** panel group name **on the CSS panel group to collapse it if necessary**

    The panel group collapses.

7. **Click the** expander arrows **and** panel tabs **to view the panels in each of the other panel groups**

    You see how easy it is to access the views and panels in Dreamweaver.

8. **Collapse all panel groups except the Files panel group**

FIGURE A-4: Code View for a blank document

Show Code View

Show Code and Design View

Show Design View

Your Property inspector might be expanded; click arrow to collapse or expand the panel

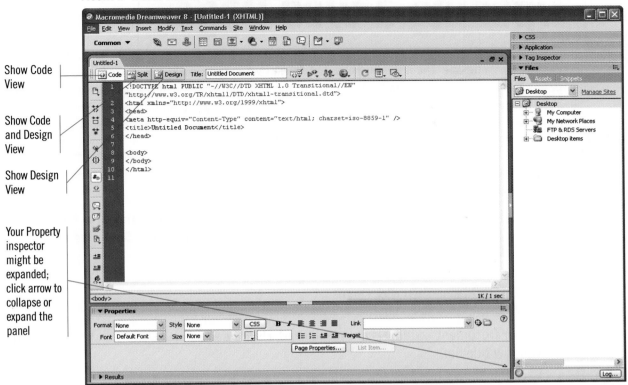

FIGURE A-5: Displaying a panel group

Drag to undock or "float" panel group

Expander arrow

CSS Styles panel

Layers panel

Panel options

CSS panel group

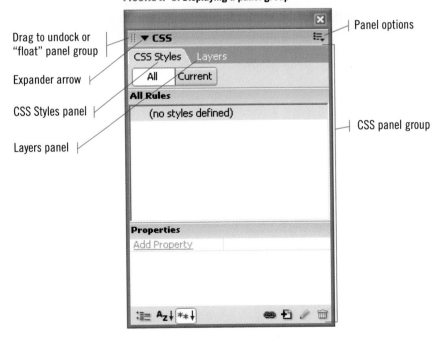

Clues to Use

Panel groups

By default, four panel groups open when you first start Dreamweaver in Windows. These are CSS, Application, Tag Inspector, and Files. The panels will retain their arrangement from one session to the next. For instance, if you open the History panel and do not close it before exiting Dreamweaver, it will be open the next time you start Dreamweaver. To close a panel group, right-click (Win) or [ctrl]-click (Mac) its title bar, then click Close Panel Group. The **panel group title bar** is the bar at the top of each panel group.

Dreamweaver 8

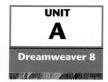

Opening a Web Page

After opening Dreamweaver, you can create a new Web site, create a new Web page, or open an existing Web site or Web page. The first Web page that appears when users go to a Web site is called the **home page**. The home page sets the look and feel of the Web site and contains a navigation structure that directs the viewer to the rest of the pages in the Web site. The resort's marketing firm has designed a new banner for The Striped Umbrella. You open the Striped Umbrella home page to view the new banner.

STEPS

1. **Click File on the menu bar, then click Open**

   The Open dialog box opens.

2. **Click the Look in list arrow ⏷ (Win) or click the arrows in the From box near the top of the window ⬍ (Mac), navigate to the drive and folder where your Data Files are stored, then double-click the unit_a folder**

   See Figure A-6.

QUICK TIP

You can also double-click a file in the Open dialog box to open it. Or click File on the menu bar, then click one of the recently opened files listed at the bottom of the menu.

3. **Click dwa_1.html, then click Open**

   The document called dwa_1.html opens in the document window in Design View.

4. **If your Document window is not maximized, click the Maximize button on the Document window title bar**

5. **Click the Show Code View button [⟨⟩ Code]**

   The HTML code for the page appears.

6. **Scroll through the code, click the Show Design View button [⬚ Design] to return to Design View, then scroll to display the top of the page if necessary**

FIGURE A-6: Open dialog box (Windows and Macintosh)

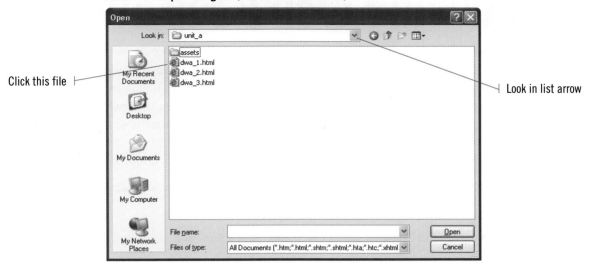

Click this file

Look in list arrow

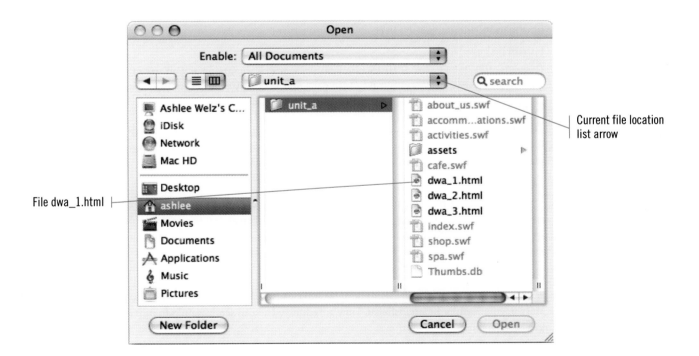

File dwa_1.html

Current file location list arrow

Clues to Use

Docked panel groups

You can move panel groups to a different area on the screen by dragging the panel group title bar. First, you must undock docked panel groups by dragging ▦ on the panel group title bar. To dock a panel group, drag the panel group back to the right side of the screen. A heavy bar indicates the position it will take when you release the mouse. When a panel group is undocked, the title bar color becomes darker.

Viewing Web Page Elements

There are many elements that make up Web pages. Web pages can be very simple, designed primarily with text, or media-rich with text, images, sound, and movies. You can use the programs shown in Table A-3 to create many Web page elements. Web page elements can be placed simply, or pages can be designed with elements placed in table cells or layers to provide for exact placement. While working through the exercises in this book, do not be concerned if your screen shows a larger or smaller area of the document. Differences in monitor size and settings affect the size of the program and document windows. You examine the various elements on the page you have open in the Document window, as shown in Figure A-7.

DETAILS

- **Text**

  Text is the most basic element on a Web page. Most information is presented with text. You type or import text onto a Web page and then format it with the Property inspector so it is easy to read. Text should be short and to the point so that viewers can easily skim it as they browse through Web sites.

- **Images**

  Images add visual interest to a Web page. However, "less is more" is certainly true with images. Too many images cause the page to load too slowly and discourage viewers from waiting. Many pages today have **banners**, images that appear across the top of the screen and incorporate the company's logo, contact information, and navigation bars.

- **Hyperlinks**

  Hyperlinks, also known as **links**, are graphic or text elements on a Web page that users click to display another location on the page, another Web page on the same Web site, or a Web page on a different Web site.

- **Tables**

  Tables, grids of rows and columns, can be used either to hold tabular data on a Web page or as a basic design tool for page layout. When used as a design tool, they can be made invisible to the viewer. Elements are then placed in table cells to control the placement of each element on the page.

- **Layers**

  Layers are another page layout tool. You can "draw" layers on the page and then use them to hold page elements, such as text or images. Because they can "float" over any page element, layers are easier to reposition than table cells and are a more flexible tool. Many designers use a combination of tables and layers for page design.

- **Flash buttons**

  Flash button objects are Flash graphic and text objects that you can insert onto a Web page without having the Macromedia Flash program installed. They are editable and can serve as links to other files. They add "pizzazz" to a Web page.

- **Flash movies**

  Flash movies are low-bandwidth animations and interactive elements created using Macromedia Flash. These animations use a series of vector-based graphics that load quickly and merge with other graphics and sounds to create short movies. Some Web sites are built entirely by using Flash. Most browsers today include the Flash player as part of the software. The Flash player is required to play these animations.

FIGURE A-7: Viewing Web page elements

Banner including logo and phone number

Table used for page layout

Flash Buttons that link to other pages in the Web site

Text

Image

Hyperlinks

TABLE A-3: Programs used to create Web page elements

source program	elements created
Macromedia Fireworks	Used to draw or edit original graphics for the Web
Macromedia Flash	Used to create animation and vector graphics
Macromedia Director	Used to create compressed Shockwave media files for downloading and playing on the Web
Macromedia ColdFusion	A feature in Dreamweaver 8 used to produce plain text code for Web server applications
Java	Used to create small applications (applets) that can be embedded on Web pages

Getting Help

Dreamweaver has an excellent Help feature that is comprehensive and easy to use. When questions or problems arise, you can use the Help menu commands, which include Dreamweaver Help, Getting Started with Dreamweaver, Dreamweaver LiveDocs, What's New in Dreamweaver 8, Using Dreamweaver, Extending Dreamweaver, Dreamweaver API Reference, Using ColdFusion, Reference, Dreamweaver Exchange, Manage Extensions, Dreamweaver Support Center, Dreamweaver Developer Center, Dreamweaver Documentation Resource Center, Macromedia Online Forums, Macromedia Training, Online Registration, Print Registration, and About Dreamweaver. The Using Dreamweaver Help window includes Contents, Index, Search, and Favorites tabs. The **Contents** tab lists Dreamweaver topics by category. You can use the **Index** tab to view topics in alphabetical order or the **Search** tab to enter a keyword to search for a topic. The **Favorites** tab lets you add topics to the Favorites window that you might want to view later without having to search again. On the Macintosh, you can choose between Index or Table of Contents view, and the Search field is always present at the top. ▓▓▓▓▓ You decide to access the Help feature to learn more about Dreamweaver.

STEPS

1. **Click Help on the menu bar**

   The Help menu appears, displaying the Help categories. See Figure A-8.

2. **Click Using Dreamweaver**

   The Dreamweaver 8 Help window opens.

   > **TROUBLE**
   > Macintosh users will not see a Search tab; proceed to the next step.

3. **Click the Search tab in the Dreamweaver 8 Help window (Win)**

   The Search tab moves to the front. You can enter one word, or several words enclosed in quotation marks in the "Type in the word(s) to search for" text box.

4. **Type saving in the keyword text box (Win) or in the text box at the top of the screen (Mac), click List Topics (Win) or press [return] (Mac), then scroll down to view the topics**

   A list of topics about saving appears in the window.

5. **Edit the search word text so it reads "save file" (including the quotation marks, Win only) in the keyword text box, then press [Enter] (Win) or [return] (Mac)**

   Fewer topics appear this time. Mac users do not need to include quotation marks.

   > **TROUBLE**
   > Macintosh users may see slightly different search results; if so, click the topic of your choice.

6. **Double-click Setting Site preference options in the topic list**

   Information on setting site preference options appears in the right frame, as shown in Figure A-9.

7. **Scroll down and scan the text**

   The search words you used are highlighted in the Help text (Win). Help will find the exact words you enter and derivatives of the words you enter.

   > **TROUBLE**
   > Depending on your printer, you may need to click Print instead of OK.

8. **Click Print on the Help toolbar (Win) or click File on the menu bar, then click Print (Mac) to print the information, then click OK (Win) or Print (Mac)**

9. **Click the Close button on the Help window title bar (Win) or click the red dot in the upper-left corner of the window (Mac)**

   The Help window closes, and you return to the Dreamweaver workspace.

FIGURE A-8: Help menu

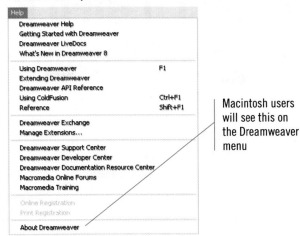

Macintosh users
will see this on
the Dreamweaver
menu

FIGURE A-9: Using the Dreamweaver Help menu

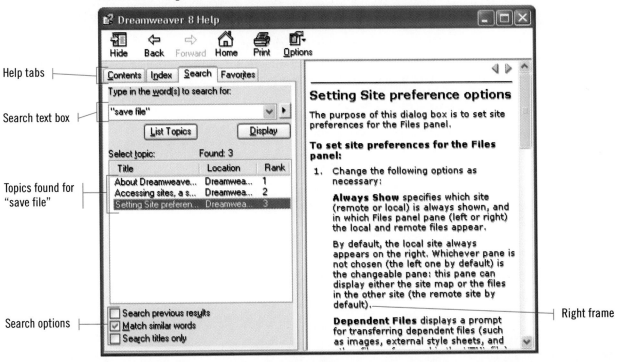

Help tabs

Search text box

Topics found for
"save file"

Search options

Right frame

Viewing a Web Page in a Browser Window

During the process of creating and editing a Web page, it is helpful to view the page in a Web browser frequently. Viewing the page in a browser provides visual feedback of what the page will look like when it is published on the Internet. It is best to view the page using different browsers and different screen sizes and resolutions to ensure the best view of your page on all types of computer equipment. It is important to remember that you cannot print a Web page in Dreamweaver except in Code View. You must go to the browser window to print the page. You decide to view the Striped Umbrella home page in your default browser.

STEPS

TROUBLE
On a Windows computer, your menu options will be dimmed if your document window is maximized.

1. Click the Restore Down button, click the Window Size shortcut menu shown in Figure A-10, then click 760 × 420 (800 × 600, Maximized) (Win)

(You may need to collapse the Property inspector to see the Window Size pop-up menu.) The screen size is set to 760 × 420, which translates to a monitor set to an 800 × 600 screen resolution. When you choose your screen size, it is important to consider the equipment your audience is using. The most common screen size that designers use today is 800 × 600. Many also use the higher resolution of 1020 × 768, so check your pages using that setting. See Table A-4 for window size options.

QUICK TIP
If you have a different default browser on your computer, your screen may differ.

2. Click the Preview/Debug in Browser button 🌐 on the Document toolbar, then click Preview in [your browser name]

The browser window opens, and the page appears in the browser, as shown in Figure A-11.

TROUBLE
Depending on your printer, you may need to click Print instead of OK.

3. Click File on the browser's menu bar, click Print, then click OK

A copy of the Web page prints. Since the print window is slightly smaller than the browser window, a small part of the text on the right side of the page may not print.

Design Matters

Choosing a window size

The 640 × 480 window size is not used by many viewers today. The 800 × 600 window setting is used on 15-inch monitors and some 17-inch monitors. Most consumers have at least a 15-inch monitor at their homes or offices, making this window size a good choice for a Web page. However, because more viewers are viewing at a 1024 resolution or higher, even if you are designing to an 800 × 600 window size, you can make sure that the pages will still view well at a higher resolution by placing the page content in a table with a fixed width. This will keep the content from spreading out too much when viewed in a larger window.

FIGURE A-10: Window Size pop-up menu

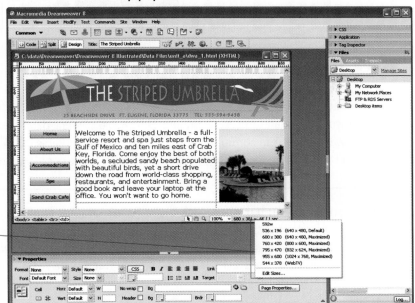

Window Size shortcut menu

FIGURE A-11: Preview in browser

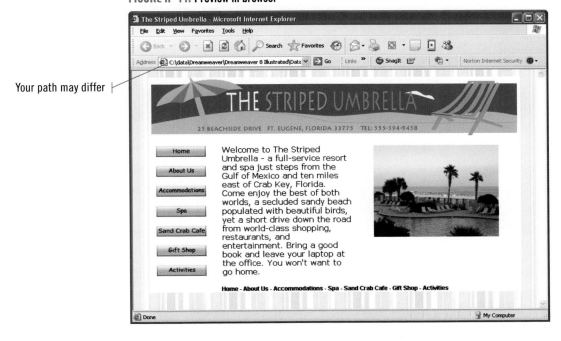

Your path may differ

TABLE A-4: Window size options

window size (inside dimensions of browser window without borders)	corresponding resolution
592	(Fixed width, variable height)
536 × 196	640 × 480, default
600 × 300	640 × 480, maximized
760 × 420	800 × 600, maximized
795 × 470	832 × 624, maximized
955 × 600	1024 × 768, maximized
544 × 378	Web TV

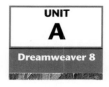

Closing a Web Page and Exiting Dreamweaver

When you are ready to stop working with a file in Dreamweaver, it is a good idea to close the current page or pages you are working on and exit the program. This should prevent data loss if power is interrupted. In some cases, power outages can corrupt an open file and make it unusable. ▓▓▓▓ You are finished for the day, so you close the browser, then close the Striped Umbrella home page, and exit Dreamweaver.

STEPS

1. **Click** File **on the menu bar, then click** Close **(Win), or click** Explorer **on the menu bar, then click** Quit Explorer **(Mac)**

   The browser closes, and your finished project is again visible in the Dreamweaver window, as shown in Figure A-12. In this book, screenshots of finished projects feature enlarged windows to display as much content as possible. You may have to scroll to see the same content.

QUICK TIP
You may need to click the Dreamweaver 8 title bar to activate the program.

2. **Click** File **on the menu bar, then click** Exit **(Win) or click** Dreamweaver **on the menu bar, then click** Quit Dreamweaver **(Mac)**

3. **When asked if you want to save the untitled page, click** No

   Dreamweaver closes.

Clues to Use

Saving and closing Dreamweaver files

It is wise to save a file as soon as you begin creating it and to save frequently as you work. A quick glance at the title bar shows whether you have saved your file. If you haven't saved the file initially, the filename shows "untitled" rather than a file name. This does not refer to the page title, but the actual filename. After you save the file and make a change to it, an asterisk appears at the end of the filename until you save it again. It is always wise to save and close a page that you are not actively working on. Keeping multiple files open can cause confusion, especially when you are working with multiple Web sites that have similarly named pages. Each open page has a tab at the top of the page with the file name. You use these tabs to switch between each open page to make it the active page.

FIGURE A-12: The finished project

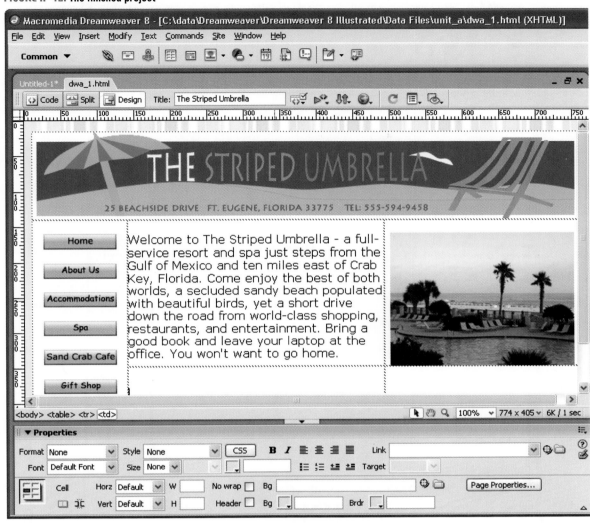

Clues to Use

Dreamweaver online support

Macromedia provides extensive help information on their Web site. The Dreamweaver Support Center is one example, and is an option in the Help menu. When you click this option, Dreamweaver opens your Internet browser and connects to the Macromedia Web site at www.macromedia.com/support/dreamweaver.

Practice

▼ CONCEPTS REVIEW

Label each element in the Dreamweaver window as shown in Figure A-13.

FIGURE A-13

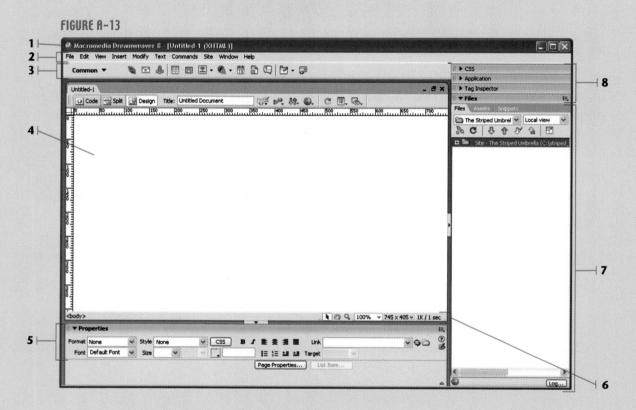

1. _____   5. _____

2. _____   6. _____

3. _____   7. _____

4. _____   8. _____

Match each of the following terms with the statement that best describes its function.

9. **Standard toolbar**

10. **Document toolbar**

11. **Code View**

12. **Tag selector**

13. **Workspace**

14. **Design View**

15. **Insert bar**

16. **Menu bar**

a. The Document window, the menu bar, toolbars, inspectors, and panels

b. Allows you to choose program commands

c. Shows the page layout

d. Contains buttons that allow you to insert objects, such as images

e. Contains buttons for some of the more commonly used options under the File and Edit menus

f. Shows the HTML coding

g. Contains buttons for changing the current viewing mode of Dreamweaver

h. Shows the HTML tags being used at the current insertion point

Select the best answer from the list of choices.

17. You display panels using the _____ menu.
    a. Window
    b. Edit
    c. Panel
    d. View

18. The tool that allows you to show the characteristics of a selected page element is the:
    a. Tool inspector.
    b. Element inspector.
    c. Insert bar.
    d. Property inspector.

19. The Dreamweaver feature that shows how the pages in a Web site relate to each other is the:
    a. Site inspector.
    b. Site panel.
    c. Site map.
    d. Site view.

20. The view that is best for designing and creating a Web page is:
    a. Code View.
    b. Design View.
    c. A combination of both Code and Design Views.
    d. Any of the above.

21. On a Windows computer, which of the following is not one of the Dreamweaver default panel groups?
    a. CSS
    b. Design
    c. Application
    d. Files

▼ SKILLS REVIEW

1. **Define Web design software.**
    a. Write a short paragraph describing at least three features of Dreamweaver; use paper or your word processing software.
    b. Add your name to the top of the page.

2. **Start Macromedia Dreamweaver 8.**
    a. Start Dreamweaver.
    b. Write a list of the panels that currently appear on the screen.

3. **View the Dreamweaver workspace.**
    a. Locate the title bar.
    b. Locate the menu bar.
    c. Locate the Document toolbar.
    d. Locate the Insert bar.
    e. Locate the Property inspector.

4. **Work with views and panels.**
    a. Switch to Code View.
    b. Switch to Code and Design Views.
    c. Switch to Design View.
    d. Expand the CSS panel group.
    e. Collapse the CSS panel group.

5. Open a Web page.

   a. Open dwa_2.html from the drive and folder where your Data Files are stored. Maximize the window if necessary. Your screen should resemble Figure A-14.

   b. Display the page in Code View.

   c. Display the page in Design View.

6. View Web page elements.

   a. Locate a banner.

   b. Locate a table.

   c. Locate a layer.

7. Get Help.

   a. Use the Using Dreamweaver command to find topics relating to the Assets panel.

   b. Display Help information on one of the topics.

   c. Print the topic information.

   d. Close the Help window.

8. View a Web page in a browser window.

   a. Note the view that is currently set in Dreamweaver.

   b. Change the window size to a different setting.

   c. Preview the page in your Web browser.

   d. Print the page.

   e. Close the browser window.

9. Close a Web page and exit Dreamweaver.

   a. Close the Web page file.

   b. Exit the Dreamweaver program.

FIGURE A-14

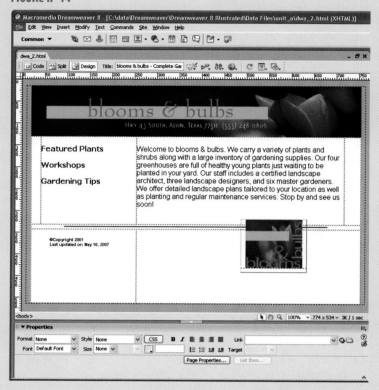

▼ INDEPENDENT CHALLENGE 1

You have recently purchased Macromedia Dreamweaver 8 and are eager to learn to use it. You open a Web page and view it using Dreamweaver.

   a. Start Dreamweaver.

   b. Open the file dwa_3.html from the drive and folder where your Unit A Data Files are stored. Your screen should resemble Figure A-15.

   c. Change to Code View.

   d. Change back to Design View.

   e. Collapse the Files panel group.

   f. Expand the Files panel group.

   g. Change the window size, then preview the page in your browser.

   h. Close the browser, then close the file and exit the Dreamweaver program.

FIGURE A-15

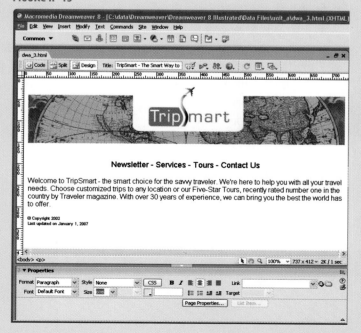

▼ INDEPENDENT CHALLENGE 2

When you work in Dreamweaver, it is important to organize your panels so that you have the information you need where you can access it quickly.

a. Start Dreamweaver.
b. Use the Dreamweaver Help feature to locate information on how to collapse or expand panel groups.
c. Read the information, noting how the Help feature highlights your search words (Win).
d. Print the information.
e. Close the Help window, then exit the Dreamweaver program.

▼ INDEPENDENT CHALLENGE 3

The Dreamweaver Support Center provides answers to common questions and suggestions for troubleshooting problems. The Support Center may help you find information and save you from placing a telephone call to Technical Support.

a. Start Dreamweaver.
b. On the Help menu, select the Dreamweaver Support Center command.
c. Click the link for Common Questions about Dreamweaver.
d. Choose a question that interests you and read the response.
e. Print the page.
f. Close the Help window, then exit the Dreamweaver program.

▼ INDEPENDENT CHALLENGE 4

The Macromedia Web site has a feature called Showcase. Showcase includes links to Web sites that were created using Macromedia software, such as Macromedia Dreamweaver, Flash, and Fireworks. The Showcase feature includes the Site of the Day and Showcase Features. The Weekly Features links provide information about the company being showcased, the challenge that was presented to the design team, the solution, and the resulting benefits to the company.

a. Connect to the Internet and go to the Macromedia Web site at www.macromedia.com.
b. Click the **Showcase** link, then click one of the companies listed under Showcase Features.
c. Read the information about the company and print the page from the browser window.
d. Close your browser window.
e. Using a word processing program or paper, write a short summary (two paragraphs) of the Web site you visited, then list three things that you learned about the Macromedia software used to create the site. For example: "I learned that Flash animation files can be inserted into Dreamweaver."

▼ VISUAL WORKSHOP

Open Dreamweaver and use the Window menu to open the panels and windows, as shown in Figure A-16. If necessary, collapse or expand the panels into the position on the screen shown in Figure A-16. Exit (Win) or Quit (Mac) the Dreamweaver program.

FIGURE A-16

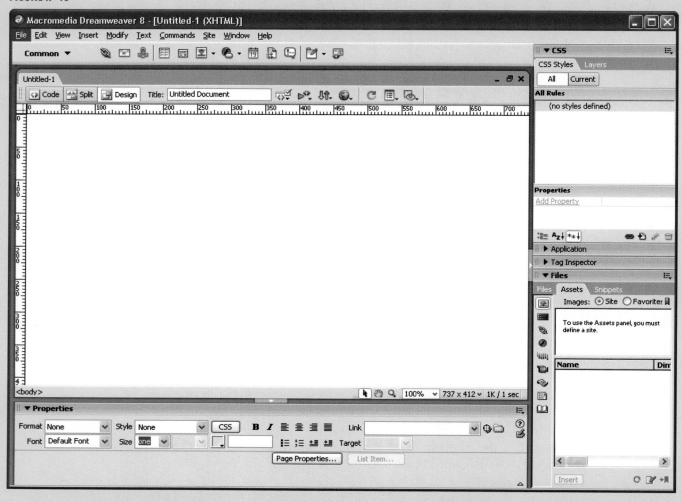

Creating a Web Site

OBJECTIVES

Plan a Web site
Create a folder for Web site management
Define a Web site
Add a folder to a Web site
Save a Web page
Set the home page and copy a new image to a Web site
Add new pages to a Web site
Create and view a site map
Select site map options

Creating a Web site requires a lot of thought and careful planning. Macromedia Dreamweaver 8 has many tools to help you plan, create, and manage your sites. In this unit, you use these tools to plan and design a new Web site. You also learn how to modify a site using Dreamweaver site management features. ▰▰▰ The owners of The Striped Umbrella meet with you to discuss their ideas for a new and improved Web site. You assure them that you can create a great site for them, using Dreamweaver.

Planning a Web Site

Developing a Web site is a process that begins with careful planning and research. Planning is an essential part of creating an effective Web site. You should plan all development phases before you begin. Figure B-1 illustrates the steps involved in Web site planning. Your plan should include how you will organize and implement your site. It should also encompass testing your pages on different types of computers and modifying the pages to handle any problems. Careful planning of your Web site may prevent mistakes that would be costly and time-consuming to correct. ▰▰▰▰ After consulting with the lead member of the Web development team, you review the steps described below to help you create a plan for the The Striped Umbrella site.

DETAILS

QUICK TIP
You can easily create a storyboard on a computer using a software program, such as Microsoft Paint, Microsoft PowerPoint, Paintshop Pro, Macromedia Freehand, or Macromedia Fireworks. A computer-created storyboard is easier to change than one created on paper.

- **Research site goals and needs**

  When you research your Web site, you determine the site's purpose and requirements. Create a checklist of questions and answer them before you begin. For example, "What are the company's or client's goals for the Web site? What software will I need to construct the site? Will the site require animations? If so, who will create them?" The more questions that you can answer about the site, the more prepared you will be to begin development. Once you have gone through your checklist, create a timeline and a budget for the site.

- **Create a storyboard**

  A **storyboard** is a small sketch that represents every page in a Web site. Like a flowchart, a storyboard shows the relationship of each page to the other pages in the site. Storyboards, like the one shown in Figure B-2, are helpful when planning a Web site because they allow you to visualize how each page in the site is linked to others.

- **Create folders**

  Before you create your Web site, you should create a system of folders for all of the elements you will use in the site. Decide where on your computer you will store your site. Start by creating a folder for the Web site with a descriptive name, such as the name of the company. Then create a subfolder in Dreamweaver called **assets** to store all of the files that are not Web pages, for example, images, audio files, and video clips. An organized folder system makes it easy to find files quickly as you develop and edit your Web site. See Figure B-3.

- **Collect the page content and create the Web pages**

  This is the fun part. After studying your storyboard, gather the files you need to create the pages, for example, text, images, buttons, videos, and animation. Some of these elements will come from other software programs, and some will be created in Dreamweaver. For example, you can create text in a word processing program and insert it into Dreamweaver, or you can create and format it directly in Dreamweaver.

- **Test the pages**

  It is important to test your Web pages using different browser software. The two most common browsers are Microsoft Internet Explorer and Netscape Navigator. Mozilla Firefox and Opera are browsers that are also gaining popularity. You should also test your Web site using different versions of each browser, a variety of screen resolutions, and various connection speeds. Today, more people are using cable modems or DSL (Digital Subscriber Line); however, some still use slower dial-up modems. Like Web site development, testing is a continuous process, so you should allocate plenty of time for it as you plan your site.

- **Modify the pages**

  After you create a Web site, you'll find that you need to change it, especially when information in the site needs updating. Each time you modify a Web site element, it is wise to test the site again.

- **Publish the site**

  To **publish** a Web site means to make it available for viewing on the Internet or on an **intranet**, an internal Web site without public access. Many companies have intranets to enable them to share information within their organizations. You publish a Web site to a **Web server**, a computer that is connected to the Internet with an **IP (Internet Protocol) address**. Until a Web site is published, you can only view the site on the storage device that contains it. For information on publishing a site, see the appendix to this text.

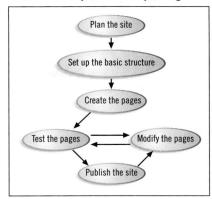

FIGURE B-1: Steps in Web site planning

FIGURE B-2: The Striped Umbrella Web site storyboard

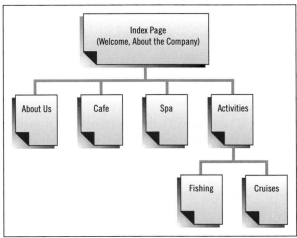

FIGURE B-3: Folder structure for The Striped Umbrella

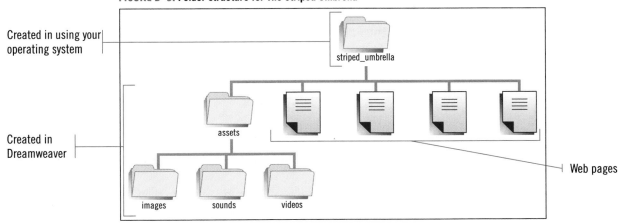

Clues to Use

IP addresses and domain names

To make a Web site accessible over the Internet, you must publish it to a Web server with a permanent IP address. An IP address is an assigned series of numbers, separated by periods, that designate an address on the Internet. To access a Web page, you can enter either an IP address or a domain name in the address box of your browser window. A **domain name** is expressed in letters instead of numbers, and it usually reflects the name of the business represented by the Web site. An example would be the Macromedia Web site. The domain name is *www.macromedia.com*, but the IP address would read something like 123.456.789.123. Because domain names use descriptive text instead of numbers, they are much easier to remember. Compare an IP address to your Social Security number and a domain name to your name. Both your Social Security number and your name are used to refer to you as a person, but your name is much easier for your friends and family to use than your Social Security number.

Creating a Folder for Web Site Management

After composing your checklist, creating storyboards, and gathering the files and resources you need for your Web site, you set up the site's folder structure. The first folder you should create for the Web site is called a local root folder. A **local root folder** is a folder on your hard drive, USB drive, or network drive that will hold all the files and folders for the Web site. Create this folder using Windows Explorer (Win) or the Finder (Mac). When naming folders, avoid using spaces, special characters, or uppercase characters to prevent problems when you publish your Web site. When you publish the Web site, you transfer a copy of the root folder contents to a remote computer, usually an Internet Service Provider (ISP). ░░░░░ You create the root folder for The Striped Umbrella Web site, and name it striped_umbrella.

STEPS

WIN

1. **Click the** Start button ░start░ **on the taskbar, point to** All Programs, **point to** Accessories, **then click** Windows Explorer

   The Windows Explorer window opens and displays the drives, folders, and files on your computer.

> **TROUBLE**
> Your Start menu command might display "Programs," depending on the version of Windows you are using.

2. **Click the** Address list arrow, **click the drive where you will save your Web site files, then navigate to the folder where you will save your Web site files**

   The drive that you select appears in the Windows Explorer Address box, and the folder contents appear in the folder list. The location where you create your root folders is very important. Be sure to check with your instructor about the best place to create and store your Web site files. It is best not to store your Web site in your Data Files folder.

3. **Click** File **on the menu bar, point to** New, **then click** Folder

   A new folder, named New Folder, appears. You can type directly over New Folder while it is still highlighted to change the folder name.

> **TROUBLE**
> If you cannot rename the folder, right-click the folder name, "New Folder," click Rename, type striped_umbrella, then press [Enter].

4. **Type** striped_umbrella **in the Folder Name text box, then press** [Enter]

   The Web site root folder is renamed striped_umbrella. See Figure B-4.

5. **Close Windows Explorer**

MAC

1. **Double-click the** Macintosh hard drive, **then double-click the drive and folder where you will save your Web site files**

   The location where you create your root folders is very important. Be sure to check with your instructor about the best place to create and store your Web site files. It is best not to store your Web site in your Data Files folder.

2. **Click** File **on the menu bar, then click** New Folder

   A new folder, named untitled folder, appears. You can type directly over untitled folder while it is still highlighted to change the folder name.

> **TROUBLE**
> If you cannot rename the folder, click the folder name, "untitled folder," to highlight it, type striped_umbrella, then press [return].

3. **Type** striped_umbrella, **then press** [return] **to rename the folder**

   The root folder is renamed striped_umbrella. See Figure B-4.

4. **Close the Finder window**

FIGURE B-4: Creating a root folder (Windows and Macintosh)

Your path may differ

Your view may differ; use the list arrow to change view options

striped_umbrella root folder

Click the drive to select it

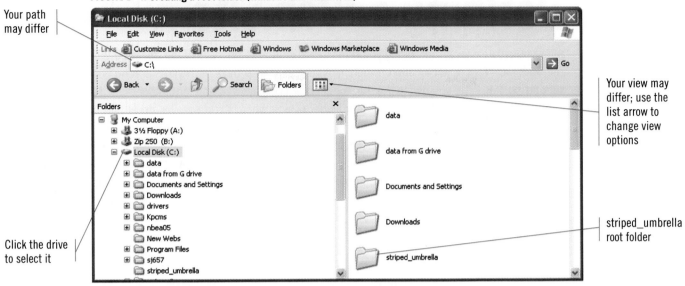

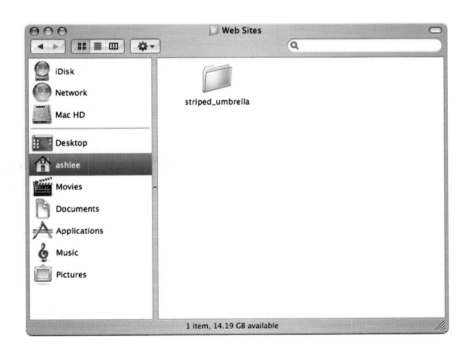

Design Matters

Managing files

It is imperative that you understand the basics of good file management before you can master Dreamweaver. You should be able to create new folders and new files in a specified location. You should also learn the basic file naming conventions for Web content: To ensure that your files are available to all viewers regardless of their operating system, do not use uppercase letters or spaces in filenames. Although files with uppercase letters or spaces in their names may look fine on your screen, they might not when they are published on a Web server and might appear as broken links. If you do not have a basic understanding of file management, a quick review will pay big dividends and shorten your Dreamweaver learning curve.

Defining a Web Site

After you create a local root folder, you must define your Web site. When you **define** a Web site, you specify the site's local root folder location to help Dreamweaver keep track of the links among your Web pages and supporting files. After you define the site, the program displays the local root folder in the **Files panel**, a window similar to Windows Explorer (Win) or Finder (Mac), where Dreamweaver stores and manages your files and folders. The Files panel contains a listing of all the folders and files in your Web site. After you define your Web site, you will no longer use Windows Explorer or Finder for file management tasks. Instead, you will use the Dreamweaver Files panel. The Files panel also helps you publish your Web site to a remote computer; see the appendix for more information on publishing your site. ▰▰▰ You define the The Striped Umbrella site.

STEPS

TROUBLE
(Mac) If a message window appears stating that the local root folder does not exist, and asks you to choose a new local root folder from the Manage Sites dialog box, click Cancel.

1. **Start** Dreamweaver

2. **Click** Dreamweaver Site **in the Create New column on the Start Screen, then click the** Advanced tab, **shown in Figure B-5, in the Site Definition dialog box if it's not already selected**
    The Site Definition for Unnamed Site 1 dialog box opens.

QUICK TIP
It is acceptable to use uppercase letters in the site name because it is not the name of a file or folder.

3. **Type** The Striped Umbrella **in the Site Name text box, replacing the existing text**

4. **Click the** folder icon 📁 **next to the local root folder text box, click the** Select list arrow ▼ **(Win) or** ▲ **(Mac) from the Choose Local Root Folder for site** The Striped Umbrella **dialog box, click the drive and folder where you created your root folder, double-click (Win) or click (Mac)** the striped_umbrella folder, **then click Select (Win) or Choose (Mac)**
    The local root folder, striped_umbrella, is designated as the location for the Web site files and folders.

5. **Click the** Document **option next to "Links relative to:"**
    The Document option will make all links document-relative. This will prevent broken links as you create new pages and import images as you work through the lessons.

6. **Verify that the** Refresh local file list automatically **and the** Enable cache **check boxes are both checked, as shown in Figure B-6, then click OK**
    Enable cache means that you want the computer system to use space on the hard drive as temporary memory, or cache, while you are working. The Refresh local file list automatically option means that the computer system automatically reflects changes made in your file listings. The Site Definition is complete. You can use the Advanced Tab at any time to edit your settings. Your Files panel should resemble Figure B-7.

Design Matters

Using the Web as your classroom

Throughout this book, you are asked to evaluate real Web sites. You learn basic design principles parallel to the new skills you learn using Dreamweaver. Learning a new skill, such as inserting an image, will not be very useful if you do not understand how to use images efficiently and effectively on a page. The best way to learn is to examine how real Web sites use page elements, such as images, to convey information. Therefore, you are encouraged to complete the E-Quest and Design Quest Independent Challenges to gain a practical understanding of the skills you learn.

FIGURE B-5: Site Definition for Unnamed Site 1 dialog box

Click Advanced tab

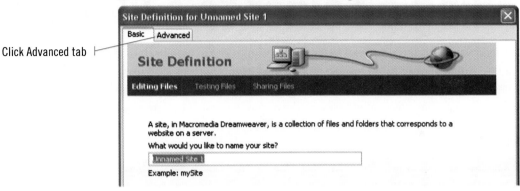

FIGURE B-6: Site Definition for The Striped Umbrella

Site name

The Striped Umbrella
local root folder (your
path may differ)

Refresh local file
list automatically
should be checked

Links relative to:
Document

Enable cache
should be checked

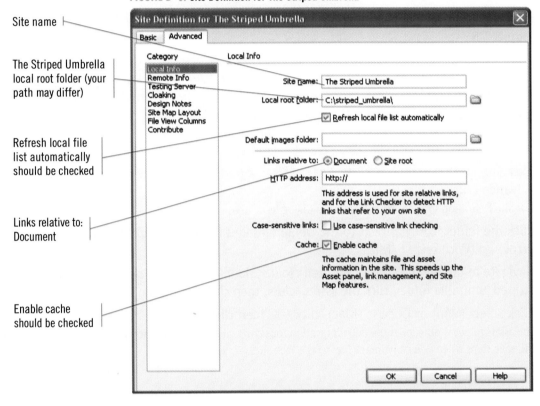

FIGURE B-7: Files panel

The Striped Umbrella
local root folder — your
path will vary

Macintosh Files
panel will vary
slightly

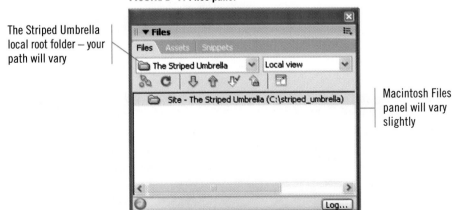

Dreamweaver 8

Adding a Folder to a Web Site

After defining your Web site, you need to create folders to contain the non-HTML files that will add content to the site. Creating a folder called assets is a good beginning. Complex Web sites with many types of multimedia files or text files may have organizing subfolders within the assets folder. For example, you might have folders for text files, image files, sound files, or video clips. You should create these folders in Dreamweaver, not in Windows Explorer or Macintosh Finder. ▰▰▰▰ You create a folder called assets for The Striped Umbrella Web site.

STEPS

1. **If necessary, expand the Files panel group and click the striped_umbrella folder in the Files panel**

   The folder is now highlighted, indicating that the site is selected.

TROUBLE

If you are using a Macintosh, you may not see the new folder if the striped_umbrella folder is collapsed. To expand it, click the triangle ▷ to the left of the striped_umbrella folder.

2. **Click the Files panel options button ▤▾, point to File, then click New Folder as shown in Figure B-8**

   A new untitled folder appears.

3. **Type assets in the folder text box, then press [Enter] (Win); or click the triangle ▷ to the left of the striped_umbrella folder to open it; if necessary, click untitled on the new folder, type assets as the folder name, then press [return] (Mac)**

   See Figure B-9. You will use the assets folder to store images and other elements used in the Web site. Next, you set the assets folder to be the default folder for the images you save in the Web site.

4. **Click Site on the menu bar, click Manage Sites, click Edit, then if necessary, click the Advanced tab**

   The Site Definition for The Striped Umbrella dialog box opens.

5. **Click the folder icon ▭ next to the Default images folder text box, click the Select list arrow ▾ (Win) or ▾ (Mac)**

6. **Navigate to display the striped_umbrella folder, double-click (Win) or click (Mac) the striped_umbrella folder, click the assets folder, then click Open (Win)**

7. **Click Select (Win) or Choose (Mac), click OK, then click Done**

   The assets folder is now set as the default location for saving all images and other multimedia elements. This will save steps when you copy image files to the Web site.

Design Matters

Organizing your Web site assets

If your Web site contains many files other than the html page files, it is wise to further subdivide the main folder in which you store them. For instance, if your default images folder is named assets, consider adding subfolders to categorize the non-html files. An images sub-folder and a sounds sub-folder are examples of how you could organize your assets folder to group the files by file type so you don't have to scroll through a long list to find a particular file. If you have relatively few assets, this would not be necessary.

FIGURE B-8: Creating a new folder in the Files panel

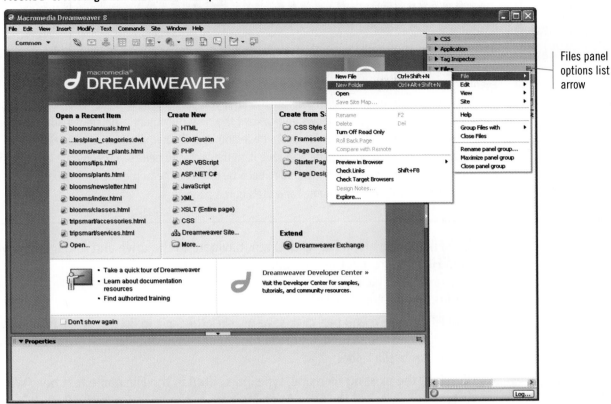

Files panel options list arrow

FIGURE B-9: The Striped Umbrella Site window with assets folder created

assets folder

Clues to Use

Using the Files panel for file management

You can use the Files panel to add, delete, move, or rename files and folders in a Web site. It is very important that you perform these file maintenance tasks in the Files panel rather than in Windows Explorer (Win) or the Finder (Mac). If you make changes to the folder structure outside the Files panel, you may experience problems. You should only use Windows Explorer (Win) or the Finder (Mac) to create the original root folder or to move or copy the root folder of a Web site to another location. You can create the root folder in the Files panel. If you move or copy the root folder to a new location, you must define the Web site again in Dreamweaver, as you did in the lesson on defining a Web site.

Saving a Web Page

It is wise to save your work frequently. A good practice is to save every five or ten minutes, before you attempt a difficult step, and after you successfully complete a step. This ensures that you do not lose any work in the event of a power outage or computer problem. To save your work, you use the Save command. In this book, you are instructed to use the Save As command after you open each Data File. The Save As command duplicates the open document and allows you to give the new document a different name. By duplicating the Data Files, you can repeat an exercise or start a lesson over if you make a mistake. ▰▰▰ You open a copy of The Striped Umbrella home page and save it to the Web site before you continue working. You save the renamed file to your striped_umbrella folder. Because it will be the home page for your site, you save it using the name index.html, the usual name for a site's home page.

STEPS

1. **Click** File **on the menu bar, click** Open, **navigate to the drive and folder where your Unit B Data Files are stored, then double-click** dwb_1.html

   The page opens in the Document window in Design View. This is the home page, the page viewers see when they first visit the striped_umbrella Web site.

2. **Click** File **on the menu bar, click** Save As, **click the** Save in list arrow **⌄ (Win) or ⬍ (Mac) to navigate to the striped_umbrella root folder, then double-click (Win) or click (Mac) the** striped_umbrella folder

QUICK TIP
You can just type the filename "index"; the program automatically adds the .html file extension to the filename after you click Save. On a Macintosh computer, there is no default extension. Because either .htm or .html is acceptable, you need to type the filename followed by .htm or .html.

3. **Highlight the existing filename, type** index.html **in the File name text box (Win) or Save As text box (Mac) of the Save As dialog box, as shown in Figure B-10, click** Save, **then click** No **in the Update Links dialog box**

   If a filename already appears in the File name text box (Win) or the Save As text box (Mac), typing the new name replaces the current one. The title bar, as shown in Figure B-11, displays the program name followed by the path to the root folder and the filename. The information within the parentheses is called the **path**, or location of the open file in relation to any folders in the Web site The page banner does not appear and is replaced by a gray box, indicating the link is broken. This means the program cannot link to the image, which is in the Data Files folder. You must indentify the image source file so Dreamweaver can copy it to the Web site assets folder. This will repair the link, and the image will then appear.

Design Matters

Choosing filenames

When you name a Web file, you should use a descriptive name that reflects the file's contents. For example, if the page is about a company's products, you could name it "products". You also must follow some general rules for naming Web pages. For example, the home page should be named "index". Most file servers look for the file named index to use as a Web site's initial page. Do not use spaces, special characters, or punctuation in Web page filenames or in the names of any images that will be inserted in your Web site. Spaces in filenames can cause errors when a browser attempts to read a file, and they may cause your images to load incorrectly. Another rule is not to use a number for the first character of a filename. To ensure that everything loads properly on all platforms, including UNIX, assume that filenames are case sensitive and use lowercase characters.

FIGURE B-10: Save As dialog box (Windows and Macintosh)

Save in striped_umbrella root folder

Type index.htm in File name text box

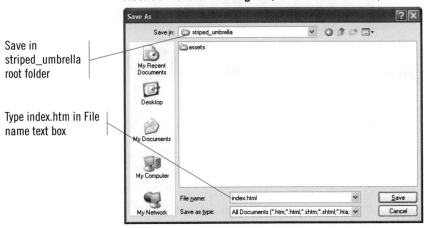

FIGURE B-11: The Striped Umbrella home page

Banner link is broken because graphic file has not been copied into Web site assets folder

Path of index.htm

Macintosh title bar placement differs

Name of open file

Name of root folder

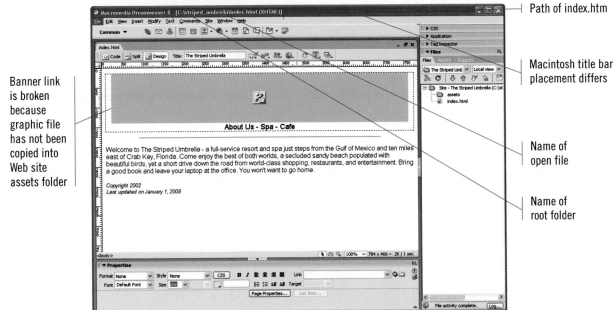

Dreamweaver 8

Setting the Home Page and Copying a New Image to a Web Site

The home page is usually the first page viewers see when they visit a Web site. Sometimes a "welcome" page precedes it. When sites use a welcome page, it will include a link to the home page. Most Web sites contain many other pages that all connect to the home page. Dreamweaver uses the home page as a starting point for creating a **site map**, a diagram of the Web pages in a Web site. On your home page, The Striped Umbrella banner is currently located in the unit_b Data Files folder; you'll need to identify its source so Dreamweaver can copy it to the site assets folder. You set the index page as your site's home page. You then identify The Striped Umbrella banner source file to copy it to the site's assets folder.

STEPS

1. **Click** index.html **in the Files panel to select it, right-click (Win) or [control] click (Mac) the** index.html filename, **then click** Set As Home Page

   The index.html file is now set as the home page for the Web site. The Striped Umbrella banner is currently in the assets folder inside the unit_b folder. You need to tell Dreamweaver to copy it to the assets folder in the striped_umbrella folder so that the program can locate it the next time it opens the home page.

2. **Click the** gray box representing the broken image **on the index page**

   Selection handles appear on the lower and right edges of the broken image. The Property inspector displays the banner's properties. The Src (Source) text box in the Property inspector displays the current location of The Striped Umbrella banner, which is the unit_b assets folder. You need to navigate to the Data Files and select the source file first. Then Dreamweaver will automatically copy it to the site's assets folder, which you have set as the default for graphics in your site.

3. **Expand the Property inspector if necessary, click the** folder icon 📁 **next to the Src text box on the Property inspector, click the** Look in list arrow ☑ **(Win) or** ☑ **(Mac) if necessary to locate the drive and folder where your Data Files are stored, double-click (Win) or click (Mac) the** unit_b folder, **double-click (Win) or click (Mac) the** assets folder, **then double-click** striped_umbrella_banner.gif **(Win) or click** striped_umbrella_banner.gif **and click** Choose **(Mac)**

   Now that you have identified the source of the image, the file is automatically copied to the site assets folder. The Src text box in the Property inspector now reads assets/striped_umbrella_banner.gif without any extra path designation in front of it.

4. **Click anywhere on the page outside of the banner, then compare your screen to Figure B-12.**

   The banner now appears correctly on the page since it has been copied to the Web site assets folder.

Design Matters

Planning the page layout

When you begin developing the content for your Web site, you must decide what to include and how to arrange each element on each page. You also must design the content with the audience in mind. What is your audience's age group? What reading level is appropriate? Should pages be simple, containing mostly text, or rich with images and multimedia files? To ensure that viewers do not get "lost" in your Web site, make sure all the pages have a consistent look and feel. This can be accomplished easily through the use of templates. **Templates** are Web pages that contain the basic layout for each page in the site.

FIGURE B-12: Property inspector showing properties of The Striped Umbrella banner

Selected Striped Umbrella banner

Lower selection handle

Source is pointing to Web site assets folder

Property inspector provides details about the selected image

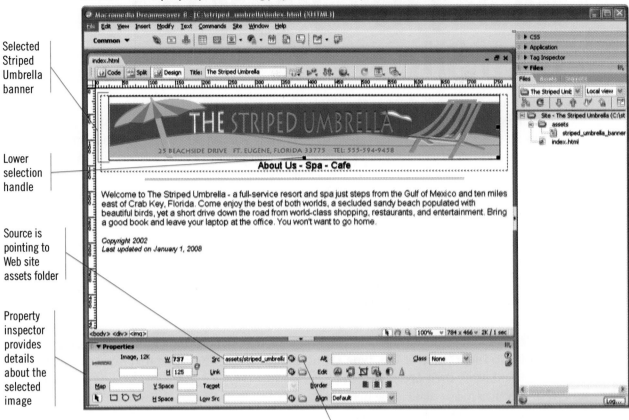

Click folder to open the Select Image Source dialog box

Making a good first impression

Since the home page is the first page viewers see as they enter a Web site, it is very important to make a good first impression. When you enter a store, you form an impression of the store by the way the merchandise is displayed, whether the staff is accessible and friendly, and by the general overall appearance and comfort of the interior. The same is true of a Web site. If you see pleasing colors and images, friendly, easy-to-understand text, and a simple navigation system, you are favorably impressed and want to explore the site. If you see poorly organized content, misspelled words, and confusing navigation, you will probably leave the site. It is much faster and easier to leave a Web site than to leave a store, so you have less time to correct a bad first impression. Have others evaluate your home page before you finalize it so you understand how others see your page.

Adding New Pages to a Web Site

Web sites may be as small as one page or contain hundreds of pages. In Dreamweaver, you can add new pages to the Web site, then add content, such as text and images, to them. The blank pages serve as place-holders for pages that you anticipate designing. That way you can set up the navigation structure of the Web site and view how each page is linked to others. When you are satisfied with the overall structure, you can then create the content for the pages. You add new pages by using the Files panel. After consulting your storyboard, you create new Web pages to add to The Striped Umbrella Web site. You create new pages called about_us, spa, cafe, activities, cruises, and fishing, and place them in the root folder.

STEPS

1. **Click the** Refresh button ⟳ **on the Files Panel, click the** plus sign (Win) **or the** triangle (Mac) **to the left of the assets folder in the Files panel to open the folder and view its contents, if not already visible**

   The striped_umbrella_banner.gif file is in the assets folder, as shown in Figure B-13.

   > **QUICK TIP**
   > When you create a new file in the Files panel, you must type the filename extension manually.

2. **Click the** root folder **to select it, then click the** Options button ⧉ **on the Files panel, point to** File, **click** New File, **type** about_us.html **in the File name text box to replace** untitled.html, **then press** [Enter]

   The about us page is added to the Web site.

3. **Repeat Step 2 to add five more blank pages to The Striped Umbrella Web site, and name the new files** spa.html, cafe.html, activities.html, cruises.html, **and** fishing.html.

   The new pages appear in the striped_umbrella root folder.

   > **TROUBLE**
   > If the site listing does not refresh, click the Files panel group options button ⧉, point to Site, then click Recreate Site Cache.

4. **Click the** Refresh button ⟳ **on the Files panel toolbar to refresh the file listing**

   The files are now sorted in alphabetical order, as shown in Figure B-14.

FIGURE B-13: Files panel showing striped_umbrella_banner.gif in the assets folder

assets folder

striped_umbrella_banner.gif file in the assets folder

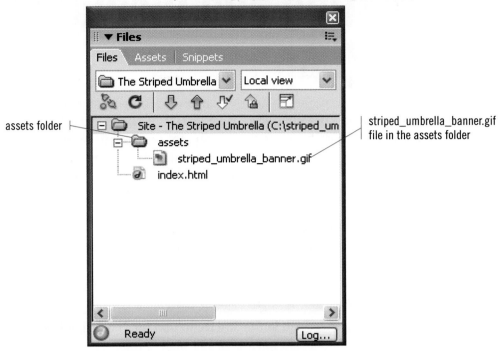

FIGURE B-14: New pages added to The Striped Umbrella Web site and sorted

Refresh icon

Your image icon for striped_umbrella_banner.gif may differ

New pages added to the striped_umbrella root folder and sorted

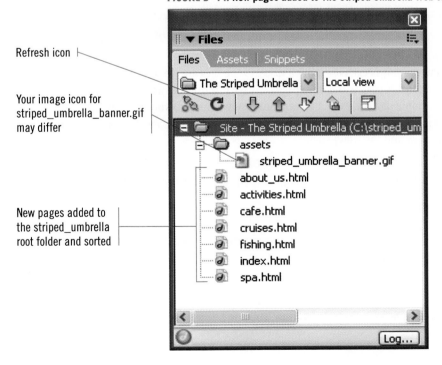

Creating and Viewing a Site Map

As you add new Web pages to a Web site, it is easy to lose track of how they all link together. Dreamweaver has a feature called a **site map**, which is a diagram of the pages in the Web site. You can find details about each page from the visual clues in the site map. For example, the site map uses different icons to indicate pages with broken links, e-mail links, or links to external Web sites. ▰▰▰▰ You create a site map for The Striped Umbrella. The site map shows only the home page because you have not yet linked other pages to it.

1. **Click Site on the menu bar, then click Manage Sites**

   The Manage Sites dialog box shows you a list of all of the Web sites on your computer. Using this dialog box, you can add, edit, duplicate, or remove Web sites.

2. **Click The Striped Umbrella if it's not already selected, then click Edit**

   The Site Definition for The Striped Umbrella dialog box opens.

3. **Click the Advanced tab in the Site Definition for The Striped Umbrella dialog box if necessary, then under Category, click Site Map Layout**

   Layout options for your site map appear in the right section of the dialog box.

4. **Verify that index.html appears as the home page in the Home page text box, as shown in Figure B-15 (if your path is long, you may need to click in the path, then press the right arrow to display the index page filename)**

5. **Click OK, then click Done**

   The Site Definition dialog box and the Manage Sites dialog box close.

6. **Click the View list arrow on the Files panel (to the right of Local View), then click Map view (Win), or click the Site map button (Mac)**

   The view changes from Local View, which displays the files and folders for the Web site, to Map View. See Figure B-16. The index page is the only page displayed in the site map. As you add more pages and link to them from the home page, the site map expands, using a tree structure to show the file relationships. As the map becomes larger when files are added, you can expand the Files panel by dragging the border between the Document window and the Files panel.

7. **Click the Expand to show local and remote sites button 🖻 on the Files panel toolbar to expand the site map (Win), click the Site Map button, then click Map and Files (if necessary)**

   The site map now appears on the left with the file list on the right.

8. **Click the Collapse to show only local or remote site button 🖻 on the Site Map window toolbar to collapse the site map**

FIGURE B-15: Options for the Site Map layout

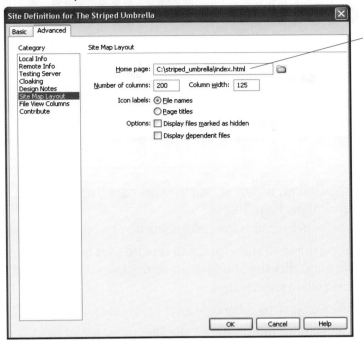

Path for
home page
(your path
may differ)

FIGURE B-16: The Striped Umbrella site map

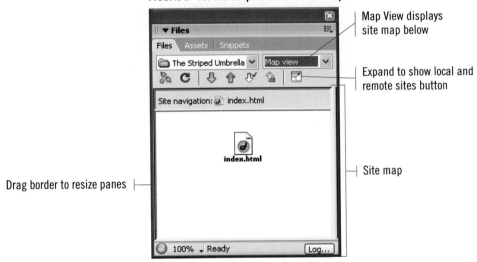

Map View displays
site map below

Expand to show local and
remote sites button

Site map

Drag border to resize panes

Clues to Use

Using site map images in Web pages

Dreamweaver lets you save a site map as an image in a Web site for printing or for viewing. Including an image of the site map in a Web site helps viewers understand the site's navigation structure. To save a site map, click the Options list arrow on the Files panel, point to File, then click Save Site Map. If you are using a Windows computer, the Save Site Map dialog box opens. Name the site map in the File name text box, then save the site map as a BMP (bitmapped) file or as a PNG file (Portable Network Graphics file). Choose BMP if you want to print the site map or insert it into a

page layout program or a slide show. Choose PNG if you plan on inserting the site map on a Web page. PNG files are capable of showing millions of colors like JPGs. Though gaining in popularity, PNG files are not available on the Macintosh platform and are not supported by older versions of browsers. If you are using a Macintosh, the Save dialog box will appear, where you can name the saved site map. Choose PICT if you want to print the site map or insert it into a page layout program or a slide show. Choose JPEG if you plan on inserting the site map on a Web page.

Selecting Site Map Options

Even after creating and publishing a Web site, a Web designer looks for ways to improve it, and frequently needs to update it with new information. There are several tasks that you can easily accomplish in the Files panel. You can double-click a file in the site map and open it in the Document window for editing. You can add new files, add new folders, and create links between files. You can also edit page titles for pages listed in the site map. The Files panel is the safest place to rename, move, and delete pages in a Web site to ensure that the page links remain intact. ▰▰▰ You explore some of the options available using the site map.

STEPS

1. **Click the** Options button 📇 **on the Files panel, point to** View, **point to** Site Map Options, **then click** Show Page Titles

   The filename, index.html, is now replaced with the page title, The Striped Umbrella.

2. **Click the** Expand to show local and remote sites button 🖼 **on the Files panel to expand the site map, click the** Site Map list arrow, **then click** Map and Files

   Your screen should resemble Figure B-17.

3. **Click the** Collapse to show only local or remote site button 🖼 **to collapse the Files panel**

TROUBLE

Be careful not to type a page title over a filename when a filename is displayed.

4. **Click the** Options button 📇 **on the Files panel, point to** View, **point to** Site Map Options, **then click** Show Page Titles **to uncheck it**

   You see the filename index.html now, rather than the page title.

5. **Click the** View list arrow **on the Files panel, then click** Local view

   The list of files in The Striped Umbrella Web site again appears.

6. **Click** File **on the menu bar, then click** Exit **(Win) or** Dreamweaver, Quit Dreamweaver **(Mac)**

   You have completed setting up the The Striped Umbrella Web site.

FIGURE B-17: Finished site map for the The Striped Umbrella Web site

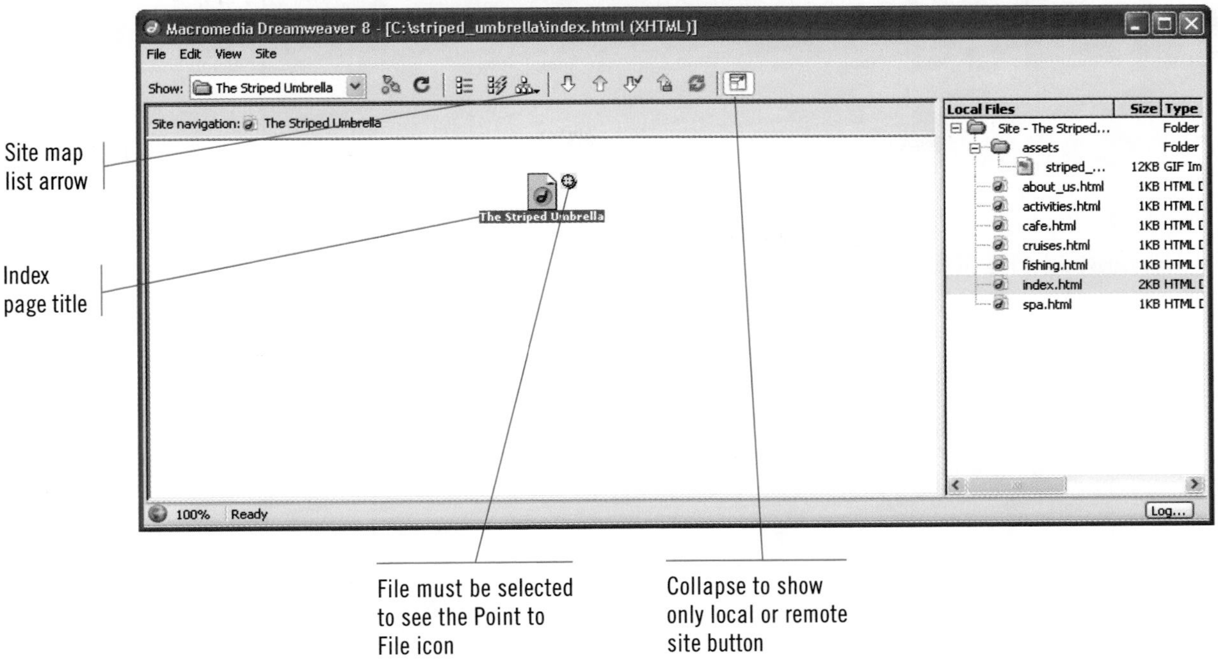

Site map list arrow

Index page title

File must be selected to see the Point to File icon

Collapse to show only local or remote site button

Dreamweaver 8

Design Matters

Choosing page titles

When users view a Web page in a browser window, the page title appears in the browser window title bar. The page title should reflect the page content and set the tone for the page. Moreover, it is important to use words in your page title likely to match keywords viewers may enter when using a search engine. Search engines compare the text in page titles to the keywords typed into the search engine. When a title bar displays "Untitled Document," the designer didn't give the page a title. To check quickly that you have included page titles on all of your Web pages, change to Map View in the Files panel, click the Options button on the Files panel, point to View, point to Site Map Options, and then verify that Show Page Titles is checked.

Practice

▼ CONCEPTS REVIEW

Label each element in the Site window in Figure B-18.

FIGURE B-18

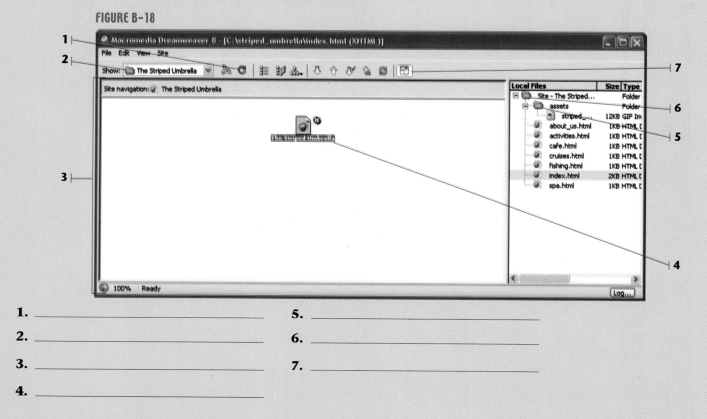

1. _____   5. _____

2. _____   6. _____

3. _____   7. _____

4. _____

Match each of the following terms with the statement that best describes its function.

8. **Expand to show local and remote sites button**

9. **Storyboard**

10. **Assets**

11. **IP address**

12. **Web server**

13. **Root folder**

14. **Site cache**

15. **Home page**

16. **Site map**

a. An address on the Web

b. Computer connected to the Internet with a permanent IP address

c. Temporary memory used to increase the speed of site management tasks

d. A small sketch showing the relationships among pages in a Web site

e. A folder that holds all the files and folders for the Web site

f. A starting point for creating a site map

g. A folder that contains non-HTML files

h. A diagram of a Web site's folder structure showing links

i. Enlarges the Files panel

Select the best answer from the following list of choices.

17. **An internal Web site without public access is called a(n):**
    a. Internet.
    b. Intranet.
    c. Domain.
    d. Extension.

18. **The first step in designing a Web site should be:**
    a. Setting up Web server access.
    b. Testing the pages.
    c. Planning the site.
    d. Creating the pages and developing the content.

19. **Which icon do you click to refresh the Files panel after you have changed files listed there?**
    a. `<?> Code`
    b.
    c.
    d.

20. **You can display page titles in the:**
    a. Site map.
    b. Assets panel.
    c. Site Definition dialog box.
    d. File menu.

▼ SKILLS REVIEW

1. **Plan a Web site.**
   a. Sketch a storyboard with five pages for a company called blooms & bulbs.
   b. Name the pages **index**, **plants**, **classes**, **newsletter**, and **tips**. (The plants, classes, newsletter, and tips pages will be links from the index page.)

2. **Create a folder for Web site management.**
   a. Open Windows Explorer or navigate to the Macintosh hard drive.
   b. Create a new folder with the name **blooms** to store your Web site files, then close Windows Explorer or the Finder.

3. **Define the Web site.**
   a. Start Dreamweaver, then create a new site using the Files panel. Name the site **blooms & bulbs**.
   b. In the Local Root Folder text box, browse to the root folder you created for the Web site.

4. **Add a folder to the Web site.**
   a. Use the Files panel to create an assets folder for the Web site.
   b. Use the Site Definition dialog box to set the assets folder as the default images folder for storing your image files.

5. **Set the home page.**
   a. Open dwb_2.html from the drive and folder where your Data Files are stored.
   b. Save the file as **index.html** in the blooms & bulbs Web site, and do not update the links.
   c. Select the gray box representing the broken banner image link on the page.
   d. Using the folder icon next to the Src text box on the Property inspector if necessary, navigate to the assets folder inside the unit_b folder where your Data Files are stored, then select blooms_banner.jpg.
   e. Refresh the Files panel, click on page, then verify that the banner was copied to the assets folder in your blooms & bulbs site.
   f. Use the Files panel to set index.html as the home page.

6. **Add new pages to a Web site.**
   a. Using the Files panel, create a new page called **plants.html**.
   b. Create three more pages, called **classes.html**, **tips.html**, and **newsletter.html.**
   c. Use the Refresh button to sort the files in alphabetical order.

7. Create a site map.

   a. Create a site map of the Web site by changing to Map view in the Files panel.

8. Modify pages from the Files panel.

   a. Display the page title, then compare your screen to Figure B-19.

   b. Turn off the Show Page Titles option.

   c. Return to Local view.

   d. Exit Dreamweaver, saving your changes.

FIGURE B-19

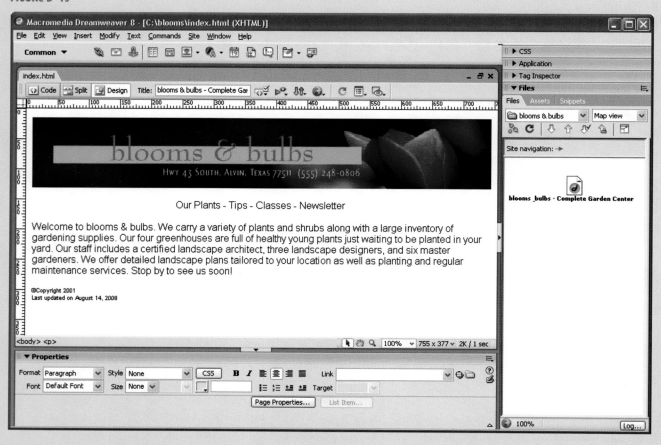

▼ INDEPENDENT CHALLENGE 1

You have been hired to create a Web site for a river expedition company named Rapids Transit, located on the Buffalo River in Arkansas. In addition to renting canoes, kayaks, and rafts, they have several types of cabin rentals for overnight stays. River guides are available, if requested, to accompany clients on float trips. The clients range from high school and college students to families to vacationing professionals. Refer to Figure B-20 as you work through the following steps:

   a. Create a Web site plan and storyboard for this site.

   b. Create a folder named **rapids** in the drive and folder where you save your Web site files.

   c. Define the Web site with the name **Rapids Transit**, setting the rapids folder as the root folder for the Web site.

   d. Create an **assets** folder and set it as the default images folder.

   e. Open dwb_3.html from the drive and folder where your Data Files are stored, then save it in the root folder of the Web as **index.html**.

   f. Set index.html as the home page.

   g. Save the rapids_banner.jpg image in the assets folder for your site. (*Hint*: Navigate to the Unit B assets folder to locate the source for the image.) Refresh the Files panel and verify that the rapids_banner.jpg image was copied to the assets folder.

▼ INDEPENDENT CHALLENGE 1 (CONTINUED)

h. Create four additional files for the pages in your site plan, and give them the following names: **guides.html**, **rentals.html**, **lodging.html**, and **before.html**. Refresh the Files panel to display the files in alphabetical order.

i. Exit Dreamweaver, saving your changes.

FIGURE B-20

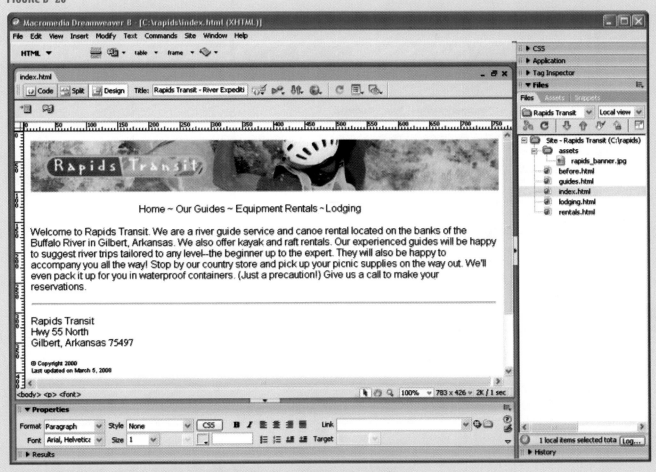

▼ INDEPENDENT CHALLENGE 2

Your company is designing a new Web site for a travel outfitter named TripSmart. TripSmart specializes in travel products and services. In addition to selling travel products, such as luggage and accessories, they sponsor trips and offer travel advice. Their clients range from college students to families to vacationing professionals. The owner, Thomas Howard, has requested a dynamic Web site that conveys the excitement of traveling. Refer to Figure B-21 as you work through the following steps:

a. Create a Web site plan and storyboard for this site to present to Thomas.

b. Create a folder named **tripsmart** in the drive and folder where you save your Web site files.

c. Define the Web site with the name **Tripsmart**, setting the tripsmart folder as the root folder for the Web site.

d. Create an **assets** folder and set it as the default images folder.

e. Open the file dwb_4.html from the drive and folder where your Data Files are stored, then save it in the root folder of the Web site as **index.html**.

f. Set index.html as the home page.

g. Save the tripsmart_banner.jpg image in the assets folder for the site and refresh the Files panel to display the image file in the assets folder.

h. Create four additional files for the pages in your plan, and give them the following names: **catalog.html**, **newsletter.html**, **services.html**, and **destinations.html**. Refresh the Files panel to display the files in alphabetical order.

i. Exit Dreamweaver, saving your changes.

FIGURE B-21

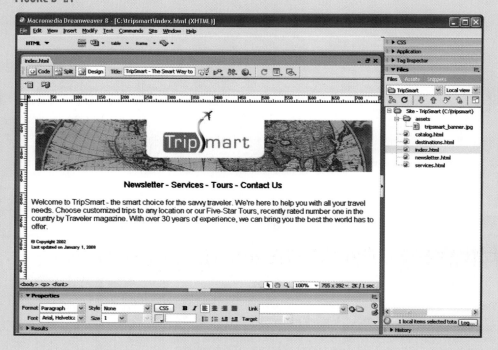

▼ INDEPENDENT CHALLENGE 3

You have been asked to design a Web site for the Over Under Dive Shop in Nevis, West Indies. This is a certified Professional Association of Diving Instructors (PADI) dive center, offering PADI certification courses. They also conduct snorkeling and dive trips to various locations around the barrier reef surrounding Nevis. Before you begin your Web site plan, you decide to find several dive sites so you can compare various Web site designs.

FIGURE B-22

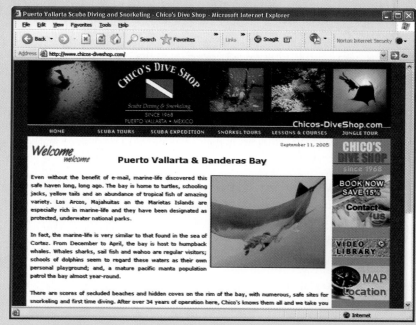

a. Connect to the Internet and go to your favorite search engine, such as www.google.com.

b. Type keywords that will help you locate dive sites, for example, **diving**, **PADI**, and **snorkeling**.

c. Find three sites like the one shown in Figure B-22 that you feel are attractive and effective, then print the home page of each site.

d. List at least two reasons why you chose each site.

e. Close your browser.

▼ INDEPENDENT CHALLENGE 4

Sharon Woods would like to buy a new car. She is considering many different makes and models, but is concentrating today on an Audi. She is looking for information on the environmental commitment of Audis in general, and for information on retail financing. Record your answers to the questions below on paper or in your word processing software. Refer to Figure B-23 as you work.

a. Connect to the Internet and go to Audi at www.audi.com.

b. Click the Site map link on the home page.

c. How has Audi organized information to help you navigate its Web site?

d. Can you find the information that Sharon needs?

e. Did you feel that the Site map helped you navigate the Web site?

f. Do you feel that this is a definite benefit for viewers?

g. Close your browser.

FIGURE B-23

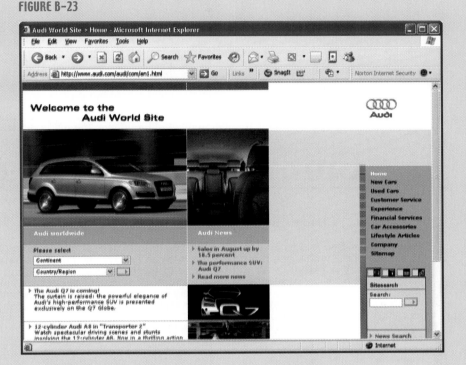

▼ INDEPENDENT CHALLENGE 5

In this assignment, you create a personal Web site entirely on your own. There will be no Data Files supplied. Each Your Site Independent Challenge will build from unit to unit, so you must do each Your Site assignment in each unit to complete your Web site.

a. Decide what type of Web site you would like to build. It can be a personal Web site about you and your family, a business Web site if you have a business you would like to promote, or a fictitious Web site. Your instructor may direct your choices for this assignment.

b. Create a storyboard for your Web site and include at least four pages.

c. Create a root folder where you store your Web site files and name it appropriately.

d. Create an assets folder in this root folder to hold your Web site assets.

e. Define the Web site with an appropriate name, using the root folder and the assets folder that you created in the site definition.

f. Begin planning the content you would like to use for the home page and plan how you would like to organize it on the page.

g. Use the Files panel to create the pages you listed in your storyboard.

h. Collect information to use in your Web site, such as pictures or text. Store these in a folder (paper, not electronic) that you can bring with you to class as you develop your site.

i. Exit Dreamweaver, saving your changes.

▼ VISUAL WORKSHOP

Your company has been selected to design a Web site for a bookstore named Emma's Book Bag, a small independent bookstore in rural Virginia. The owner of the bookstore, Emma Claire, specializes in children's books, although she stocks a large variety of other books. She has a small cafe in the store that serves beverages and light snacks. Create the Web site pictured in Figure B-24, using the files dwb_5.html for the index page and book_bag_banner.jpg for the banner. Name the site Emma's Book Bag and name the root folder bookbag. The files are located in the drive and folder where your Data Files are stored.

FIGURE B-24

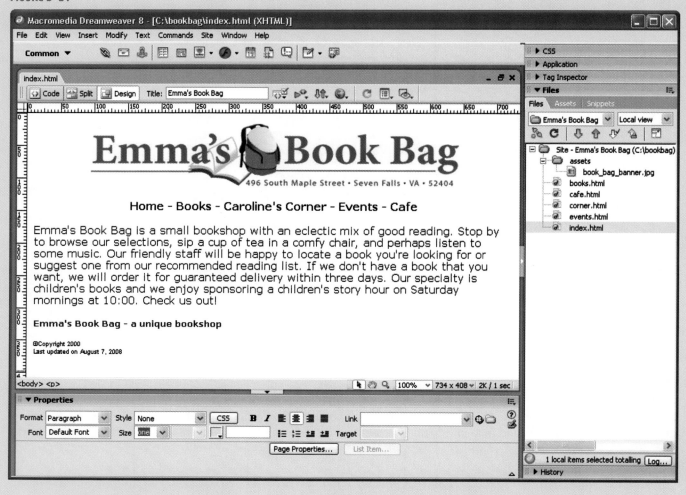

Developing a Web Page

OBJECTIVES

| Plan the page layout |
| Create the head content |
| Set Web page properties |
| Create and format text |
| Add links to Web pages |
| Use the History panel |
| View HTML code |
| Test and modify Web pages |

When you begin developing Web pages, you should choose the page content with the audience in mind. A Web site designed for a large professional corporation is designed quite differently from an educational Web site for children. You can use colors, font types and sizes, and images to set a formal or casual tone. In this unit, you learn about planning a Web site, modifying a Web page, and linking it to other pages. Finally, you'll use Code View to modify some of the page code, and test the links to make sure they work. ▓▓▓▓ The Striped Umbrella Web site should appeal to families, singles, and maturing baby boomers with leisure time and money to spend. You improve the design and content of the home page to attract this broad target audience.

Planning the Page Layout

When people visit your Web site, you want them to feel "at home," as if they know their way around the pages in your site. You also want to ensure that viewers will not get "lost" due to layout inconsistencies. When you plan your Web site, consider the layout of all of the Web site pages so that they have a consistent look and feel. To help maintain a common look for all pages, you can use templates. **Templates** are Web pages that contain basic layouts you can apply to your Web site pages, such as the location of a company logo or a menu of buttons. As you will learn in Unit D, **Cascading Style Sheets (CSS)** provide a way to easily format objects or entire pages by providing common formatting characteristics that can be applied to multiple objects. And, as you will learn in Unit G, many designers use **tables**, simple grids of cells in rows and columns, as a page layout tool to position elements on the page easily. Tables can contain headings, text, and/or images, and you can adjust their layout to provide exact placement on the page. 🔲🔲 Before you begin working on The Striped Umbrella home page, you identify key concepts that govern good page layout.

DETAILS

- **Use white space effectively**

  Too many text blocks, links, and images can confuse viewers, and actually make them feel agitated. Consider leaving some white space on each page. **White space**, which is not necessarily white, is a Web page area that is not filled with text or graphics. Using white space effectively creates a harmonious balance for the page. Figure C-1 shows how white space can help emphasize strong visual page elements, yet still achieve a simple, clean look for the page.

- **Limit multimedia elements**

  The expression "less is more" is especially true of Web pages. Too many multimedia elements, such as graphics, video clips, or sounds, may result in a page that takes too long to load. Viewers may tire of waiting for these elements to appear and leave your Web site before the entire page finishes loading. In addition, placing an unnecessary multimedia element on your page may make your Web site seem unprofessional.

- **Keep it simple**

  Often the simplest Web sites are the most appealing. Plus, Web sites that are simple in layout and design are the easiest to create and maintain. A simple Web site that works is far superior to a complex one with errors.

- **Use an intuitive navigation structure**

  A Web site's navigational structure should be easy to use. It can be based on text links or a combination of text and graphic links. Viewers should always know where they are in the Web site, and be able to find their way back to the home page quickly. If viewers get "lost" in your Web site, they may leave the site rather than struggle to find their way around.

- **Apply a consistent theme using templates**

  A theme can be almost anything—from the same background color on each page to common graphics, such as buttons or icons that reflect a nautical, western, automotive, or literary theme. Common design elements, such as borders, can also be considered a theme. Templates are a great way to easily incorporate consistent themes in Web sites. See the appendix for information on using templates.

- **Use tables for page layout**

  When you use tables as the basis for page layout, you can control both how the entire page appears in the browser window and how the various page elements are positioned on the page in relation to each other. This allows a page to look the same, regardless of the size of a viewer's screen.

- **Be conscious of accessibility issues**

  There are several techniques you can use to ensure that your Web site is accessible to individuals with disabilities. These techniques include using alternate text with graphic images, avoiding certain colors on Web pages, and supplying text as an alternate source for information that is presented in an audio file. Dreamweaver can display Accessibility dialog boxes to prompt you to insert accessibility information for the page objects, as shown in Figure C-2.

FIGURE C-1: An effective Web page layout

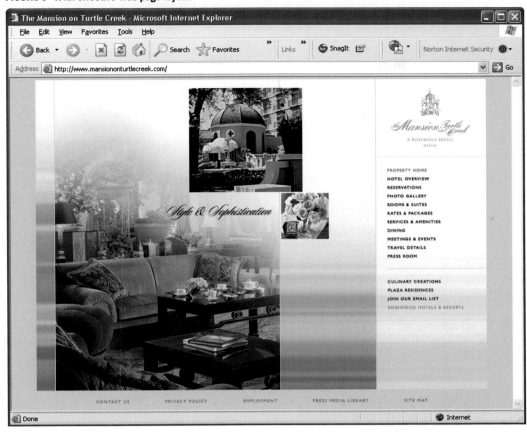

FIGURE C-2: Accessibility attributes for page design

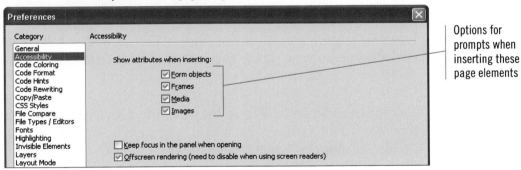

Options for prompts when inserting these page elements

Design Matters

Designing for accessibility

It is extremely important to design your Web site so that individuals with disabilities can successfully navigate the Web site and read the page content. In fact, government Web sites must be made accessible pursuant to Section 508 of the Workforce Investment Act of 1998, based on the Americans with Disabilities Act (ADA). On May 5, 1999, the Web Content Accessibility Guidelines were published by the World Wide Web Consortium (W3C). Macromedia provides much information about Web site compliance with Section 508 accessibility guidelines. For more information, visit the accessibility page at the Macromedia Web site: Go to the Student Online Companion for this book, then locate the link for this unit.

Creating the Head Content

A Web page consists of two sections: the head section and the body. The **body** contains all the page content viewers see in their browser window, such as text, graphics, and links. The **head section** contains the **head content**, including the page title that is displayed in the browser title bar, as well as some very important page elements that are not visible in the browser. These items are called meta tags. **Meta tags** are HTML codes that include information about the page, such as keywords and descriptions. **Keywords** are words that relate to the content of the Web site. Search engines find Web pages by matching the title, description, and keywords in the head content of Web pages with keywords viewers enter in search text boxes. A **description** is a short summary of Web site content. ▰▰▰ Before you work on page content for the home page, you modify the page title and add a description and keywords that will draw viewers to The Striped Umbrella Web site.

1. **Start Dreamweaver, click the** Site list arrow **on the Files panel, then click** The Striped Umbrella**, if it isn't already selected**
   The Striped Umbrella Web site opens.

> **TROUBLE**
> If you don't see the index.html file listed, click the plus sign next to the striped_umbrella folder to expand the folder contents.

2. **Double-click** index.html **in the Files panel, make sure the Document window is maximized, click** View **on the menu bar, then click** Head Content**, if it isn't already checked**
   The head content section appears at the top of The Striped Umbrella home page, as shown in Figure C-3. The head content section includes the Title icon 🔲 and the Meta tag icon 🔳.

> **QUICK TIP**
> You can also change the page title using either the Title text box on the Document toolbar or the Page Properties dialog box.

3. **Click the** Title icon 🔲 **in the head section, place the insertion point after the current title in the Title text box on the Property inspector, press the spacebar, type** beach resort and spa, Ft. Eugene, Florida**, then press** Enter **(Win) or** return **(Mac)**
   The new title replaces the old title. See Figure C-4. The new title uses the words beach and resort, which are words that potential customers may use as keywords when using a search engine.

4. **Click the** Insert bar list arrow**, click** HTML**, click the** Head list arrow 🔲 ▾**, then click** Keywords
   Some buttons on the insert bar include a list arrow, indicating that there is a menu of choices beneath the current button. The button that was selected last appears on the Insert bar until you select another.

5. **Type** beach resort, spa, Ft. Eugene, Florida, Gulf of Mexico, fishing, dolphin cruises **(including the commas) in the Keywords text box, as shown in Figure C-5, then click** OK
   The Keywords icon 🔳 appears in the head section, indicating that keywords have been created for the Web page. Keywords should always be separated by commas.

6. **Click the** Head list arrow 🔳 ▾ **on the Insert bar, click** Description**, then type** The Striped Umbrella is a full-service resort and spa just steps from the Gulf of Mexico in Ft. Eugene, Florida.**, as shown in Figure C-6, then click** OK
   The Description icon 🔳 appears in the head section, indicating that a description has been entered.

7. **Click the** Show Code View button 🔳 Code **on the Document toolbar, click anywhere in the code, view the head section code, as shown in Figure C-7, click the** Show Design View button 🔳 Design**, then save your work**
   The title, keywords, and description appear in the HTML code.

Clues to Use

Checking your screen against book figures

To show as much of the Document window as possible, most figures appear with the Standard toolbar hidden. Keep in mind that Dreamweaver will "remember" the screen arrangement from the last session when it opens each time. This may mean that you must open, close, collapse, or expand the various panels, toolbars, and inspectors to match your screens to the figures in the book.

FIGURE C-3: Viewing the head content

Meta tag icon

Head content section

Page title icon

FIGURE C-4: Property inspector displaying new page title

New page title

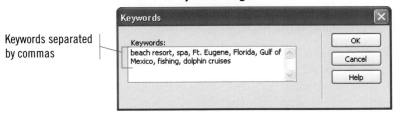

FIGURE C-5: Keywords dialog box

Keywords separated by commas

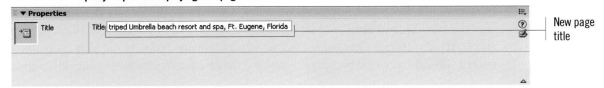

FIGURE C-6: Description dialog box

Description

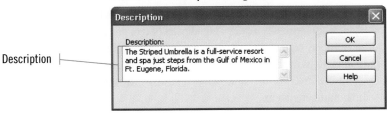

FIGURE C-7: Code View displaying the head content

Title

Keywords

Description

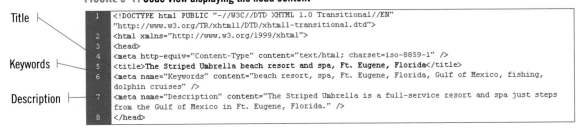

```
1  <!DOCTYPE html PUBLIC "-//W3C//DTD XHTML 1.0 Transitional//EN"
   "http://www.w3.org/TR/xhtml1/DTD/xhtml1-transitional.dtd">
2  <html xmlns="http://www.w3.org/1999/xhtml">
3  <head>
4  <meta http-equiv="Content-Type" content="text/html; charset=iso-8859-1" />
5  <title>The Striped Umbrella beach resort and spa, Ft. Eugene, Florida</title>
6  <meta name="Keywords" content="beach resort, spa, Ft. Eugene, Florida, Gulf of Mexico, fishing,
   dolphin cruises" />
7  <meta name="Description" content="The Striped Umbrella is a full-service resort and spa just steps
   from the Gulf of Mexico in Ft. Eugene, Florida." />
8  </head>
```

Design Matters

Entering titles, keywords, and descriptions

Search engines use titles, keywords, and descriptions to find pages after the user enters search terms. Therefore, it is very important to anticipate what your potential customers will use for search terms, and to try to include those in the keywords, description, or title. Many search engines print the page titles and descriptions when they list pages in their search results. Some search engines limit the number of keywords that they will index. Keep your keywords and description short and to the point to avoid being ignored by search engines that limit the number of words you can use. It is usually sufficient to enter keywords and a description only for the home page or any other page you want viewers to find, rather than for every page on the Web site.

Dreamweaver 8

Setting Web Page Properties

One of the first design decisions that you should make is the background color of your Web page. The **background color** is the color that fills the entire Web page. This color should complement the colors used for text, links, and graphics you place on the page. A strong contrast between the text and background colors makes it easier for viewers to read the text. You can choose a light background color and a dark text color, or a dark background color and a light text color. A white background, though not terribly exciting, is the easiest to read for most viewers, and provides good contrast in combination with dark text. The next step is to choose the default font color and default link color. The **default font color** and the **default link color** are the colors the browser uses to display text, links, and visited links. The default color for links that the viewer has not previously clicked is blue. **Visited links** are links that the user has previously clicked. The default color for visited links is purple. You can change these default settings in your browser; however, not all browsers recognize link color settings. You set the background color and the default font color for The Striped Umbrella home page.

1. **Click Modify on the menu bar, then click Page Properties**

    The Page Properties dialog box opens. This dialog box is where you set page properties, such as the background color and default font color.

2. **Click the Background color box ▢▾, as shown in Figure C-8**

    The color picker opens, and the pointer changes to an eyedropper 🖋. Initially, the color boxes are set to gray, which represents the default colors. This does not mean that the color gray will be applied. After you select a color, it appears in the appropriate color box.

3. **Click the blue color swatch, #66CCFF, the next to the last color in the sixth row, as shown in Figure C-8**

    Each color is assigned a **hexadecimal value**, a value that represents the amount of red, green, and blue in the color. For example, white, which is made of equal parts of red, green, and blue, has a hexadecimal value of FFFFFF. Each pair of numbers represents the red, green, and blue values. The hexadecimal number system is based on 16, rather than 10 as in the decimal number system. Since you run out of digits after you reach the number 9, you begin using letters of the alphabet. A represents the number 10, and F represents the number 15 in the hexadecimal number system.

4. **Click Apply in the Page Properties dialog box**

    The background color of the Web page changes to blue. The text color is set to the default color, which is black. The Apply button allows you to see changes that you have made to the page without having to close the Page Properties dialog box. The black text against the blue background is difficult to read. You decide to leave the text black, but change the page background back to white.

5. **Click the Background color box ▢▾, click the white color swatch, the rightmost color in the bottom row, then click Apply**

6. **Click the Links color box, shown in Figure C-9, then use 🖋 to select a shade of red for the color of the links on the home page**

    You decide that red would clash with the other page elements.

7. **Click the Links color box again, then click the Strikethrough button at the top of the color picker ▢**

    The color for links is set back to the default color. Your screen should resemble Figure C-9. The strikethrough button returns the links to the default color.

8. **Click OK to close the Page Properties dialog box**

    The colors for the page have been set.

9. **Save your work**

FIGURE C-8: Color picker

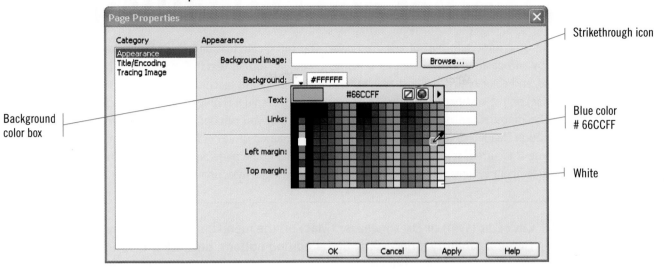

Strikethrough icon

Background color box

Blue color # 66CCFF

White

FIGURE C-9: Page Properties dialog box

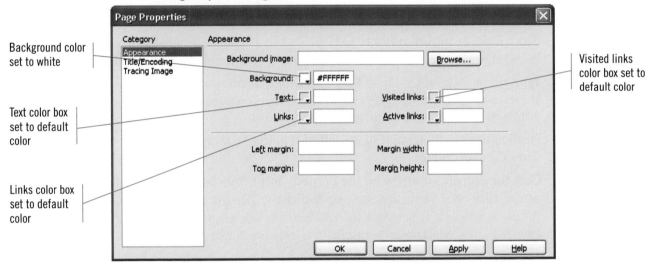

Background color set to white

Text color box set to default color

Links color box set to default color

Visited links color box set to default color

Design Matters

Web-safe colors

The colors that you choose for your Web page elements should be Web safe. **Web-safe** colors will display consistently in all browsers, and on Macintosh, Windows, and Unix platforms. Netscape defined Web-safe colors in 1994 as a set of 216 colors that are uniformly recognized by all operating systems. (In actuality only 212 of the 216 colors are truly Web safe.) Before Web-safe colors were established, designers didn't know which colors were displayed differently on different platforms. If a designer chose a color, such as red, on a Windows computer, he or she could not be certain that it would look like the same shade of red on a Macintosh computer. Dreamweaver has two Web-safe color palettes: Color Cubes and Continuous Tone. Each palette contains the 216 Web-safe colors. Color Cubes is the default color palette; however, you can choose

another one by clicking Modify on the menu bar, clicking Page Properties, clicking the Background, Text, or Links color box, clicking the color palette list arrow, then clicking the desired color palette. Figure C-10 shows the list of color palette choices. See the Macromedia Help files for more information about Web-safe colors.

FIGURE C-10: Color palettes

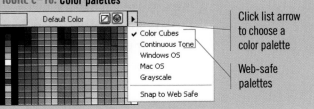

Click list arrow to choose a color palette

Web-safe palettes

Creating and Formatting Text

Text is an important part of any Web page. You can create text directly in Dreamweaver, import text, or copy and paste text from another document. You can format text in Dreamweaver by changing the font, size, and color of the text, just as in other software programs. Each time you press [Enter] (Win) or [return] (Mac) on the keyboard, you create a new paragraph, even if it is only a few words long. You can format text as headings. **Headings** are six different text styles that you can apply to text: Heading 1 (the largest size) through Heading 6 (the smallest size). A **style** is a named group of formatting characteristics. You revise the current text links on The Striped Umbrella home page and format them using a heading style. You temporarily turn off the option to automatically generate styles until you learn about Cascading Style Sheets.

STEPS

1. **Click** Edit **(Win) or** Dreamweaver **(Mac) on the menu bar, click** Preferences, **click the** General **category if necessary; under editing options, uncheck the option** Use CSS instead of HTML tags, **then click** OK

   Unchecking this box will temporarily turn off the option to create Cascading Style Sheet styles automatically when you are formatting text. You will turn this option back on in Unit D, where you will learn to use Cascading Style Sheets.

> **QUICK TIP**
> Be careful with selected text or objects on the page because the next keystroke will replace the selected items, and you may inadvertently delete page elements that you want to keep.

2. **Position the insertion point to the left of** A **in** About Us, **then drag to select** About Us – Spa – Cafe, **as shown in Figure C-11**

   You select text in order to delete it. If text is not selected, you can use [Backspace] or [Delete].

3. **Type** Home - About Us - Spa - Cafe - Activities, **using spaces on either side of the hyphens**

   The text you typed forms the page's new navigation bar. A **navigation bar** is a set of text or graphic links that viewers use to navigate to other pages in your Web site.

4. **Position the insertion point to the left of** H **in** Home, **then drag to select** Home - About Us - Spa - Cafe - Activities

5. **Click the** Format list arrow **on the Property inspector,click** Heading 4, **click the** Font list arrow, **click** Arial, Helvetica, sans-serif, **click the** Size list arrow, **then click** None

   The Heading 4 format and the Arial, Helvetica, sans-serif font family is applied to the line of text, as shown in Figure C-12. You should not use both a Font size and a Heading size on the same text.

6. **Position the insertion point after the period following** …want to go home, **as shown in Figure C-12, press** [Enter] **(Win) or** [return] **(Mac), then type** The Striped Umbrella

> **QUICK TIP**
> Line breaks are useful when you want to apply the same formatting to text but place it on separate lines. The HTML code for a line break is <br>, which stands for break.

7. **Press and hold** [Shift], **press** [Enter] **(Win) or** [return] **(Mac) to create a line break, then enter the following information, using a line break at the end of each line:**

   25 Beachside Drive
   Ft. Eugene, Florida 33775
   (555) 594-9458

   A **line break** places text on separate lines without creating new paragraphs. You are now ready to format the address and telephone number.

8. **Position the pointer to the left of** The Striped Umbrella, **click and drag until the entire** address and telephone number **are selected, click the** Italic button I **on the Property inspector to italicize the text, click the** Font list arrow, **click** Arial, Helvetica, sans-serif, **click the** Size list arrow, **click** Size 2, **then click anywhere to deselect the text; see Figure C-13**

9. **Save your work**

FIGURE C-11: Deleting the current navigation bar

Click insertion point here, then drag to select the text

Welcome to The Striped Umbrella - a full-service resort and spa just steps from the Gulf of Mexico and ten miles east of Crab Key, Florida. Come enjoy the best of both worlds, a secluded sandy beach populated with beautiful birds, yet a short drive down the road from world-class shopping, restaurants, and entertainment. Bring a good book and leave your laptop at the office. You won't want to go home.

FIGURE C-12: Formatting the new navigation bar

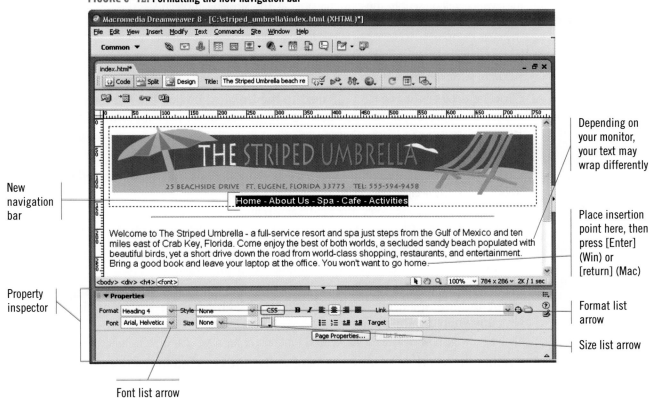

Depending on your monitor, your text may wrap differently

New navigation bar

Property inspector

Place insertion point here, then press [Enter] (Win) or [return] (Mac)

Format list arrow

Size list arrow

Font list arrow

FIGURE C-13: Creating and formatting the address and telephone number

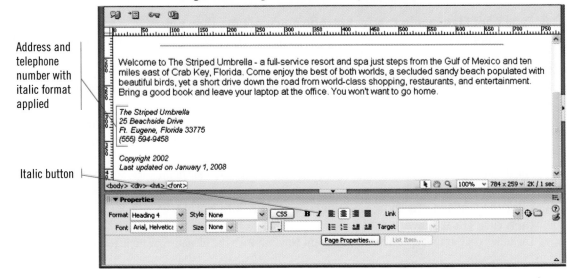

Address and telephone number with italic format applied

Italic button

Dreamweaver 8

Adding Links to Web Pages

Hyperlinks, or links, are specially formatted text or images that users click to navigate, or move, through the pages in Web sites. Viewers are more likely to return to Web sites that have a user-friendly navigation system. Viewers also enjoy Web sites that have interesting links to other Web pages or other Web sites. When creating Web pages it is important to avoid **broken links**, links that cannot find the intended destination file. You should also provide a **point of contact**, a place on a Web page that gives viewers a means of contacting the company if they have questions or problems. A **mailto: link**, an e-mail address for viewers to contact someone at the Web site's headquarters, is a common point of contact.  You enter the links for the navigation bar for The Striped Umbrella home page. You also create an e-mail link for viewer inquiries, which will be sent to the club manager at The Striped Umbrella.

STEPS

1. **Double-click Home to select it**
   You must select the text that you want to attach a link to.

QUICK TIP

If your Browse for File icon is behind the Panel Groups window, click the triangle on the splitter bar to close and then reopen it as necessary.

2. **Click the Browse for File icon 📁 next to the Link text box on the Property inspector, as shown in Figure C-14, then navigate to the striped_umbrella root folder if necessary**
   The Select File dialog box opens, showing the striped_umbrella root folder contents for The Striped Umbrella Web site.

3. **Click index.html, as shown in Figure C-15, verify that Document is selected next to Relative to, then click OK (Win) or Choose (Mac)**
   The Select File dialog box closes. The word Home is linked to the index.html page in The Striped Umbrella Web site. When users click the Home link in a browser window, the index.html page opens.

QUICK TIP

When text is selected, you cannot see the text color.

4. **Click anywhere on the home page to deselect Home**
   Notice that Home is underlined and blue, the default color for links.

5. **Repeat Steps 1–4 to create links for About Us, Spa, Cafe, and Activities, using about_us.html, spa.html, cafe.html, and activities.html as the corresponding files, then click anywhere on the page**
   All five links are now created for The Striped Umbrella home page. Your screen should resemble Figure C-16.

QUICK TIP

If you don't put the insertion point immediately after the last digit in the telephone number, you will not retain the formatting.

6. **Position the insertion point immediately after the last digit in the telephone number, press and hold [Shift], then press [Enter] (Win) or [return] (Mac)**

7. **Click the Insert bar list arrow, click Common if it's not already selected, then click the Email Link button 🖾 on the Insert bar**
   The Email Link dialog box opens.

8. **Type Club Manager in the Text text box, press [Tab], then type manager@thestripedumbrella.com in the E-Mail text box, as shown in Figure C-17, click OK, then italicize the Club Manager link text if necessary**
   You must enter the correct e-mail address in the E-Mail text box for the link to work; however, you can use a descriptive name, such as Customer Service, in the Text text box. The links you created will now show in Map view.

TROUBLE

If you don't see the pages in Map view, return to the Files panel if necessary, then press [F5] to refresh the panel.

9. **Click the View list arrow in the Files panel, click Map view, click the Expand to show local and remote sites button 🖻 on the Files panel toolbar, click the Site list arrow, then click Map and Files**
   The site map shows the e-mail link and the pages that are linked to the home page, and the file list appears on the right side of the screen.

10. **Click the Collapse to show only local or remote site button 🖻, click the View list arrow, then click Local view**
    The index page again appears in the document window, with the filenames again listed in the Files panel.

FIGURE C-14: **Creating a link using the Property inspector**

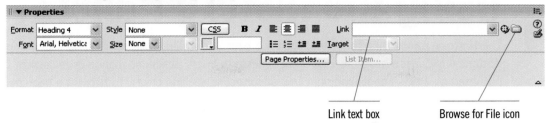

Link text box Browse for File icon

FIGURE C-15: **Select File dialog box**

striped_umbrella root folder

index page

Make sure that Relative to: is set to Document

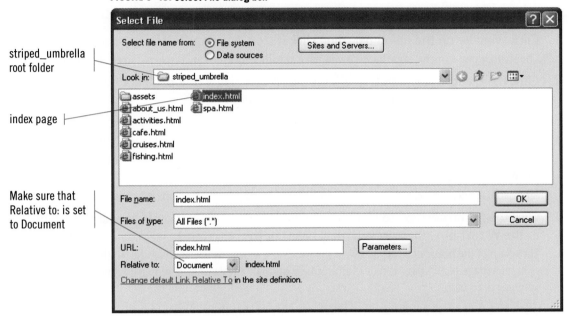

FIGURE C-16: **Links added to navigation bar**

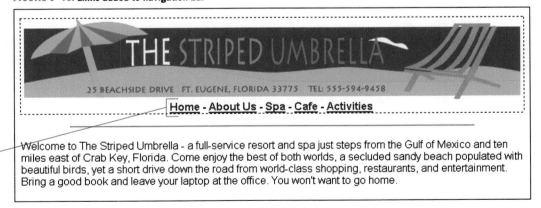

Links to Home, About Us, Spa, Cafe, and Activities pages

FIGURE C-17: **Email Link dialog box**

Text for e-mail link on the page

Link information

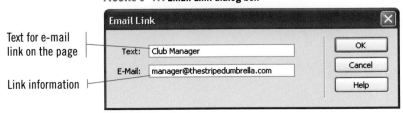

Using the History Panel

The **History panel** shows the steps that you have performed while editing and formatting a particular document in Dreamweaver. To **edit** a page means to insert, delete, or change page content by, for example, inserting a new image, adding a link, or correcting spelling errors. To **format** a page means to make adjustments in the appearance of page elements by, for example, resizing an image or changing the color of text. Formatting does not change the content of a page; it simply makes it look better. The History panel records all tasks that you perform and displays them in the order in which you completed them. You experiment with the History panel by inserting, and then formatting, a horizontal rule.

STEPS

1. **Click Window on the menu bar, then click History to open the History panel**

   The History panel opens, and the steps you have already performed are displayed in the panel window.

2. **Click the Options menu button on the History panel title bar, click Clear History, as shown in Figure C-18, then click Yes in the warning box**

   The History panel is empty.

3. **Position the insertion point to the left of the words The Striped Umbrella in the first address line, click the Insert bar list arrow, click HTML, then click the Horizontal Rule button on the Insert bar**

   A horizontal rule, or line, appears on the page above the address and remains selected.

4. **Click the list arrow next to pixels on the Property inspector, click % if necessary, type 90 in the W text box, then press [Enter] (Win) or [return] (Mac)**

   The width of the horizontal rule is 90% of the width of the page. It is wise to set the width of a horizontal rule as a percentage of the page rather than in pixels so that it resizes itself proportionately when viewed on different-sized monitors.

5. **Click the Align list arrow on the Property inspector, then click Center**

   Your horizontal rule is centered on the page. Compare your Property inspector settings to those shown in Figure C-19.

6. **Using the Property inspector, change the width of the rule to 80% and the alignment to Left**

   The rule is now 80% of the width of the window and is left aligned. You prefer the way the rule looked when it was centered, so you decide to undo the last two steps.

7. **Drag the slider on the History panel up until it is pointing to Set Alignment: center, as shown in Figure C-20, then release the mouse button**

   The bottom two steps in the History panel appear gray, indicating that these steps have been undone, and the horizontal rule returns to the centered, 90% width settings.

8. **Save your work**

FIGURE C-18: History panel

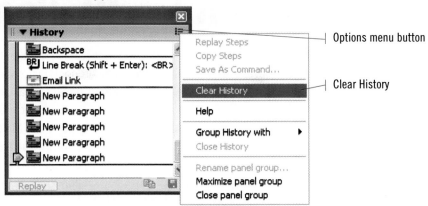

Options menu button

Clear History

FIGURE C-19: Property inspector settings for rule

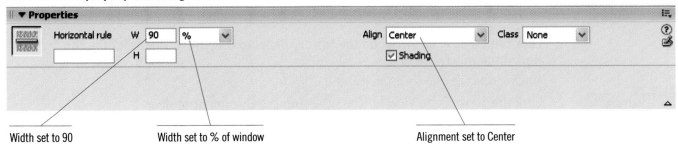

Width set to 90

Width set to % of window

Alignment set to Center

FIGURE C-20: Undoing steps using the History panel

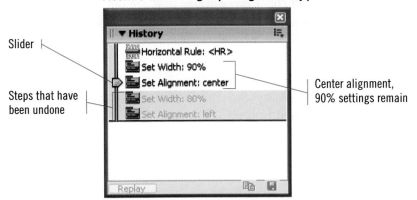

Slider

Steps that have
been undone

Center alignment,
90% settings remain

Clues to Use

The History panel

Dragging the slider up and down in the History panel is a quick way to undo or redo steps. However, the History panel offers much more. It can "memorize" certain steps and consolidate them into one command. This is a useful feature for steps that you need to perform repeatedly. Note that some Dreamweaver features, such as steps performed in the Files panel, cannot be recorded in the History panel. The default number of steps that the History panel will record is 50, unless you specify otherwise in the General Preferences dialog box. Setting this number too high requires additional memory, and may affect the speed at which Dreamweaver functions.

Viewing HTML Code

Although the default files created in Dreamweaver are XHTML files, the file extension is .html, and the code is referred to as "HTML." XHTML is the newest standard for HTML code. It is often helpful to view the code while editing or formatting a Web page. Some designers prefer to make changes to their pages by typing directly into the code, rather than working in Design View. Features, such as JavaScript functions, are often added to pages by copying and pasting code into the existing page's HTML code. **JavaScript** is code that adds user-driven or state-driven functionality, such as rollovers or interactive forms, to a Web page. **Rollovers** are screen elements that change in appearance as the pointer rests on them. You can view the HTML code in Dreamweaver by using Code View or Code and Design View. In these views, you can view the HTML code and the page content in different colors, highlight HTML code that contains errors, and **debug**, or correct, HTML errors. You can use the **Reference panel** to find answers to coding questions covering topics such as HTML, JavaScript, and Accessibility. Dreamweaver also has a feature that tells you the last date that changes were made to a Web page. ⬛⬛⬛ You view the home page HTML code in Code View, use the HTML Reference panel to find out how to change the color of a rule, and then insert the date on the home page.

STEPS

1. **Click the collapse arrow ▼ on the History panel to collapse it, then click the top horizontal rule to select it**

   After you select an object, you can change it.

QUICK TIP

[Ctrl] [P] (Win) or [command] [P] (Mac) prints the HTML code for an open page.

2. **Click the Show Code View button ◀▷ Code on the Document toolbar**

   The highlighted HTML code represents the selected horizontal rule on the page. Notice the Coding toolbar that is docked along the left side of the document window.

3. **Click the View Options button 📄, on the Document toolbar, then click Word Wrap, if necessary, to select it**

   The code appears within the width of the window, making it easier to read.

TROUBLE

If you don't make a change in the options, click off the menu to make sure you don't accidentally uncheck one of the items.

4. **Click 📄, again and check any options that are unchecked, as shown in Figure C-21**

   If Syntax Coloring is not checked, the color of the HTML code and the text on the Web page are both black, making it harder to differentiate between the two. Next, you would like to find out how to change the color of the horizontal rule. You'll use one of the built-in electronic reference books supplied with Dreamweaver.

5. **Click Window on the menu bar, click Reference, choose the O'REILLY HTML Reference in the Book list if necessary, click the Tag list arrow, then scroll to and click HR in the Tag text box, as shown in Figure C-22**

   HR is the HTML code for horizontal rule. You find out that the color of rules can be changed by using style sheets, then decide to leave the horizontal rule alone. (Style sheets will be covered in the next unit.)

6. **Click the collapse arrow ▼ to collapse the Results panel group**

   Dreamweaver lets you insert a date that updates automatically each time you save the file.

TROUBLE

You may have to scroll to see the date at the bottom of the window.

7. **Highlight January 1, 2008 at the bottom of the Code window, press [Delete], click the Insert Bar list arrow, click Common, click the Date button 📅 on the Insert bar, click March 7, 1974, if necessary, in the Date Format text box, click the Update automatically on save check box to select it, as shown in Figure C-23, then click OK**

   March 7, 1974 is an example of a date format. The manually entered date on the page is replaced with a date that will automatically update each time the page is opened and saved. Notice how the HTML code for the date has changed.

8. **Click the Show Design View button 🔲 Design to return to Design View**

   Today's date appears at the bottom of the page.

9. **Save your work**

FIGURE C-21: Code View options

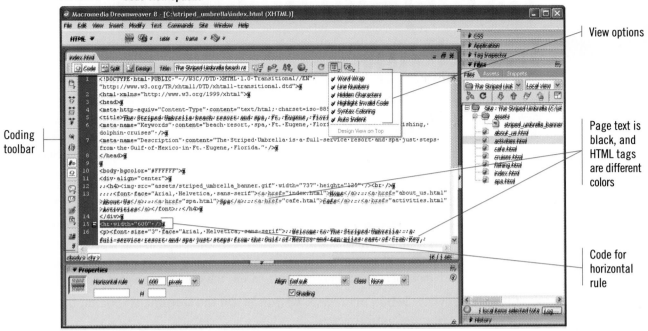

View options

Coding toolbar

Page text is black, and HTML tags are different colors

Code for horizontal rule

FIGURE C-22: Viewing the Reference panel

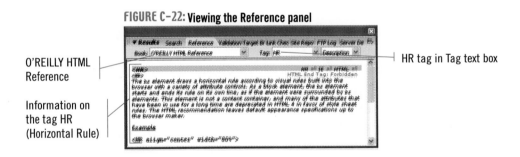

O'REILLY HTML Reference

Information on the tag HR (Horizontal Rule)

HR tag in Tag text box

FIGURE C-23: Insert Date dialog box

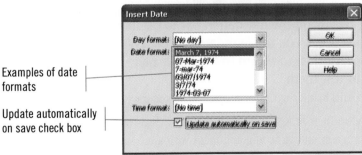

Examples of date formats

Update automatically on save check box

Clues to Use

Understanding XHTML vs. HTML

You can save Dreamweaver files in many different file formats, including XHTML, HTML, JavaScript, CSS, or XML, to name a few. XHTML is the acronym for eXtensible HyperText Markup Language, the current standard language used to create Web pages. XHTML, which is based on XML (eXtensible Markup Language), is an extension of HTML 4. Using XHTML rather than HTML combines the advantages of both HTML and XML content and is the next step in the evolution of the Internet. You can still use HTML (HyperText Markup Language) in Dreamweaver; however, it is no longer considered the standard language. In Dreamweaver 8 you can easily convert existing HTML code to XHTML-compliant code. Although the default files created in Dreamweaver 8 are XHTML files, the file extension is .html, and the code is still referred to as "HTML code."

Testing and Modifying Web Pages

As you develop your Web pages, you should test them frequently. The best way to test a Web page is to preview it in a browser window to make sure it appears the way you expect it to. You should also check to see that the links work properly, that there are no typographical or grammatical errors, and that you have included all of the necessary information for the page. You view The Striped Umbrella home page in Dreamweaver, preview it using the default browser, and make adjustments to the page.

STEPS

QUICK TIP

You cannot resize a document in the Document window if it is maximized. Click the Document window Restore Down button before attempting to resize the window. If, due to your monitor size, you cannot see the status bar, try hiding some toolbars or the Property inspector.

1. **Restore down your Document window, click the** Window Size list arrow **on the Status bar, click** 760 × 420 (800 × 600, Maximized), **then view the page in the Document window**
   The 800 × 600 window setting is used on 15-inch monitors and some 17-inch monitors. Most consumers have at least a 15-inch monitor at their homes or offices, making this window size a good choice for a Web page.

2. **Click the** Preview/Debug in Browser button 🔘 **on the Document toolbar, then click** Preview in [your default browser]
   The page opens in the browser window. You decide to replace the period after "...go home" with an exclamation point.

3. **Close your browser, highlight the period after** "...go home." **then type** ! **(an exclamation point)**
   You now decide that the horizontal rules need adjusting to better balance the page

4. **Click the** top horizontal rule **to select it, type** 55 **in the W text box of the Property inspector, click the** Width list arrow, **then click** %.

5. **Repeat step 4 to resize the second horizontal rule to** 100%.
   The horizontal rules look more balanced on the page with the rest of the page objects.

QUICK TIP

It is a good idea to make a back-up copy of the Web site fairly frequently. Save the back-up copy to a different drive or folder other than the one where the original Web site is stored.

6. **Save the file, then use** 🔘 **to view the changes in your browser**
   With your finishing touches, the home page should resemble Figure C-24.

7. **Click the** About Us link **on the navigation bar to display the blank page you created earlier, click the** Back button **on the Standard toolbar (Win) or the** Back button **on the Navigation toolbar (Mac) to return to the home page, then click the** Spa, Cafe, **and** Activities links **to test them**
   Each link should open a blank page in the browser since you haven't placed any text or images on them yet.

TROUBLE

If you are asked to configure your default e-mail client, answer the questions in the series of dialog boxes that appears.

8. **Click the** Club Manager **link, then close the Untitled message window that appears**
   The default mail program on your computer opens with a message addressed to The Striped Umbrella club manager.

9. **Close the browser, close the file, then** Exit **(Win) or** Quit **(Mac) the Dreamweaver program**

FIGURE C-24: The finished page

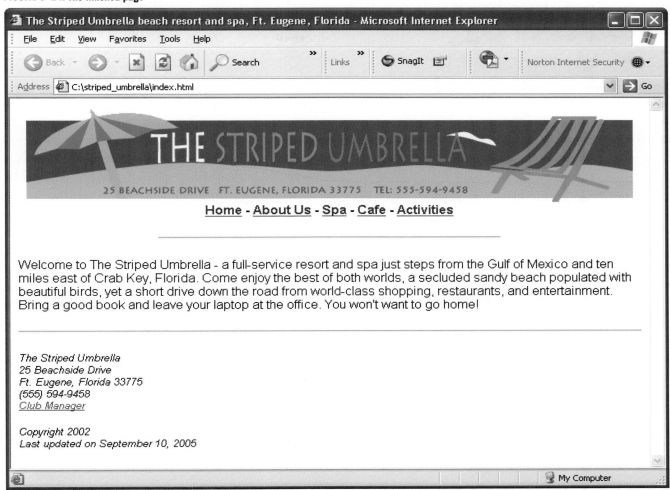

Practice

▼ CONCEPTS REVIEW

Label each element in the Dreamweaver window shown in Figure C-25.

FIGURE C-25

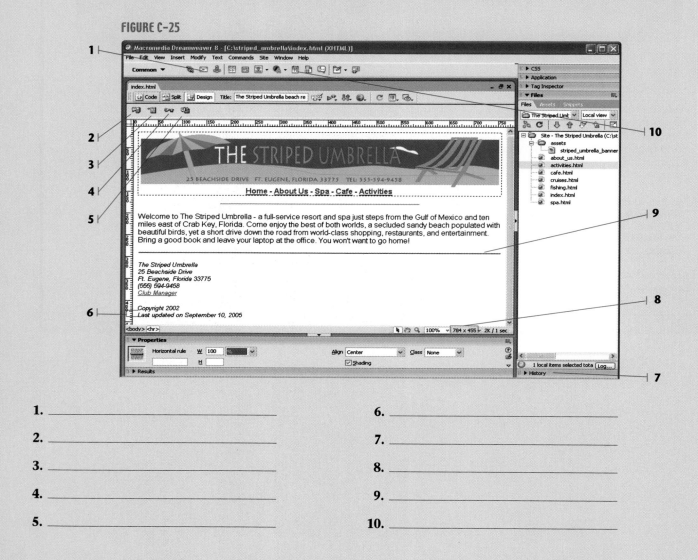

1. _____   6. _____

2. _____   7. _____

3. _____   8. _____

4. _____   9. _____

5. _____   10. _____

Match each of the following terms with the statement that best describes its function.

11. **Style**

12. **Head section**

13. **Body section**

14. **Page Properties dialog box**

15. **Heading 1**

16. **Heading 6**

17. **Edit a page**

18. **Format a page**

a. The part of a Web page that includes text, graphics, and links

b. A named group of formatting characteristics

c. Includes the default Web page settings

d. The smallest heading size

e. Make adjustments in the appearance of page elements

f. Insert, delete, or change page content

g. The largest heading size

h. The part of a Web page that includes the page title and meta tags

Select the best answer from the following list of choices.

19. **The head section of a Web page can include:**
    a. Keywords.
    b. Descriptions.
    c. Meta tags.
    d. All of the above.

20. **Links that have been previously clicked are called:**
    a. Active links.
    b. Links.
    c. Visited links.
    d. Broken links.

21. **The Web-safe palette contains _____ colors.**
    a. 256
    b. 216
    c. 125
    d. 250

22. **The _____ on the History panel is used to undo or redo several steps.**
    a. Scroll bar
    b. Pointer
    c. Slider
    d. Undo/Redo Tool

23. **An example of a point of contact is a:**
    a. Heading.
    b. Title.
    c. Mailto: link.
    d. Keywords.

24. **The Dreamweaver default color palette is the:**
    a. Continuous Tone.
    b. Color Cubes.
    c. Windows OS.
    d. Mac OS.

Dreamweaver 8

▼ SKILLS REVIEW

Important: If you did not create the Web sites used in the following exercises in Unit B, you need to create a root folder for each Web site and define the Web sites using files your instructor provides. See the "Read This Before You Begin" section for more detailed instructions.

1. **Plan the page layout.**
   a. Using a word processor or a piece of paper, list three principles of good page design that you have learned, and list them in order of most important to least important to you, based on your experiences.
   b. Explain why you chose these three concepts and why you selected the order you did.

2. **Create the head content.**
   a. Start Dreamweaver.
   b. Use the Files panel to open the blooms & bulbs Web site.
   c. Open the index page and view the head content.
   d. Insert the following keywords: **garden**, **plants**, **nursery**, **flowers**, **landscape**, and **greenhouse**.
   e. Insert the description **blooms & bulbs is a premier supplier of garden plants for both professional and home gardeners**.
   f. Switch to Code View to view the HTML code for the head section.
   g. Switch to Design View.
   h. Save your work.

3. **Set Web page properties.**
   a. View the page properties.
   b. Change the background color to a color of your choice and apply it to the page, leaving the dialog box open.
   c. Reset the background color to white.
   d. Save your work.

4. **Create and format text.**
   a. Replace the hyphens in the current navigation bar with a split vertical bar (the top of the backslash key) separated by a space on either side to separate the items.
   b. Using the Property inspector, apply the Heading 4 style to the navigation bar.
   c. Place the insertion point at the end of the last sentence and add a paragraph break.
   d. Type the following text, inserting a line break after each line. (*Hint*: To create a line break, press and hold [Shift], then press [Enter] (Win) or [return] (Mac).)
      blooms & bulbs
      Hwy 43 South
      Alvin, Texas 77511
      (555) 248-0806
   e. Delete the date in the "Last updated" line and replace it with a date that will update automatically each time the page is saved, using the March 7, 1974 format.
   f. Using the Property inspector, italicize the company name and address information.
   g. Save your work.

5. **Add links to Web pages.**
   a. Link Our Plants to plants.html.
   b. Link Tips to tips.html.
   c. Link Classes to classes.html.
   d. Link Newsletter to newsletter.html.
   e. Using the Insert bar, create an e-mail link under the telephone number, using a line break; type **Customer Service** in the Text text box and **mailbox@blooms.com** in the E-Mail text box, then italicize Customer Service.

6. Use the History panel.

  a. Open and clear the History panel.

  b. Using the Insert bar, insert a horizontal rule under the paragraph about blooms & bulbs.

  c. Using the Property inspector, center the rule and set the width to 80% of the width of the window.

  d. Use the History panel to return the horizontal rule to its original width.

  e. Set the horizontal rule width to 75% of the window width.

  f. Collapse the History panel.

  g. Save your work.

7. View HTML code.

  a. Use Code View to examine the code for the horizontal rule properties, the e-mail link, and the date in the "Last updated" statement.

  b. Return to Design View.

8. Test and modify Web pages.

  a. Using the Window Size pop-up menu on the status bar, view the page at two different sizes. (*Hint:* Recall that if you select a size that is larger than your monitor, you may need to hide toolbars or the Property inspector to see your status bar.)

  b. Preview the page in your browser.

  c. Verify that all links work correctly, then close the browser.

  d. Add the text **We are happy to ship your orders by FedEx.** to the end of the paragraph, using the same formatting settings that you used for the paragraph.

  e. Save your work, preview the page in your browser, compare your screen to Figure C-26, then close your browser.

  f. Close the page, then exit Dreamweaver.

FIGURE C-26

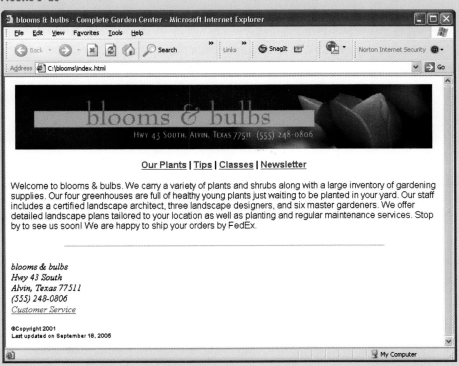

Dreamweaver 8

Important: *If you did not create the Web sites used in the following exercises in Unit B, you need to create a root folder for each Web site and define the Web sites using files your instructor provides. See the "Read This Before You Begin" section for more detailed instructions.*

▼ INDEPENDENT CHALLENGE 1

You have been hired to create a Web site for a river expedition company named Rapids Transit, located on the Buffalo River in Arkansas. In addition to renting canoes, kayaks, and rafts, they have several types of cabin rentals for overnight stays. River guides are available, if requested, to accompany clients on float trips. The clients range from high school and college students to families to vacationing professionals. The owner's name is Mike Andrew.

a. Use the Files panel to open the Rapids Transit Web site.

b. Open the index page in the Rapids Transit Web site.

c. Create the following keywords: **river**, **rafting**, **Buffalo**, **Arkansas**, **kayak**, **canoe**, and **float**.

d. Create the following description: **Rapids Transit is a river expedition company located on the Buffalo River in Arkansas**.

e. Change the page title to **Rapids Transit - Buffalo River Outfitters**.

f. Edit the navigation bar below the Rapids Transit banner by changing **Our Guides** to **River Guides**.

g. Apply the Heading 5 style to the navigation bar, and add any additional formatting you wish.

h. Enter the telephone number **(555) 365-5228** below the address, with a line break between the lines.

i. Italicize the company information, then after the phone number, enter a line break and create an e-mail link (not italicized, but using the same font family), using **Mike Andrew** for the text and **mailbox@rapidstransit.com** for the e-mail link.

j. Add links to the entries in the navigation bar, using the files index.html, guides.html, rentals.html, and lodging.html in the rapids root folder. (Recall that these files don't have any content yet, but you can still link to them. You will add content to the pages as you work through the remaining units of the book.)

k. Delete the horizontal rule.

l. Delete the date in the last updated statement and change it to a date that will be automatically updated when the page is saved, using the March 7, 1974 data format. Reformat the date to match the rest of the line if necessary.

m. View the HTML code for the page, noting in particular the code for the head section.

n. View the page in two different window sizes, save your work, then test the links in your browser window, as shown in Figure C-27.

o. Close the page, and exit Dreamweaver.

FIGURE C-27

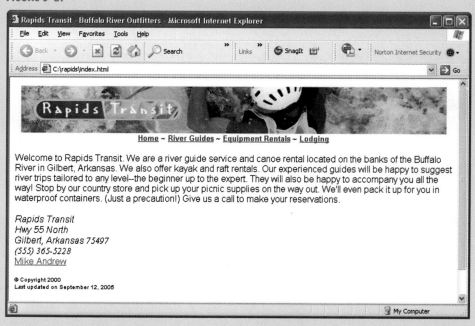

▼ INDEPENDENT CHALLENGE 2

Your company is designing a new Web site for a travel outfitter named TripSmart. TripSmart specializes in travel products and services. In addition to selling travel products, such as luggage and accessories, they sponsor trips and offer travel advice. Their clients range from college students to families to vacationing professionals. The owner, Thomas Howard, has requested a dynamic Web site that conveys the excitement of traveling. Refer to Figure C-28 as you work through the following steps.

a. Open the TripSmart Web site, then open its index page.

b. Create the following keywords: **travel, traveling, tours, trips, vacations**.

c. Create the following description: **TripSmart is a comprehensive travel store. We can help you plan trips, make the arrangements, and supply you with travel gear.**

d. Change the page title to read **TripSmart: Serving all your travel needs**.

e. Change the navigation bar below the banner to read **Home - Destinations - Newsletter - Services - Catalog**.

f. Remove the text size formatting and apply a heading style to the text links in the navigation bar.

g. Add links to the navigation bar entries, using the files index.html, destinations.html, newsletter.html, services.html, and catalog.html. (Recall that these files don't have any content yet, but you can still link to them. You will add content to the pages as you work through the remaining units of the book.)

h. Replace the date in the "Last updated" statement with a date that will update automatically when the file is saved, using the format of your choice. Reformat the date to match the rest of the last updated line if necessary.

i. Add the following contact information between the paragraph and copyright statement: **TripSmart, 1106 Beechwood, Fayetteville, AR 72604, (555) 848–0807**, and format the contact information with the settings of your choice.

j. Immediately beneath the telephone number, place an Email link using **Contact Us** as the text and **associate@tripsmart.com** for the link.

k. View the HTML code for the page, noting in particular the head section code.

l. View the page in two different window sizes, save your work, then test the links in your browser window.

m. Close the page and exit Dreamweaver.

FIGURE C-28

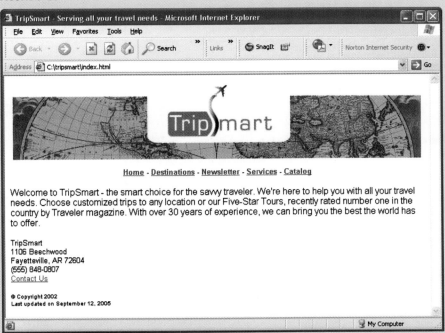

Dreamweaver 8

▼ INDEPENDENT CHALLENGE 3

The World Wide Web Consortium (W3C), created in October 1994, develops guidelines, software tools, and other technology "to lead the World Wide Web to its full potential," as its Web site states. The W3C home page, as shown in Figure C-29, includes the most current Web accessibility guidelines.

a. Open your browser and go to the World Wide Web Consortium: Go to the Student Online Companion for this book, then locate the link for this unit.
b. Search to find information about accessibility guidelines for Web pages, especially the Priority 1 guidelines.
c. Using a word processing program or a sheet of paper, list the major guidelines covered.
d. Make a checklist of the steps you would take when developing a Web site to ensure that your Web site would be compliant with the Priority 1 standards.
e. Save your work, close your files, and exit all programs.

FIGURE C-29

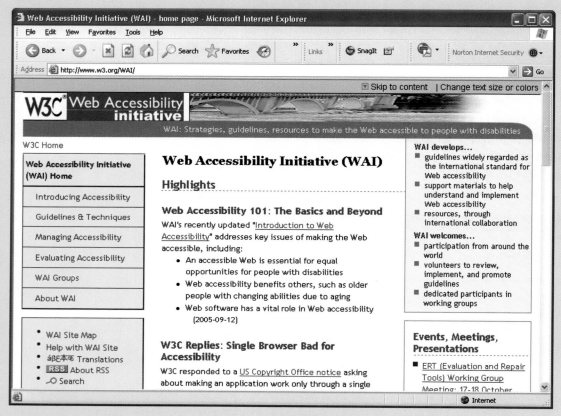

 ▼ INDEPENDENT CHALLENGE 4

Kory Clark is a freelance photographer. He is searching the Internet for a particular type of paper to use in processing his prints. He knows that Web sites use keywords and descriptions in order to receive "hits" with search engines. He is curious as to how keywords and descriptions work with search engines. Write your answers to the questions below on paper or using your word processor.

▼ INDEPENDENT CHALLENGE 4 (CONTINUED)

a. Go to the Student Online Companion for this chapter, then click the link for the Kodak Web site.

b. View the page source by clicking View on the menu bar, then clicking Source (Internet Explorer) or Page Source (Netscape Navigator or Communicator).

c. Can you locate a description and keywords?

d. How many keywords do you find?

e. How many words are in the description?

f. In your opinion, is the number of keywords and words in the description about right, too many, or not enough?

g. Go to the Student Online Companion for this book, locate the links for this unit, then click the link for the Google search engine. Type **photography** and **paper** in the search text box.

h. Click the first link in the list of results and view the source code for that page. Do you see keywords and a description? Do any of them match the words you used in the search?

i. If you don't see the search words in keywords or descriptions, do you see them in the body of the pages?

j. Save your work and exit all programs.

▼ INDEPENDENT CHALLENGE 5

This assignment will continue to build on the personal Web site that you created in Unit B. In this lesson, you will work with your home page.

a. Insert a brief description and a list of meaningful keywords for your home page in the appropriate locations.

b. Insert an effective title for your home page.

c. Format the home page attractively, creating a strong contrast between your page background and your page content.

d. Add links from the home page to your other pages.

e. Insert an e-mail link.

f. Insert a "Last updated" statement that includes a date that updates automatically when you save the file.

g. Preview the home page in your browser, verifying that each link works correctly.

h. Check the page for errors in content or format and edit as necessary.

i. Save your work, close the page, and exit the program.

▼ VISUAL WORKSHOP

Your company has been selected to design a Web site for a bookstore named Emma's Book Bag, a small independent bookstore in rural Virginia. The owner of the bookstore, Emma Claire, specializes in children's books, although she stocks a large variety of other books. She has a small cafe in the store that serves beverages and light snacks. Open your Emma's Book Bag Web site and modify the index page to duplicate Figure C-30. (*Hint:* Remember to add an appropriate description and keywords and revise the last updated statement so it will automatically update when the page is saved. Also, have the e-mail link create an e-mail addressed to emma_claire@emmasbookbag.com.)

FIGURE C-30

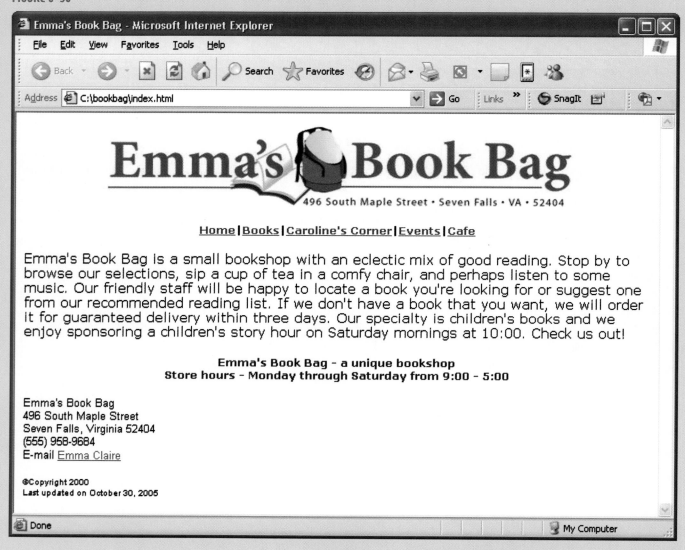

Formatting Text and Using Cascading Style Sheets

OBJECTIVES

Import text

Set text properties

Create an unordered list

Change Preferences for Cascading Style Sheets

Create a Style in a new Cascading Style Sheet

Apply and edit a Style

Add styles to a Cascading Style Sheet

Attach a Cascading Style Sheet to a Page

Insert rollovers with Flash text

The content of most Web pages is based on text. Because text on a computer screen is more tiring to read than text on a printed page, you should strive to make your Web page text attractive and easy to read. Dreamweaver has many options for enhancing text, including font properties, styles you can apply to paragraphs and lists, and Cascading Style Sheets. Cascading Style Sheets are used to assign sets of common formatting characteristics to page elements, such as text and tables. You can also insert text created in Macromedia Flash, a Macromedia software program used to create Web page animations. Your current focus is on the spa page for The Striped Umbrella Web site. You have decided to use lists to group content on the page to make the page more readable. You will use styles to make the formatting throughout the Web site more consistent.

Importing Text

Entering text in Dreamweaver is as easy as entering text in a word processing program. The Dreamweaver text editing features, listed in Table D-1, are similar to those in word processing programs. If you have text that you want to place on a Dreamweaver page, you can either copy and paste it, or save the file in the source program and then import it into Dreamweaver. Keep in mind that viewers must have the same fonts installed on their computers as the fonts that you apply to your text. Otherwise, the text may appear incorrectly. Some software programs, such as Adobe Photoshop and Adobe Illustrator, can convert text into graphics, which eliminates this problem. When text is converted to a graphic, it retains the same appearance, but is no longer editable. The spa has given you a list of the services they want to include on their Web page. The document, which contains a list of spa services and descriptions, was created in Microsoft Word, then saved as a Word document. You open the spa Web page, import the text, and format the text.

STEPS

1. **Start Dreamweaver, open The Striped Umbrella Web site, open dwd_1.html from the drive and folder where your Unit D Data Files are stored, then save it as spa.html in the striped_umbrella root folder, overwriting the existing file and not updating links**

   The small image under the banner appears as a broken link. This is an example of text that has been converted to a graphic. The source of this graphic file, named the_spa.jpg, is in the unit_d Data Files folder. You must copy it to the assets folder in the striped_umbrella root folder by selecting the original image source in the Property inspector. Then Dreamweaver automatically copies it to the Web site's assets folder and displays the graphic file correctly. The banner at the top of the page is already displayed correctly since it resides in the Web site assets folder.

2. **Click the gray image box, click the Browse for File icon 📁 next to the Src text box on the Property inspector, navigate to the Unit D Data Files assets folder, double-click the_spa.jpg, then click on the page to deselect the image**

   The file is now copied to the assets folder of The Striped Umbrella Web site. You are ready to import the Word text file into the Web site to place the text onto the spa page.

   QUICK TIP
   You may need to maximize your spa.html window to match the figure.

3. **Expand the assets folder on the Files panel if necessary, then if the newly copied file is not visible, click the Refresh button C on the Files panel**

   You see two graphics saved in the assets folder, striped_umbrella_banner.gif and the_spa.jpg, as shown in Figure D-1.

4. **(Win) Click to the right of The Spa, press [Enter], click File on the menu bar, point to Import, click Word Document, navigate to the drive and folder where your Unit D Data Files are stored, then double-click spa.doc**

   (Mac) Navigate to the Unit D Data Files folder, double-click spa.doc, select all, copy, close spa.doc, then paste the copied text on the spa page in Dreamweaver.

5. **Click Commands on the menu bar, then click Clean up Word HTML; in the Clean Up word HTML dialog box, click OK, then click OK again**

   The text from the Word file is copied to the page, as shown in Figure D-2.

6. **Click File on the menu bar, then click Save**

Clues to Use

Saving a Word file for importing into Dreamweaver

When you create text in Microsoft Word that you know will eventually be used on a Web page, you should not format the text. Formatting should be applied *after* the text is imported into Dreamweaver. Some formatting, such as creating new paragraphs, is OK; however, you should avoid applying styles to the text or aligning it. Creating text, importing it into Dreamweaver, and then applying styles for formatting is a much better plan. This practice will save both time and unnecessary frustration.

FIGURE D-1: The Striped Umbrella Web site with two image files in the assets folder

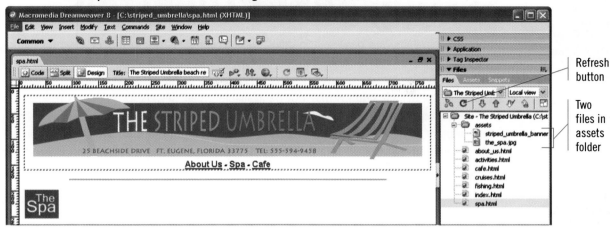

Refresh button

Two files in assets folder

FIGURE D-2: Imported Word text

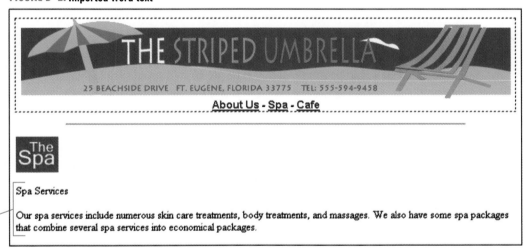

Text is placed below text image

TABLE D-1: Dreamweaver text editing features

feature	menu	function	feature	menu	function
Find and Replace	Edit	Finds and replaces text on the current Web page, the entire Web site, or in selected files	Style	Text	Sets various styles, such as bold and italic
Indent and Outdent	Text	Indents selected text to the right or left	CSS Styles	Text	Gives you the choice of creating a new CSS Style, editing a style sheet, attaching a style sheet, and applying Design Time Style Sheets
Paragraph Format	Text	Used to set paragraph (H1 through H6) and preformatted text			
			Size	Text	Sets text size from 1 to 7
Align	Text	Aligns text with the left or right margin, or centers it on the page	Size Change	Text	Changes the font size to the next smaller or larger font size
			Color	Text	Sets text color
List	Text	Creates unordered, ordered, or definition list settings	Check Spelling	Text	Runs a spell check on the page
Font	Text	Sets font combinations to be used by a browser			

Dreamweaver 8

Setting Text Properties

You can manipulate Web page text in many ways to enhance its appearance. Text formatting attributes, such as paragraph formatting, heading formatting, fonts, size, color, alignment, indents, and styles, are easy to change using the Property inspector. (Using fonts within the default settings is wise because fonts set outside the default settings may not be available on all viewers' computers.) To apply formatting to words or sentences, you must select them first. When formatting paragraphs, you can simply position the insertion point anywhere inside the paragraph that you want to format. Avoid mixing too many different fonts or formatting attributes on a Web page. This can lead to pages that are visually confusing and may be difficult to read. ▰▰▰▰ Now that you have the text on the spa page, you decide to apply some formatting to improve its appearance.

STEPS

1. **Click to place the insertion point anywhere within the words** Spa Services

   Spa Services is a paragraph; therefore you can format it with a paragraph format by clicking the insertion point in it instead of selecting the text. (Character formats, on the other hand, require you to select the text.) You are going to apply a paragraph format. The Property inspector shows the settings for the paragraph with the insertion point.

2. **Click the** Format list arrow **on the Property inspector, then click** Heading 4

   The text changes to the Heading 4 style. You decide to set the font to the font combination Arial, Helvetica, sans-serif. **Font combinations** are used so that if one font is not available, the browser will use a similar one. The browser will first look on the viewer's system for Arial, then Helvetica, then a sans-serif font to apply to the text. Since the font format is a character format, rather than a paragraph format, you must select the text before you apply it.

3. **Select the** Spa Services **heading, click the** Font list arrow **on the Property inspector, click** Arial, Helvetica, sans-serif, **as shown in Figure D-3, then deselect the text to see the new font applied**

   The text is now set to the combination of these three fonts. You decide to change the color of the heading to navy blue.

4. **Select the heading again, click the** Text Color button 🔲 **on the Property inspector, use the eyedropper** 🖊 **to click** #000066 **from the Color Picker, as shown in Figure D-4, then deselect the text to see the new color applied**

   The Color Picker closes, and the new color is applied to the heading. You are now ready to format the rest of the text on the page. You begin by setting the font and size.

5. **Click to place the insertion point before the** O **in** Our spa services, **scroll to the end of the text, press and hold** [Shift], **click after the end of the last sentence, then release** [Shift]

   The entire passage of text is selected.

6. **Click the** Font list arrow **on the Property inspector, then click** Arial, Helvetica, sans-serif

   The font list is applied to the text selection.

7. **Click the** Size list arrow **on the Property inspector, then click** 3, **as shown in Figure D-5**

   Size 3 is the default size for body text, so the text will not appear to change on the screen.

8. **Click anywhere on the page to deselect the text, save your work, click the** Preview/Debug in Browser button 🖾 **on the Document toolbar, click** Preview in [your browser name], **examine the page, then close the browser**

FIGURE D-3: Property inspector

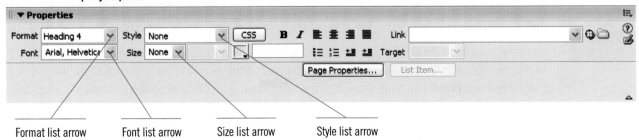

Format list arrow Font list arrow Size list arrow Style list arrow

FIGURE D-4: Color picker

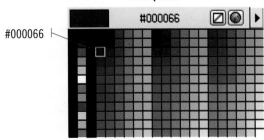

#000066

Size list arrow

FIGURE D-5: Property inspector

Clues to Use

Font sizes

There are two ways to change text size. You can select a font size between 1 and 7, 7 being the largest, or you can change the font size relative to the default basefont. The **default basefont** is size 3. When you choose +1 in the size list, you increase the basefont size from 3 to 4. If you choose –1, you decrease the basefont size from 3 to 2. See Figure D-6. Do not confuse the font size number system with the paragraph style number system, which uses Headings from 1 to 6, with 6 being the smallest. Font sizes on Windows and Macintosh computers may differ slightly.

FIGURE D-6: Font size menus

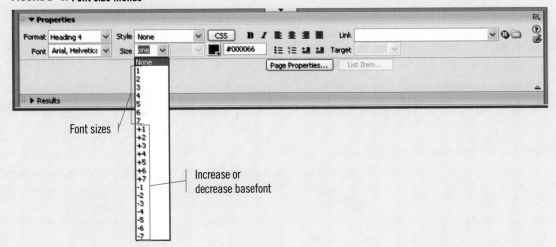

Font sizes

Increase or decrease basefont

Creating an Unordered List

You may need to create a list of products or services on your Web pages. Dreamweaver provides three types of lists: bulleted lists, numbered lists, and definition lists. **Bulleted lists**, or unordered lists, are lists of items that do not need to be placed in a specific order. Each item is usually preceded by a **bullet**, a small filled circle, or a similar icon. Bullets make lists easier to read than unformatted lists. Numbered lists, or **ordered lists**, are lists of items that must be placed in a specific order, and each item is preceded by a number or a letter. Definition lists are similar to unordered lists, but do not use leading characters, such as numbers or bullets. ⬛⬛⬛ You decide to create an unordered list from the list of spa services, to make the item list easier to read.

STEPS

1. **Select the three items under the Skin Care Treatments heading.**
   The three items are selected.

2. **Click the Unordered List button ▤ on the Property inspector to create an unordered list**
   The list of items becomes an unordered list. You can extend the list to add more bullets by pressing [Enter] (Win) or [return] (Mac) once at the end of an unordered list. To end an unordered list, press [Enter] (Win) or [return] (Mac) twice.

3. **Repeat step 2 to create unordered lists of the items under the Body Treatments, Massages, and Spa Packages headings.**

4. **Click to place the insertion point in any of the items in the first unordered list, click the expander arrow ▾ in the lower-right corner of the Property inspector to expand the Property inspector if necessary, then click List Item**
   The List Properties dialog box opens.

5. **Click the Style list arrow, click Square, as shown in Figure D-7, then click OK**
   The bullets now appear as squares rather than circles.

6. **Repeat step 5 to format the other three unordered lists.**

7. **Click to place the insertion point before the first item in the unordered list, click the Show Code View button [▣ Code] on the Document toolbar to view the code for the unordered list, click the View Options list arrow, then uncheck the Hidden Characters option**
   The HTML codes, or **tags**, surrounding the unordered list are <ul> and </ul>. Each of the items is surrounded by a <li> and </li> tag, as shown in Figure D-8. The first tag in each pair begins the code, and the last tag ends the code.

8. **Click the Show Design View button [▣ Design] on the Document toolbar to return to Design View, then save your work**

Design Matters

Choosing fonts

There are two classifications of fonts: sans-serif and serif. **Sans-serif** fonts, such as the font you are reading now, are plain characters without the small strokes at the top and bottom of letters. They are used frequently for headings and subheadings in printed text. Examples of sans-serif fonts are Arial, Verdana, and Helvetica. **Serif** fonts are more ornate, with small extra strokes at the top and bottom of the characters. They are generally easier to read in printed material because the extra strokes lead your eye from one character to the next. Examples of serif fonts are Times New Roman, Times, and Georgia. Many designers feel that a sans-serif font is preferable when the content of a Web site will be read on the screen. However, if the content is frequently printed and then read from the printed material, a serif font is preferable. When choosing fonts, limit each Web site to not more than three font variations. Using more than this may make your Web site appear unprofessional and leans toward the "ransom note effect." The ransom note effect implies that fonts have been randomly used in the document window without regard to style, comparing it to a ransom note in which words from various sources have been cut and pasted onto a page.

FIGURE D-7: List Properties dialog box

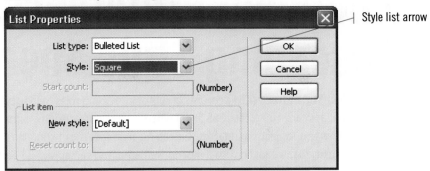

Style list arrow

FIGURE D-8: Code View

Unordered list tag

List item tag

Close list item tag

```
25   <p><font size="3" face="Arial, Helvetica, sans-serif">Body Treatments </font></p>
26   <ul type="square">
27     <li><font size="3" face="Arial, Helvetica, sans-serif">Salt Glow<br />
28       Imported sea salts are massaged into the skin, exfoliating  and cleansing the pores. </font></li>
29     <li><font size="3" face="Arial, Helvetica, sans-serif">Mud Body Wrap<br />
30       Relief for your aches and pains.</font></li>
31     <li><font size="3" face="Arial, Helvetica, sans-serif">Seaweed Body Wrap<br />
32       Seaweed is a natural detoxifying agent that also helps  improve circulation.</font></li>
33   </ul>
34   <p><font size="3" face="Arial, Helvetica, sans-serif">Massages</font></p>
35   <ul type="square">
36     <li><font size="3" face="Arial, Helvetica, sans-serif">Sports Massage<br />
37       Our deepest massage for tense and sore muscles.</font></li>
38     <li><font size="3" face="Arial, Helvetica, sans-serif">Swedish Massage<br />
39       A gentle, relaxing massage.</font></li>
40     <li><font size="3" face="Arial, Helvetica, sans-serif">Hot Stone Massage<br />
41       Good for tight, sore muscles. Advance notice required. </font></li>
```

Clues to Use

Ordered lists

Numbered lists, or ordered lists, contain numbered or lettered items that should appear in a particular order, such as listing the steps to accomplish a task. For example, if you followed directions to drive from point A to point B, each step would have to be executed in order or you would not successfully reach your destination. For sequential items such as this, ordered lists can add more emphasis than bullets. Dreamweaver uses several options for number styles, including Roman and Arabic.

Changing Preferences for Cascading Style Sheets

A **Cascading Style Sheet (CSS)** consists of sets of formatting rules called **styles** that determine how your Web page content appears. You create CSS Styles when you want to apply the same formatting attributes to page elements, such as text, objects, and tables. Cascading style sheets can contain many different styles, such as heading or body text, that are saved with a descriptive name. You can apply CSS Styles to any element in a document and to all of the documents in a Web site. If you edit an existing CSS style, all the page elements you have formatted with that style automatically update. CSS Styles save a lot of time and help create continuity in a Web site. A separate file that contains formatting code for such rules is called an **external style sheet**. External style sheets can be attached to multiple Web pages to quickly apply formatting to the Web page content and are saved with a .css file extension. External style sheets are stored in the directory structure of the Web site. When you want to use a Cascading Style Sheet in your Web sites, you should verify that the Property inspector is set to automatically use CSS styles instead of HTML tags. This makes applying styles effortless. ▰▰▰▰ You decide to change the preferences in the Property inspector to use Cascading Style Sheets. This is the default setting for the Property inspector, but you changed it earlier so you could use HTML styles. While HTML styles can be useful and easy to learn, you will find that CSS styles save you more time and give a more consistent look to your site.

STEPS

1. **Click Edit (Win) or Dreamweaver (Mac) on the menu bar, then click Preferences**
2. **Click the General category if necessary, click the check box Use CSS instead of HTML tags to select it, as shown in Figure D-9, then click OK**
   This option allows you to quickly access the styles you create through the Styles list on the Property inspector. This preference remains the same for all of your Web sites unless you change it. With this option selected, if you attempt to format text using the Property inspector, a style will automatically be created with a default name.

Clues to Use

Understanding Cascading Style Sheet files

For most people beginning to learn about Cascading Style Sheets, the terms are very confusing. A Cascading Style Sheet is a file that is attached or linked to a page in a Web site and that determines the formatting for various page objects. This single file can contain many individual styles. For instance, if you have a cascading style sheet with ten styles, you will have only one file, not ten files. Do not create a separate style sheet file for each style. Then you can attach this single file to the rest of the pages in the same Web site or additional pages in other Web sites and choose from the various styles the Cascading Style Sheet contains. There are also different types of styles that are embedded in the code for a single Web page and styles that redefine HTML tags.

General preferences category

Use CSS instead of HTML tags check box

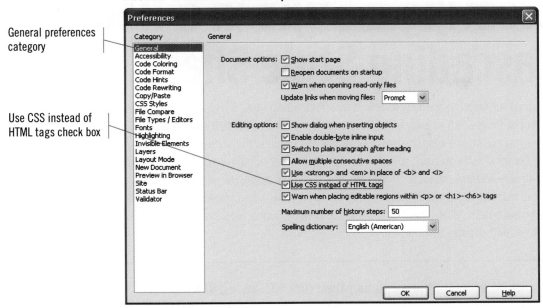

Clues to Use

Using styles without a Cascading Style Sheet

If you have checked the preference to use CSS Styles rather than HTML styles, but do not create a style sheet, Dreamweaver will create styles for you automatically as you format text. These styles will be named style1, style2, etc., and will be embedded in your HTML document file. You can rename these styles with more meaningful names to help you identify them. Figure D-10 is an example of what the HTML code would look like in this case. The disadvantage to this method of creating styles is that they are not external files and, therefore, cannot be attached to other pages.

FIGURE D-10: Embedded styles

```
1   <!DOCTYPE html PUBLIC "-//W3C//DTD XHTML 1.0 Transitional//EN"
    "http://www.w3.org/TR/xhtml1/DTD/xhtml1-transitional.dtd">
2   <html xmlns="http://www.w3.org/1999/xhtml">
3   <head>
4   <meta http-equiv="Content-Type" content="text/html; charset=iso-8859-1" />
5   <title>The Striped Umbrella</title>
6   <style type="text/css">
7   <!--
8   .style1 {
9       font-family: Verdana, Arial, Helvetica, sans-serif;
10      font-size: medium;
11  }
12  -->
13  </style>
```

Code for automatically created style

Clues to Use

Using Cascading Style Sheets

Cascading Style Sheets are great timesavers because once you apply them, you can change the style definition, which will change all the items to which you've applied it. Cascading Style Sheets are not limited to one Web site. They can be exported into other Web sites, which makes them quite a powerful tool. Unfortunately, not all browsers can read Cascading Style Sheets. Versions of Internet Explorer that are 4.0 or lower do not support Cascading Style Sheets. For Netscape Navigator, only version 6.0 or higher dependably supports Cascading Style Sheets. Most people today, however, are using browsers that do support Cascading Style Sheets.

Creating a Style in a New Cascading Style Sheet

The steps for creating the first style in a new Cascading Style Sheet are different from the steps for creating additional styles in an already existing style sheet. Creating the first style in a new CSS is a two-step process. When you create the first style, you have not yet created the style sheet, so you must first name the style sheet file in which you want to save the first style. After you have named and saved the style sheet file, you then simply add new styles to it. ▓▓▓▓ You decide to apply the same formatting to the names of each spa service. Instead of formatting each item one at a time, you create a Cascading Style Sheet and apply the style to each item. That way, if you decide to change it later, you only have to change the CSS Style, and all the items will change automatically.

STEPS

1. **Click Window on the menu bar, then click CSS Styles, if necessary**
   The CSS Styles panel opens in the CSS panel group. This panel is where you can add, delete, edit, and apply styles.

2. **Click the New CSS Rule button ▣ on the CSS Styles panel, then verify that the Class (can apply to any tag) and the (New Style Sheet File) option buttons are both selected**
   The Class option creates a new custom style that can apply to any tag and places it in the CSS Styles panel. The New Style Sheet File option makes the CSS Style available to use in the entire Web site, not just the current document. See Figure D-11.

3. **Type spa_names in the Name text box, then click OK**
   The Save Style Sheet File As dialog box opens. This dialog box prompts you to name the Cascading Style Sheet file and store it in the Web site's root folder. The name of the new style is spa_names. You will save the style spa_names in the Cascading Style Sheet file called su_styles.css.

4. **Type su_styles.css in the File name text box (Win) or the Save As text box (Mac), then click Save**
   The CSS Rule Definition for .spa_names in the su_styles.css style sheet dialog box opens. The .css extension stands for Cascading Style Sheet. This dialog box allows you to choose attributes, such as font color and font size, for the CSS Style.

5. **Click the Font list arrow, then click Arial, Helvetica, sans-serif**

6. **Click the Size list arrow, click 14, leave the size measurement unit as pixels, click the Style list arrow, click normal, click the Weight list arrow, then click bold**
   Using a measurement of pixels rather than points will help keep the text from distorting in browser windows.

QUICK TIP
Click the plus sign next to the css file in the Styles panel to expand it and see the styles saved in the file. If the styles do not appear, make sure that All is selected.

7. **Click the Color list button ▢, click #000066, as shown in Figure D-12, then click OK**
   The CSS Style named spa_names appears in the CSS Styles panel as a style for the Striped Umbrella Web site, preceded by a period in the name. Notice, also, that the style sheet is an open file in Dreamweaver. You will save it as you would an .html file.

QUICK TIP
To switch between open documents, click the tab for the document you wish to view.

8. **Click the Refresh button ↻ on the Files panel if necessary to view the su_styles CSS style file**
   The su_styles.css file appears in the file listing for the Web site, as shown in Figure D-13, with a different file extension from the HTML files. You also see that the Cascading Style Sheet is an open document in Dreamweaver that you can view and edit by clicking the su_styles.css file tab.

9. **Click the Show Code View button [◀▶ Code] on the Document toolbar to view the HTML code linking to the su_styles.css file, click File on the menu bar, then click Save All to save your changes to both the page and the style sheet file**
   The code linking to the su_styles.css file appears in the Head section, as shown in Figure D-14, and the spa_names style is indented under the file su_styles.css in the CSS Style panel.

FIGURE D-11: New CSS Rule

Selector Type = Class option button

Enter name of style here

New Style Sheet File option button

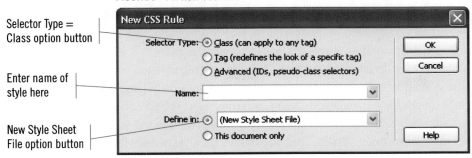

FIGURE D-12: CSS Rule Definition for .spa_names

Size list arrow

Style list arrow

Font list arrow

Weight list arrow

Color list arrow

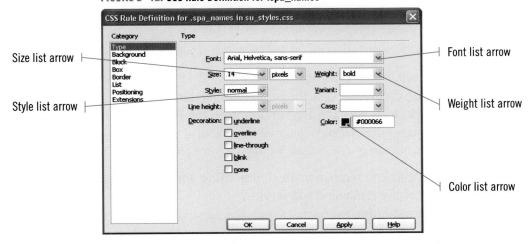

FIGURE D-13: The Striped Umbrella site with the su_styles.css file listed

su_styles.css style sheet file

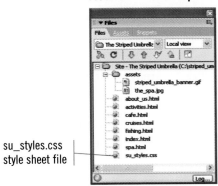

FIGURE D-14: Code view showing link to style sheet file

Head section

HTML code for su_styles.css

Click the plus sign next to su_styles.css file to see the styles saved in the file

spa_names style

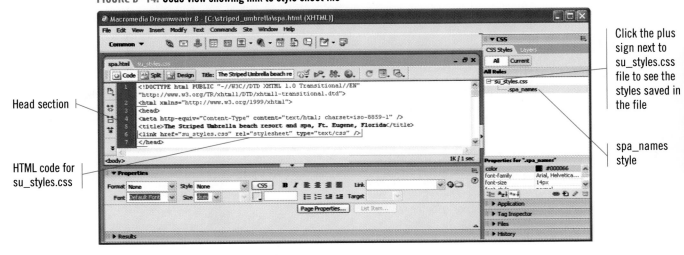

Dreamweaver 8

Applying and Editing a Style

After creating a Cascading Style Sheet, it is easy to apply the styles in it to Web page elements. If, after applying a style, the results are not satisfactory, you can edit the style to change the formatting of all items to which that style applies. To apply a CSS Style, you select the text or page element to which you want to apply the style, remove any manual formatting, and then select the CSS Style from the Property inspector. You are ready to apply the spa_names style to each item in the list of spa services, to emphasize them and to make them easier to read. Then you modify the style and see its effect on the items.

STEPS

1. **Click the** Show Design View button [🖳 Design] **on the Document toolbar to return to Design View**

   You are ready to apply the new CSS Style to the list of bulleted items.

2. **Select** Revitalizing facial, **as shown in Figure D-15, click the** Format list arrow **in the Property inspector, click** None, **click the** Font list arrow, **click** Default Font, **click the** Size list arrow, **then click** None, **click the** Style list arrow **on the Property inspector, then click** spa_names

   The spa_names style is applied to the Revitalizing Facial text. The Font, Size, Color, and Style text boxes all reflect the spa_names style settings. You apply it to the rest of the items in the list.

3. **Repeat Step 2 to remove manual formatting and apply the spa_names style to the names of each of the remaining spa services**

   The spa_names style is now applied to each item name. You decide that the text is too small.

4. **Click the** spa_names style **in the CSS Styles panel, then click the** Edit Style button [📝] **on the CSS Styles panel**

   The CSS Rule Definition for .spa_names in su_styles.css dialog box opens, as shown in Figure D-16. You can use this dialog box to edit a .css file. This is the same dialog box you used to create the original .spa_names style.

5. **Click the** Size list arrow, **click** 16, **then click** OK

   The spa_names style now includes a larger text size, as shown in Figure D-17.

6. **Save your work using the Save All command**

   This saves both the changes to the Web page and the changes to the style sheet.

Clues to Use

CSS Style Sheet settings

You can also use Cascading Style Sheets to format page content other than text. For example, you can use them to format a background, borders, lists, and boxes. A CSS Style consists of two parts: the selector and the declaration. The **selector** is the name or the tag to which the style declarations have been assigned. The **declaration** consists of the property and the value. An example of a property would be font family. An example of a value would be Arial. If you open the file su_styles.css, you will see the coding for the two CSS Styles in the su_styles.css file. See Figure D-18.

FIGURE D-18: Code for su_styles.css file

Code for
.spa_names

Code for
.heading

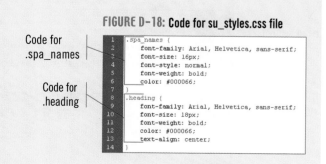

FIGURE D-15: Applying a CSS style to text

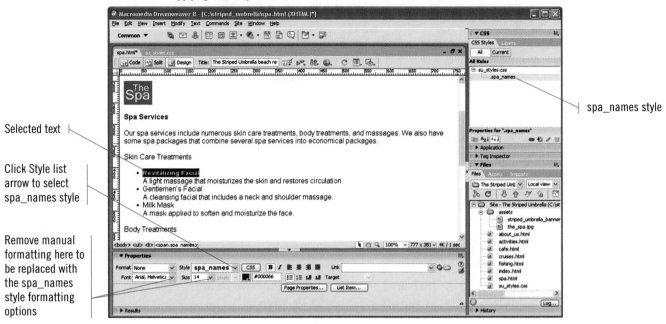

Selected text

Click Style list arrow to select spa_names style

Remove manual formatting here to be replaced with the spa_names style formatting options

spa_names style

FIGURE D-16: CSS Rule Definition for .spa_names in su_styles.css

Change the Size to 16

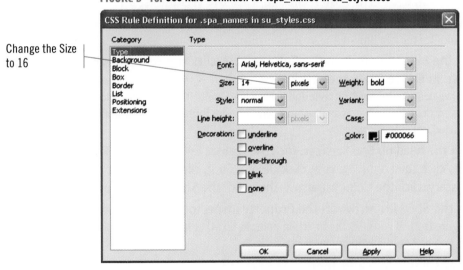

FIGURE D-17: Viewing text with .spa_names style applied to it

Formatted text with the spa_names style

Dreamweaver 8

Adding Styles to a Cascading Style Sheet

Once you have created a Cascading Style Sheet, it is easy to add styles to it. Generally, the more styles you have defined in a Style Sheet, the more time you can save in formatting text. You add styles by using the Add CSS Styles button in the Styles panel. When you have several pages in a Web site, you will probably want to use the same style sheet for each page to ensure that all your elements have a consistent appearance. ▰▰▰▰ You decide to create two new styles, one for the Spa Services heading and one for the service categories, to add to the su_styles.css file.

STEPS

1. **Click the** New CSS Rule button 🔁 **on the CSS Styles Panel**
   The New CSS Rule dialog box opens.

2. **Type** heading **in the Name Text box, verify that the Define In text box is set to the** su_styles.css **file, as shown in Figure D-19, then click** OK
   The CSS Rule Definition for .heading in su_styles.css dialog box opens.

3. **Click the** Font list arrow, **then click** Arial, Helvetica, sans-serif

4. **Click the** Size list arrow, **then click** 18, **click the** Weight list arrow, **then click** bold

5. **Click the** Color list button 🔲, **then select color** #000066
   The color for the heading style is set to navy blue.

6. **Click the** Block **category in the Category list, click the** Text Align list arrow, **click** center, **as shown in Figure D-20, then click** OK
   You have defined the heading style and are ready to apply it to the page headings. Manual or HTML formatting overrides CSS Styles, so you must first remove prior formatting before applying a CSS Style. Two styles are now listed in the Styles panel.

7. **Select the heading** Spa Services, **click the** Format list arrow **in the Property inspector, click** None, **click the** Font list arrow, **click** Default Font, **click the** Size list arrow, **then click** None; **if necessary, click the** Color list arrow, **then click the** Strikethrough button 🔲

TROUBLE
If the style does not apply correctly, you may have to remove the formatting codes in Code View.

8. **Click the** Style list arrow **on the Property inspector, then click** heading
   See Figure D-21. If you click the insertion point in text that has an applied CSS Style, that style appears in the Styles text box on the Property inspector.

9. **Repeat steps 1–5 to add another style called subheading with the Arial, Helvetica, sans-serif font, size 16, normal style, color #000066.**

10. **Apply the subheading style to each category of spa services, then save your work using the File, Save All command**

FIGURE D-19: New CSS Rule dialog box

Name of new style

This style will be added
to the su_styles.css file

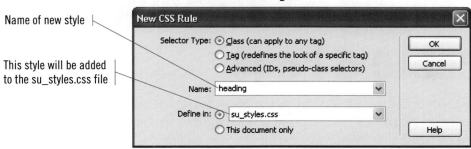

FIGURE D-20: Block category in the CSS Rule Definition

Block Category

Text Align: Center

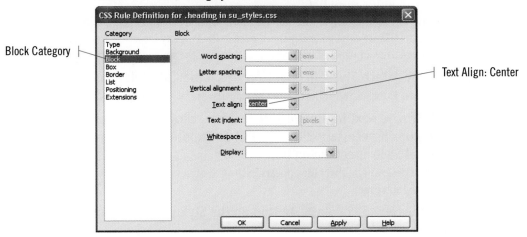

FIGURE D-21: Heading style applied to the Spa Services text

Spa Services
text with heading
style applied

heading style

heading style

Format is removed

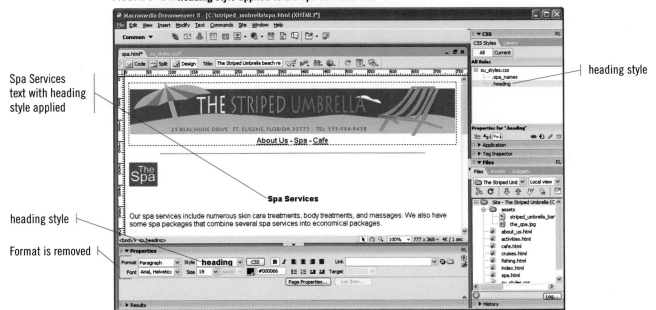

Dreamweaver 8

Attaching a Cascading Style Sheet to a Page

You see the power of Cascading Style Sheets as you quickly format text using styles. You can also edit styles and see the changes automatically applied to text to which you have applied that style. An even greater advantage of using Cascading Style Sheets is that you can attach an existing style sheet to a different page and use its styles there, either within the same Web site or in a different Web site.  You decide to attach the su_styles.css file to the home page and use it to add another style to format the body text on the home page and the spa page.

1. **Open the index.html page**

   You have not created a style sheet for the index page. When you open the index page, you do not see the style sheet in the CSS Styles panel or any styles listed in the Property inspector. You need to attach it to pages other than the original page for which it was created (in this case, the spa page) to use its styles in other locations.

2. **Click the Attach Style Sheet button on the CSS Styles panel**

   The Attach External Style Sheet dialog box opens, as shown in Figure D-22.

3. **Click Browse next to the File/URL text box, click su_styles.css in the Select Style Sheet File dialog box if necessary, click OK (PC) or Choose (Mac), then click OK to close the Attach External Style Sheet dialog box.**

   The su_styles.css style sheet file appears in the CSS Styles panel. It is now attached to the index page, in addition to the spa page.

4. **Click the New CSS Rule button on the Styles panel, type body_text in the Name text box, then click OK**

   The CSS Rule Definition for body_text in the su_styles.css dialog box opens.

5. **Use the settings shown in Figure D-23 to format the new body text style, then click OK**

   The new body_text style appears in the CSS Styles panel as part of the su_styles.css style sheet file.

6. **Select the paragraph of text, click the Font list arrow on the Property inspector, click Default font, click the Size list arrow, then click None to remove the manual formatting from the paragraph**

7. **Click the Style list arrow on the Property inspector, then click body_text to apply the body_text style**

   The Property inspector reflects the settings of the body_text style.

8. **Switch to the spa file by clicking its page tab, clear all prior formatting from the paragraphs of text without an assigned style, then apply the body_text style to them.**

9. **Compare your screen to Figure D-24, then use the File, Save All command to save all open files.**

FIGURE D-22: Attach External Style Sheet dialog box

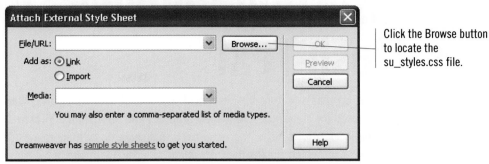

Click the Browse button to locate the su_styles.css file.

FIGURE D-23: CSS Rule Definition for .body_text in su_styles.css

Font = Arial, Helvetica, sans-serif

Size = 14 pixels

Style = normal

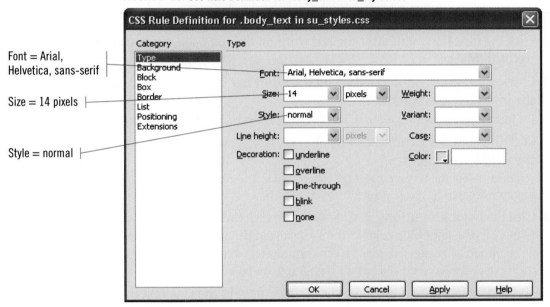

FIGURE D-24: CSS Styles panel with four styles listed

body_text style applied to text

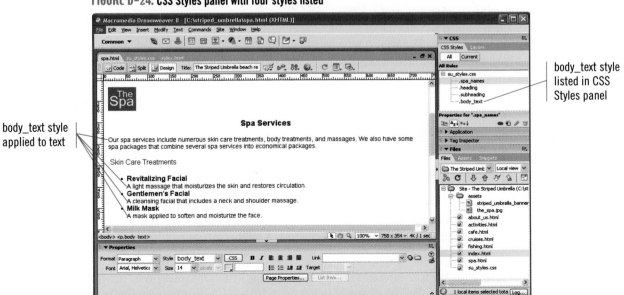

body_text style listed in CSS Styles panel

Dreamweaver 8

UNIT
D

Dreamweaver 8

Inserting Rollovers with Flash Text

The Insert bar has a feature for inserting Flash text onto a Web page. **Macromedia Flash** is a software program used for creating vector-based graphics and animations. **Vector-based graphics** are based on mathematical formulas rather than the pixels that make up bitmap images. They have a smoother look and smaller file size, which means they download quickly. Flash files have the .swf extension, for Shockwave Flash. The **Macromedia Flash Player** is a free program that you must have installed on your computer to view movies created with Macromedia Flash. Most browsers today include the Flash player. You add Flash text to the spa page to provide a link that viewers can click to return to the home page.

STEPS

1. **Click the insertion point after the last word on the spa page, then press [Enter] (Win) or [return] (Mac)**

2. **Change to the Common category on the Insert bar if necessary, click the Media button on the Insert bar, then click Flash Text**

   The Insert Flash Text dialog box opens. This dialog box allows you to set the formatting options for the Flash text.

3. **Click the Font list arrow, click Arial if necessary, leave the Size text box as 30, then click the Bold button** B

   You next choose the text color and the rollover color. The **rollover color** is the color in which the text appears whenever the mouse pointer is "rolled over" it.

TROUBLE

If you choose the wrong color for the text or the rollover text, you can click the Strikethrough button to start over.

4. **Click the Color list button ☐, click #000066, click the Rollover Color list arrow, then click #66CCFF (the light blue color in the sixth row in the second column from the right)**

   When the mouse pointer rolls over the Flash text, the text will change from dark blue to light blue. You are ready to type the Flash text and link the Flash text to the home page.

5. **Type Home in the Text text box, click Browse next to the Link text box, then double-click index.html**

   The index.html file is linked to the Flash text button.

QUICK TIP

Flash text files must be saved in the same folder as the page file in which they are placed.

6. **Click the Target list arrow, click _self, if necessary, type home.swf in the Save As text box, as shown in Figure D-25, then click OK**

   The Flash text file is saved in the root folder for the Web site. The Flash text appears on the page, but the rollover effect works only in a browser window or when you click the Play button in the Assets panel or the Property inspector. Setting the target to _self opens the index page in the same browser window, rather than a new window.

7. **Type Link to home page in the Title text box in the Flash Accessibilities dialog box, as shown in Figure D-26, then click OK**

   This is similar to alternate text for graphics. It is a title that will be read by screen readers to make the Flash text meet accessibility standards.

QUICK TIP

If your Flash text does not display in the browser, you may need to adjust your security settings to allow active content to play on your computer.

8. **Save the file, then preview it in your browser, as shown in Figure D-27**

9. **Scroll to the bottom of the page, roll your mouse pointer over Home, click Home, then close the browser**

   When you point to Home, the text changes from dark blue to light blue. Clicking the Home button opens the home page.

10. **Close your files, then Exit (Win) or Quit (Mac) the Dreamweaver program**

FIGURE D-25: Insert Flash text dialog box

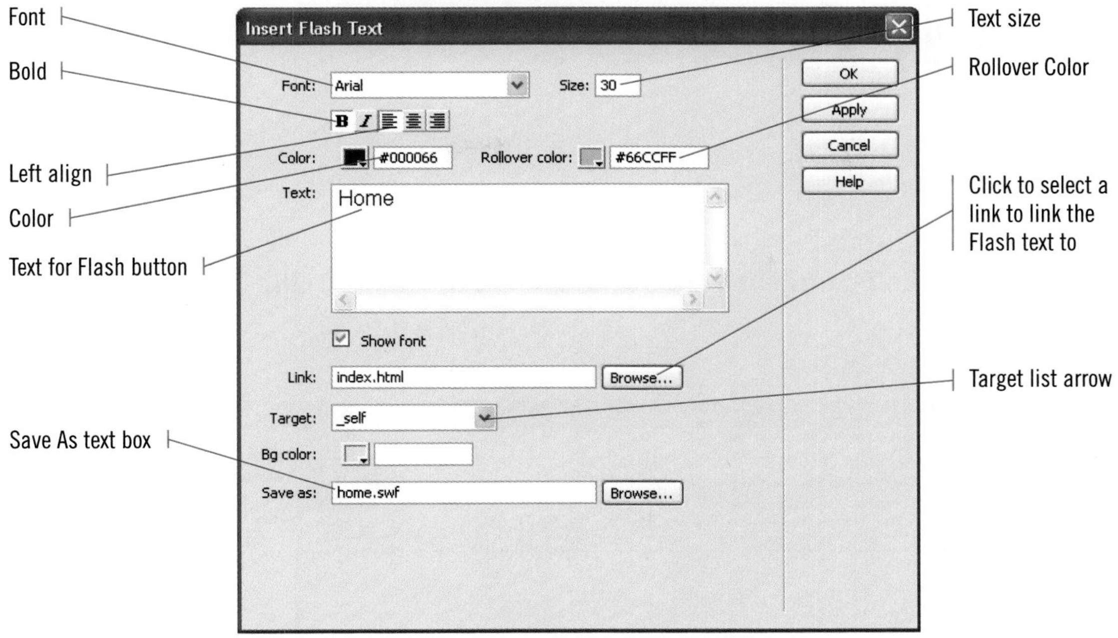

Font

Bold

Left align

Color

Text for Flash button

Save As text box

Text size

Rollover Color

Click to select a link to link the Flash text to

Target list arrow

FIGURE D-26: Flash Accessibility Attributes dialog box

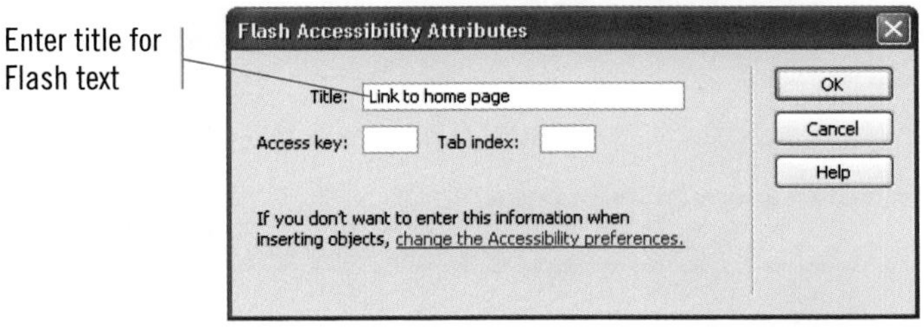

Enter title for Flash text

FIGURE D-27: The finished product

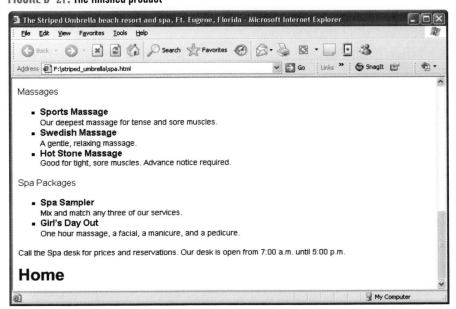

Dreamweaver 8

Practice

▼ CONCEPTS REVIEW

Label each element in the Document window, as shown in Figure D-28.

FIGURE D-28

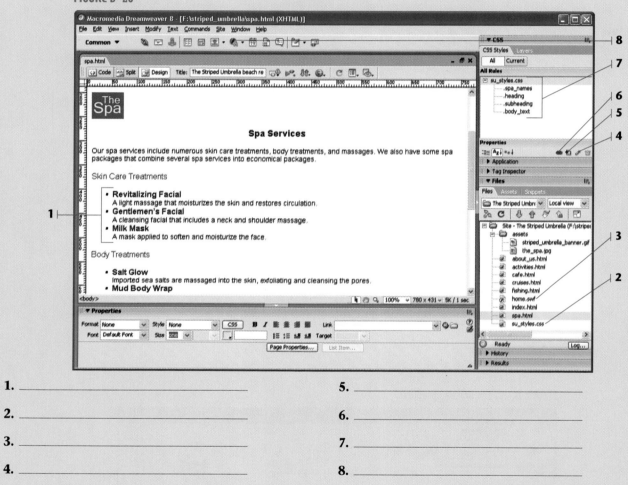

1. _____   5. _____

2. _____   6. _____

3. _____   7. _____

4. _____   8. _____

Match each of the following terms with the statement that best describes its function.

9. Sans-serif font
10. Property inspector
11. Ordered lists
12. Unordered lists
13. CSS Styles
14. Macromedia Flash
15. HTML Styles
16. Vector-based graphic
17. Bitmap graphic
18. Serif font

a. Numbered lists
b. Font without extra strokes at top and bottom
c. Program that creates vector-based animation
d. Used to change the format of HTML tags
e. Based on mathematical formulas
f. Bulleted lists
g. The tool used for formatting text
h. Based on pixels
i. Font with extra strokes at the top and bottom
j. Sets of formatting attributes to format page elements

Select the best answer from the following list of choices.

19. The button used to select color is:
    a.
    b.
    c.
    d.

20. Flash files are saved with the filename extension:
    a. PNG.
    b. JPG.
    c. SWF.
    d. GIF.

21. A CSS Style in the Styles palette name is preceded by a:
    a. Pound sign.
    b. Period.
    c. Dash.
    d. Number.

22. The color of Flash text that appears when you move the mouse pointer over it is called the:
    a. Flash color.
    b. Rollover color.
    c. Button color.
    d. Hyperlink color.

23. The default font is size _____.
    a. 2
    b. 4
    c. 1
    d. 3

▼ SKILLS REVIEW

Important: If you did not create this Web site in Unit B and maintain it in Unit C, you will need to create a root folder for this Web site and define the Web site using files your instructor will provide. See the "Read This Before You Begin" section for more detailed instructions.

1. **Import text.**
   a. Start Dreamweaver.
   b. Open the blooms & bulbs Web site and uncheck the General Preference Use CSS instead of HTML styles. You will leave this unchecked until you begin using Cascading Style Sheets.
   c. Open dwd_2.html from the drive and folder where your Unit D Data Files are stored.
   d. Save the file as **tips.html** in the root folder of your blooms & bulbs Web site, overwriting the existing file, and not updating links.
   e. Verify that the path for the blooms banner is linked to the banner in the assets folder of the blooms & bulbs Web site.
   f. Set the path for the garden_tips.jpg to the assets folder of the blooms & bulbs Web site.
   g. With the insertion point below the garden tips graphic text, change the alignment to Left if necessary, then import (Win) or copy and paste (Mac) the gardening_tips.doc file from the drive and folder where your Unit D Data Files are stored.
   h. Save the changes to the page.

2. Set text properties.

   a. Select the Seasonal Gardening Checklist heading.

   b. Use the Property inspector to center the text.

   c. Format the text with the Heading 4 style.

   d. Apply the color #003366 to the text.

   e. Set the font to Arial, Helvetica, sans-serif.

   f. Save your work.

3. Create an unordered list.

   a. Select the items in the Seasonal Gardening Checklist.

   b. Format the list of items as an unordered list.

   c. Save your work.

4. Change Preferences for Cascading Style Sheets.

   a. Edit the General Preferences to Use CSS instead of HTML tags.

   b. Save your work.

5. Create a Style in a new Cascading Style Sheet.

   a. Open the CSS Styles panel, if necessary.

   b. Create a new style.

   c. Make sure that the Class option button is checked and that the New Style Sheet File option button is checked in the New CSS Rule dialog box.

   d. Name the new style seasons.

   e. Save the style sheet file with the name blooms_styles.css in the blooms folder.

   f. Set the font for the seasons style as Arial, Helvetica, sans-serif.

   g. Set the font size as 12 pixels, the style as normal, and the weight as bold.

   h. Set the font color as #003399.

   i. Save your work. (You should be using the File, Save All command to include saving the blooms_styles.css file.)

6. Apply and edit a Style.

   a. Apply the seasons style to the words Fall, Winter, Spring, and Summer.

   b. Edit the style to increase the text size to 14 pixels.

   c. Save your work. (You should be using the File, Save All command to include saving the blooms_styles.css file.)

7. Add a style to a Cascading Style Sheet.

   a. Remove all formatting from the text Seasonal Gardening Checklist.

   b. Set the format to Paragraph.

   c. Create a new style named headings.

   d. Set the font as Arial, Helvetica, sans-serif.

   e. Set the font size as 16 pixels, the style as normal, set the color as #003366, and the weight as bold.

   f. Use the Block category to set the text alignment to center.

   g. Apply the headings style to the text Seasonal Gardening Checklist.

   h. Add a style named body_text to the style sheet.

   i. Set the font as Arial, Helvetica, sans-serif.

   j. Set the font size as 14 pixels and the style as normal.

   k. Apply the body_text style to the rest of the text on the page.

   l. Save your work. (You should be using the File, Save All command to include saving the blooms_styles.css file.)

8. Attach a Cascading Style Sheet to a page.

   a. Open the index page in the blooms & bulbs Web site.

   b. Attach the blooms_styles.css file to the index page.

   c. Remove the manual formatting from the paragraph and apply the style body_text to it.

   d. Save your work. (You should be using the File, Save All command to include saving the blooms_styles.css file.)

9. Insert Flash text.

  a. Close the index page and return to the tips page, place your insertion point at the end of the last line of text on the page, then press [Enter] (Win) or [return] (Mac) twice.

  b. Using the Insert bar, insert Flash text.

  c. Set the font to Arial, size 18.

  d. Set the font color to #000066, and the rollover color to #0000CC.

  e. Type **Home** in the Text text box.

  f. Use the Browse button to navigate to the blooms root folder and select the index.html page for the link on the Flash text button.

  g. Set the target to _self.

  h. Save the Flash text as **home.swf**.

  i. Type **Link to home page** in the Accessibilities Attributes dialog box.

  j. Click in a blank area to deselect the Flash text, save your work, and compare your display and file list to Figure D-29.

  k. Preview the page in your Web browser and test the Home Flash text.

  l. Close your browser, then Exit (Win) or Quit (Mac) Dreamweaver.

FIGURE D-29

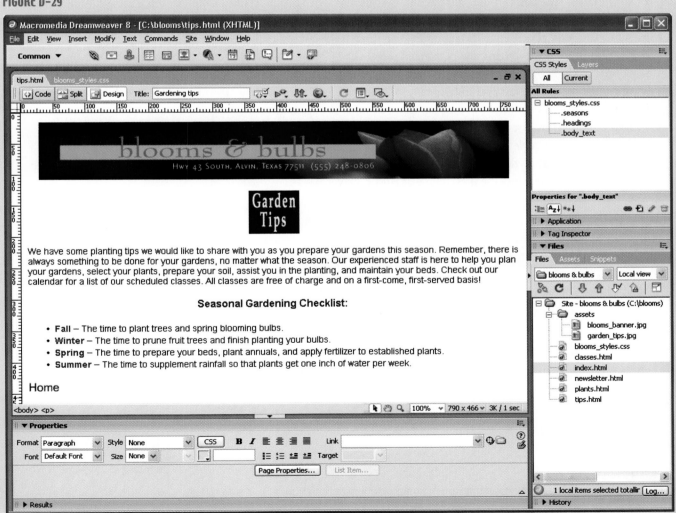

Dreamweaver 8

Important: *If you did not create the following Web sites in Unit B and maintain them in Unit C, you will need to create a root folder for the Web sites in the following exercises and define the Web sites using files your instructor will provide. See the "Read This Before You Begin" section for more detailed instructions.*

▼ INDEPENDENT CHALLENGE 1

You have been hired to create a Web site for a river expedition company named Rapids Transit, located on the Buffalo River in Arkansas. In addition to renting canoes, kayaks, and rafts, they have several types of cabin rentals for overnight stays. River guides are available, if requested, to accompany clients on float trips. The clients range from high school and college students to families to vacationing professionals. The owner's name is Mike Andrew. Mike has asked you to add a page to the Web site that will describe the lodge, cabins, and tents that are available for their customers.

    a. Start Dreamweaver.

    b. Open the Rapids Transit Web site.

    c. Open the file dwd_3.html from the drive and folder where your Unit D Data Files are stored and save it as **lodging.html** in the Rapids Transit Web site, replacing the existing file and not updating links.

    d. Verify that the rapids banner path is set to the assets folder in the Web site. Also verify that your Preferences are set to use CSS instead of HTML styles.

    e. Create an unordered list from the four types of lodging and their rates.

    f. Create a new style named **body_text** and save it in a new style sheet file named rapids_styles.css using the following settings: Arial, Helvetica, sans-serif, normal Style, size 14.

    g. Apply the body_text style to all text on the page except the navigation bar.

    h. Create a style for the lodging choices named **lodging**.

    i. Format the lodging style as Arial, Helvetica, sans-serif; normal Style; bold Weight; size 14 pixels; color #0033CC.

    j. Apply the style to the text The Lodge, Jenny's Cabins, and John's Camp at the beginning of the first three paragraphs.

    k. Add Flash text at the bottom of the page that will link the page to the index page. Format the Flash text as shown in Figure D-30. (Hint: Use #000066 for the color and #0099FF for the rollover color.)

    l. Attach the rapids_styles.css file to the index page, then use it to format the paragraph of text on the page.

    m. Save your work using the Save All command on the File menu, and preview the page in the browser.

    n. Close your browser, close the files, then exit Dreamweaver.

FIGURE D-30

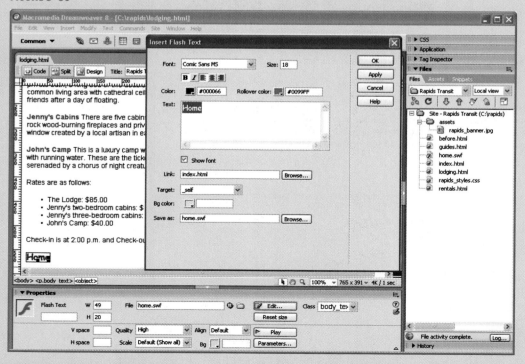

▼ INDEPENDENT CHALLENGE 2

Your company is designing a new Web site for a travel outfitter named TripSmart. TripSmart specializes in travel products and services. In addition to selling travel products, such as luggage and accessories, they sponsor trips and offer travel advice. Their clients range from college students to families to vacationing professionals. You are now ready to work on the newsletter page.

   a. Start Dreamweaver and open the TripSmart Web site.

   b. Open the file dwd_4.html and save it as **newsletter.html** in the TripSmart Web site, replacing the existing file, but not updating links.

   c. Verify that the banner path is set to the assets folder of the Web site.

   d. Create an ordered list from the ten items on the page starting with Expandable clothesline and clothespins.

   e. Create a new style called **body_text** and save it in a new style sheet named **tripsmart_styles.css**.

   f. Choose a font, size, style, color, and weight of your choice for the body_text style.

   g. Apply the body_text style to all the text on the page.

   h. Create another style called **heading** with a font, size, style, color, and weight of your choice and apply it to the Ten Packing Essentials heading.

   i. Type **Travel Tidbits** in the page title text box.

   j. Attach the style sheet to the index page and apply the body_text style to the paragraph of text, then save and close the page.

   k. Save your work, preview the page in the browser, then compare the newsletter page to Figure D-31.

   l. Close your browser, close the file, then exit Dreamweaver.

FIGURE D-31

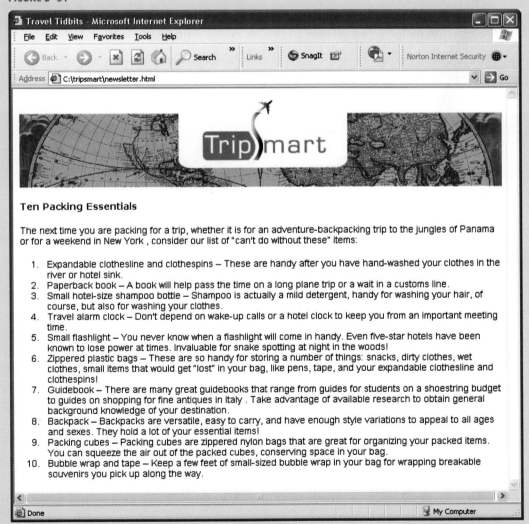

Dreamweaver 8

▼ INDEPENDENT CHALLENGE 3

You are a student in Dr. Michael Wasylewski's Web Design I class. He would like your class to learn more about Cascading Style Sheets. He has directed you to go to the Web site for The World Wide Web Consortium, the origin of the definition of the Cascading Style Sheet specification.

   a. Connect to the Internet and go to The World Wide Web Consortium at www.w3.org, shown in Figure D-32.

   b. Search the Web site for the most current definition of Cascading Style Sheets.

   c. Copy and paste the definition into a document you create in a word processing program.

   d. List four topics that are covered in the Cascading Style Sheets Table of Contents.

   e. Exit the browser.

FIGURE D-32

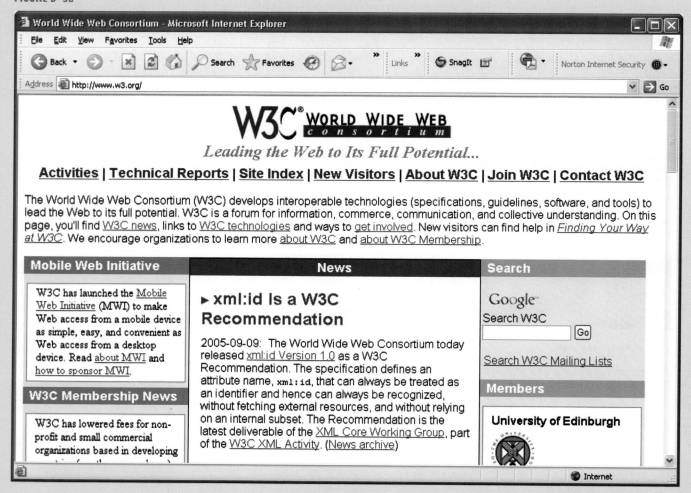

▼ INDEPENDENT CHALLENGE 4

Dr. Chappel is a government historian who is conducting research on the separation of church and state. He has gone to the Library of Congress Web site to look for information he can use. Write your answers to the questions below on paper or in your word processor.

a. Connect to the Internet and go to The Library of Congress Web site at www.loc.gov, shown in Figure D-33.

b. Do you see text that was created and saved as a graphic? If so, on which page or pages? Was the use effective?

c. What font or fonts are used on the pages for the main text? Are the same fonts used consistently on the other pages in the Web site?

d. Do you see an ordered or unordered list on the Web site? If so, how was it used?

e. View the source to see if Cascading Style Sheets were used on any pages in the Web site.

f. Use the search engine of your choice to find another Web site of interest. Compare the use of text on that site with the Library of Congress Web site.

FIGURE D-33

▼ INDEPENDENT CHALLENGE 5

This assignment will continue to build on the personal Web site that you created in Unit B and modified in Unit C. You have created and developed your index page. In this lesson, you will work with one of the other pages in your Web site.

a. Consult your storyboard and decide which page you would like to develop in this lesson.

b. Create content for this page and format the text attractively on the page using settings for font, size, text color, style, and alignment.

c. With CSS styles turned off, format some of the text on the page as either an ordered or unordered list.

d. Turn on the CSS styles preference, then create a CSS Style Sheet with a minimum of two styles and apply each style to selected text on the page.

e. Create Flash text for the page that will link to the index page.

f. Save the file and preview the page in the browser.

After you are satisfied with your work, verify the following:

a. Each completed page has a page title.

b. All links work correctly.

c. The completed pages view well using a screen resolution of 800×600.

d. All graphics are properly set showing a path to the assets folder of the Web site.

e. A cascading style sheet is used to format text.

Your company has been selected to design a Web site for a bookstore named Emma's Book Bag, a small independent bookstore in rural Virginia. Open your Emma's Book Bag Web site. Open the file dwd_5.html and save it as **books.html** in the Emma's Book Bag Web site, replacing the original file. Format the page using styles so it looks similar to Figure D-34. If you have not maintained this Web site from the previous unit, then contact your instructor for assistance.

FIGURE D-34

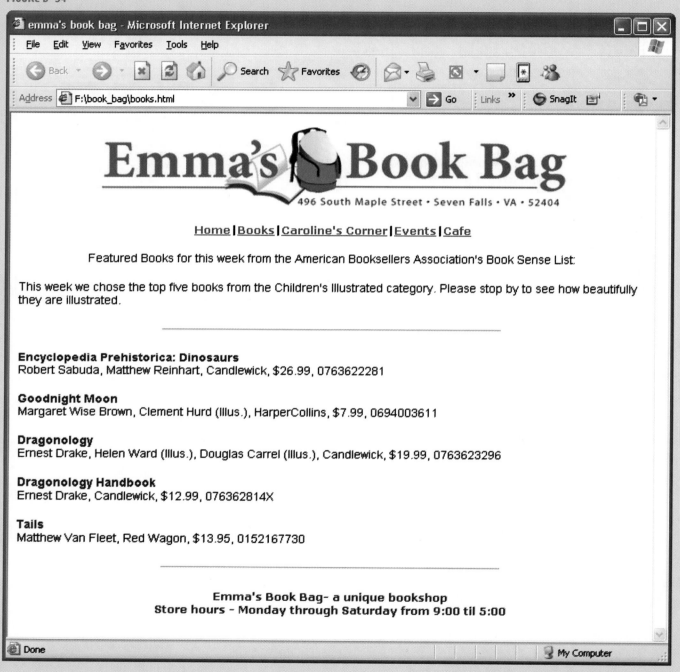

Using and Managing Images

OBJECTIVES

Insert an image
Align an image
Enhance an image
Use alternate text and set Accessibility preferences
View the Assets panel
Use the Assets panel to insert Flash text
Insert a background image
Delete image files from a Web site
Create and find images for a Web site

Images can make Web pages more exciting than pages with just text. You can position images on your Web pages, then resize them, add borders, and customize the amount of space around them. You can also use images as a Web page background. In this unit you learn how to incorporate images into a Web site and how to manage them effectively using the Assets panel. ▄▄▄▄ You have been asked to develop the page that describes the resort. You decide to incorporate several photographs taken around the property to illustrate the text.

Inserting an Image

Images you import into a Web site are automatically added to the Assets panel. The **Assets panel**, located with the other panels on the right side on your screen, lists the assets, such as images and colors, in the Web site. As you add images to a Web page, the page **download time** (the time it takes to transfer the file to a viewer's computer) increases. The Status bar displays the download time for the current Web page. As you may remember from earlier units in this book, the three primary Web image file formats are GIF, JPEG, and PNG. You selected several photos for the about us Web page. As you place each graphic on the page, you check the file size in the Assets panel.

STEPS

TROUBLE

Your download time shown may vary according to the Connection Speed preferences set for your Status bar. To change your settings, click Edit (Win) or Dreamweaver (Mac) on the menu bar, click Preferences, then click Status Bar.

1. **Open The Striped Umbrella Web site, open** dwe_1.html **from the drive and folder where your Unit E Data Files are stored, then save it as** about_us.html **in the striped_umbrella root folder, overwriting the existing file, and not updating the links**

   As shown in Figure E-1, the Status bar shows that the page will take one second to download at your current connection speed setting.

2. **Click the** Attach Style Sheet button ⬛ **in the CSS Styles panel, attach the** su_styles.css style sheet, **then apply the** body_text **style to all of the paragraph text on the page**

   The style sheet for the Web site is attached to the page, and the body_text style is applied to the paragraph. Using the same style sheet for all pages in a Web site is the fastest way to format text for a consistent look across your site.

TROUBLE

If you see a dialog box requesting alternate text, click Cancel. This dialog box relates to Dreamweaver accessibility features, which you will learn about shortly.

3. **Click to place the insertion point in front of** When **in the first paragraph, click the** Insert bar list arrow, **click** Common, **click the** Images list arrow **in the Insert bar, then click** Image **to open the Select Image Source dialog box, navigate to the Unit E Data Files assets folder, double-click** club_house.jpg, **open the Files panel if necessary, then click the** Refresh button ⬛ **on the Files panel toolbar**

   The picture appears at the beginning of the first paragraph, as shown in Figure E-2. The club house graphic is now located in the Web site assets folder, which is now the location that will be used to load the graphic in the browser when the page is viewed.

TROUBLE

You need to select club_house.jpg to see the thumbnail.

4. **Save the file, click the** Assets panel tab, **click the** Images button ⬛ **on the Assets panel if necessary, then click the** Refresh Site List button ⬛ **at the bottom of the Assets panel**

   After you click the Refresh Site List button, you should see the three images you added to The Striped Umbrella Web site listed: club_house.jpg, striped_umbrella_banner.gif, and the_spa.jpg. The Assets panel, as shown in Figure E-3, is split into two windows. The lower window lists the images in the Web site, and the top window displays a thumbnail of the image selected in the list.

5. **Repeat steps 3 and 4 to insert the** boardwalk.jpg **image at the beginning of the second paragraph**

   The picture appears on the page at the beginning of the second paragraph, and the boardwalk.jpg is added to the list of images in the Asset panel.

6. **Repeat steps 3 and 4 to add the** pool.jpg, sago_palm.jpg, **and** sports_club.jpg **files at the beginning of each of the next paragraphs**

   Your Assets panel should list the seven images shown in Figure E-4.

FIGURE E-1: Status bar displaying page download time

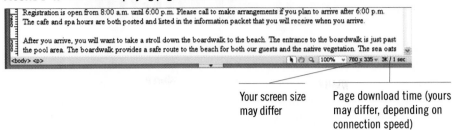

Your screen size may differ

Page download time (yours may differ, depending on connection speed)

FIGURE E-2: About us page with image inserted

Image inserted

Image saved in assets folder

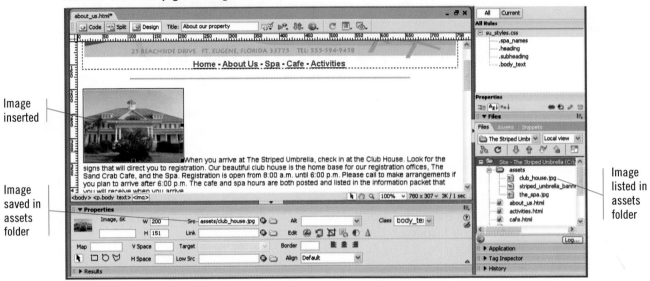

Image listed in assets folder

FIGURE E-3: Assets panel listing for the The Striped Umbrella Web site

The Images icon displays the images in the current Web site

List of graphic images in The Striped Umbrella Web site

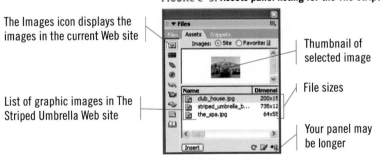

Thumbnail of selected image

File sizes

Your panel may be longer

FIGURE E-4: Assets panel with seven images

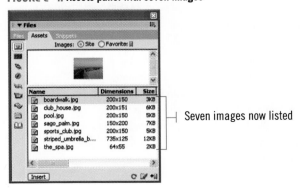

Seven images now listed

Dreamweaver 8

Aligning an Image

Like text, images can be positioned on the page in relation to other page elements in the same line or paragraph. Positioning an image is called **aligning** the image. When an image is selected, the Property inspector displays options for aligning images, instead of for aligning text. You can align an image on the same line as text by using one of the alignment options in the Property inspector. See Table E-1 for a description of each alignment option. You should experiment with the options to find the best alignment for your image. When you first place an image on a page, it has the **Default** alignment, which aligns the bottom of the image with the text **baseline**, the bottom of the line of text, not including descending characters such as "y" or "g". ▓▓▓▓▓ After experimenting with several alignment options, you decide to stagger the alignment of the images on the page, to make the page more visually appealing.

STEPS

1. **Scroll to the top of the page, click the club house image to select it, click the Property inspector expander arrow ▽ to expand it if necessary, then click the Align list arrow on the Property inspector**
   The expanded Property inspector displays additional settings, including those for the image map, horizontal and vertical spacing, border size, and additional alignment settings. Notice the ten alignment options in the list, as shown in Figure E-6.

2. **Click Left**
   The club house photo is aligned to the left side of the paragraph. The text is repositioned to align with the top and right of the photo.

3. **Scroll down the page, click the boardwalk image to select it, click the Align list arrow on the Property inspector, then click Right**
   The boardwalk photo is aligned to the right of the paragraph. The text is repositioned to align with the top and left of the photo.

4. **Repeat steps 1 through 3 to align the next three images, alternating the alignment between left and right**
   The photos are all now aligned in staggered positions on the page, as shown in Figure E-7.

5. **Save your work**
   The file is saved with the alignment settings.

6. **Click the Preview/Debug in Browser button 🌐 on the Document toolbar, then click Preview in [your browser name]**
   The about us page appears in the browser window.

7. **Close the browser**
   The about us page reappears in Design View.

Design Matters

Using dynamic images

To make a page even more interesting, you can place images on the page that change frequently, called **dynamic images**. To insert dynamic images, you first must create a **recordset**, or database stored on a server. The recordset will contain the image files. You then insert the images on the page using the Data Sources option, rather than the File System option, in the Select Image Source dialog box, as shown in Figure E-5. You can also use dynamic images to display multiple items with a similar layout. For example, a Web site for a retail store might display images of current sale items in one window on a Web page, one item at a time.

FIGURE E-5: Using the Data sources option

Select this option ⎯⎯

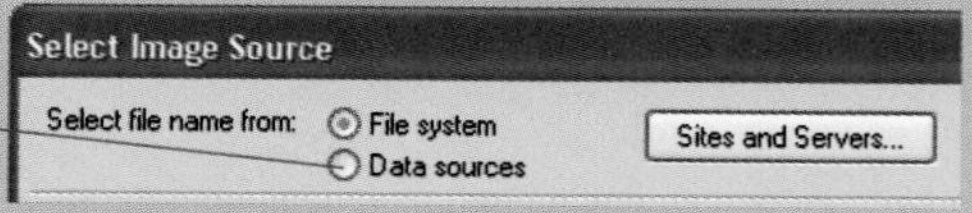

Select Image Source

Select file name from: ⦿ File system   [Sites and Servers...]
                        ◯ Data sources

FIGURE E-6: Alignment options for images

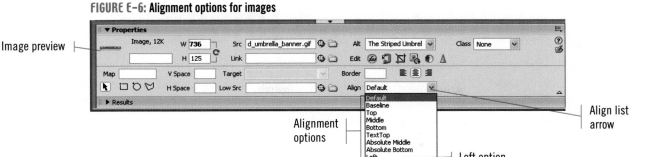

Image preview

Alignment options

Align list arrow

Left option

FIGURE E-7: Aligned images on the about us page

Left-aligned images

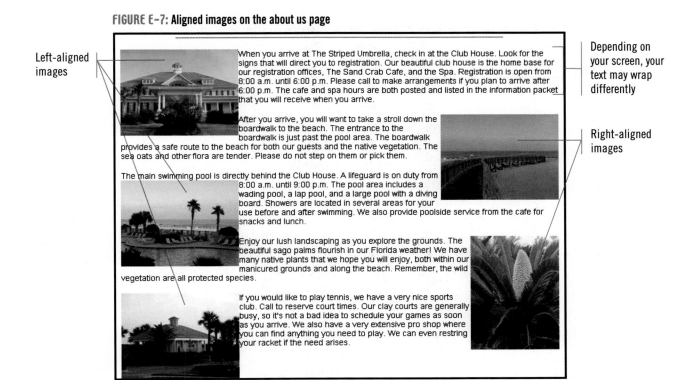

Depending on your screen, your text may wrap differently

Right-aligned images

TABLE E-1: Aligning text to elements

alignment option	description
Default	This is the default setting. The element is aligned with the text baseline. The default can vary by browser.
Baseline	The element is aligned with the baseline of the text.
Top	The element is aligned with the top of the tallest item, whether that item is text or another object.
Middle	The element is aligned with the text baseline or another object at the vertical middle of the image.
Bottom	The bottom of the item is aligned with the bottom of the text.
TextTop	The element is aligned with the top of the tallest character in a line of text.
Absolute Middle	The element is aligned with the absolute middle of the current line.
Absolute Bottom	The element is aligned with the bottom of a text line or another object. This applies to letters that fall below the baseline, such as the letter y.
Left	The element is placed on the left margin with text wrapping to the right.
Right	The element is placed on the right margin with text wrapping to the left.

Enhancing an Image

After you select, place, and align an image on a Web page, you can enhance it to improve its appearance. You'll need to use an image editor, such as Macromedia Fireworks, Adobe Illustrator, or Adobe Photoshop, to change the image itself, for example, to remove scratches from it or significantly resize it. However, you can enhance an image in Dreamweaver using borders, cropping or resizing, adjusting its brightness, and adjusting the horizontal and vertical space around an image. **Borders** are like frames that surround an image to make it stand out on the page. **Cropping** an image removes part of the image, both visually (on the page) and physically (the file size). A cropped image is smaller and takes less time to download. **Horizontal** and **vertical space** refers to blank space above, below, or on the sides of an image that separates the image from the text or other elements on the page. You decide to enhance the images on the about us page by adding borders around the images, and adjusting the horizontal and vertical space around each image.

STEPS

QUICK TIP

You can click the expander arrow ⬜ on the Property inspector again to return it to its original size.

1. **Click the club house image to select it**

2. **Type 1 in the Border text box, then press [Tab] to apply the border size, as shown in Figure E-8**

   A black border with a thickness of 1 pixel appears around the image, replacing the default size of zero.

3. **Repeat Steps 1 and 2 for the other four images**

   All images now have black borders. You notice that the surrounding text wraps closer to the sides of the images than to the bottoms of the images.

4. **Click the club house image to select it, type 10 in the V Space text box on the Property inspector, press [Tab], type 10 in the H Space text box, press [Tab], then deselect the image**

   V Space refers to the space around the top and bottom of the image. H Space refers to the space on either side of the image. You like the way the text is more evenly wrapped around the image, so you decide to apply the same option to the other images.

5. **Repeat Step 4 for the rest of the images**

   The five images reflect the horizontal and vertical space settings.

6. **Click the sago palm image to select it, click the Crop button ⬚ on the Property inspector, then click OK to close the warning message that you are about to permanently alter the image**

   See Figure E-9.

7. **Position the pointer over the bottom-center resizing handle, slowly move the handle up toward the center of the image to remove part of the lower leaves, then double-click the image to crop it**

   The image now appears smaller on the page, and the Property inspector shows that the file size has decreased.

8. **Click Edit on the menu bar, click Undo Crop to restore the image to the original size, then save the file**

   The image is restored to its original size.

Clues to Use

Resizing an image using the Property inspector

When you crop an image, you remove part of it. If you want to resize the whole image rather than crop it, you can select the image, then drag a selection handle toward the center of the image. Dragging a selection handle distorts the image; to resize an image while retaining its original proportions, press and hold [Shift], then drag a corner selection handle. (You can also enlarge an image using these methods.) After you drag an image handle to resize it, the image dimensions in the Property inspector appear in bold and a blue Refresh icon appears to the right of the dimensions. If you click the Refresh icon, the image reverts to its original size.

FIGURE E-8: Changing the border size

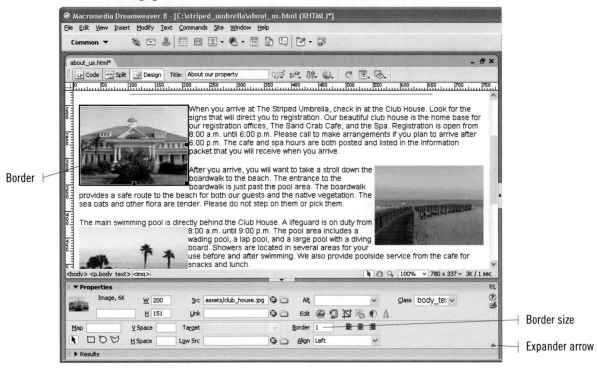

Border

Border size

Expander arrow

FIGURE E-9: Cropping an image

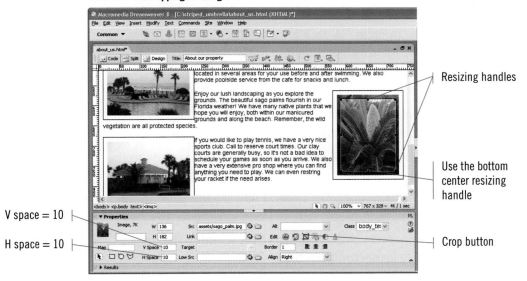

Resizing handles

Use the bottom center resizing handle

Crop button

V space = 10

H space = 10

Design Matters

Resizing graphics using an external editor

Each image on a Web page takes a specific number of seconds to download, depending on the size of the file. Larger files (in kilo-bytes, not width and height) take longer to download than smaller files. You should determine the smallest acceptable size that an image can be for your Web page, and then, if you need to resize the image, use an external image editor, instead of resizing it in Dreamweaver. You can use the H Size (height) and W Size (width) settings on the Property inspector to resize the image on the screen, but these settings do not affect the file size. If you decrease the size of an image using the Property inspector settings, you are not reducing the time it will take the file to download unless you use the crop tool. The ultimate goal is to use graphics that have the smallest file size and the highest quality possible. Many designers feel that an ideal page will download in five to ten seconds.

Using Alternate Text and Setting Accessibility Preferences

One of the easiest ways to make your Web page viewer-friendly and handicapped-accessible is through the use of alternate text. **Alternate text** is descriptive text that can be set to appear in place of an image while the image is downloading or when users place the mouse pointer over an image. Some browsers can be set to display only text and to download images manually. In such instances, alternate text is used in place of graphic images. Alternate text can be read by a **screen reader**, a device used by the visually impaired to convert written text on a computer monitor to spoken words. Using a screen reader and alternate text, visually impaired viewers can have an image described to them in detail. In a new installation, Macromedia has turned all accessibility preferences on by default. In this lesson you will check that your computer has the correct accessibility settings. You add alternate text that describes each of the images on the about us page. You also set the Images option in the Accessibility preferences so Dreamweaver will prompt you to enter alternate text each time you add an image to the Web site.

STEPS

1. **Click the** club house image **to select it, type** The Striped Umbrella Club House **in the Alt text box on the Property inspector, press** [Tab]**, then save the file**

   The alternate text is entered for the image, as shown in Figure E-10.

TROUBLE

If you are using a Macintosh and do not see the alternate text, contact your instructor or technical support person. If you are using a Windows computer with Mozilla Firefox, you may not see the alternate text.

2. **Preview the page in your browser, then place your pointer over the club house image**

   When the pointer is over the image, a small text box containing the alternate text appears on the screen, as shown in Figure E-11.

3. **Close your browser window**

4. **Click the** boardwalk image **to select it, type** Boardwalk to the beach **in the Alt text box on the Property inspector, then press** [Tab]

5. **Click the** pool image **to select it, type** The pool area **in the Alt text box on the Property inspector, then press** [Tab]

6. **Click the** palm image **to select it, enter** Sago palm **in the Alt text box on the Property inspector, then press** [Tab]

7. **Click the** sports club image **to select it, enter** The Sports Club **in the Alt text box on the Property inspector, then press** [Tab]

   You decide to set Dreamweaver to prompt you to enter alternate text each time you add a new image.

QUICK TIP

Once you set the Accessibility preferences, they will be in effect for all of your Web sites. You will not have to set each Web site separately.

8. **Click** Edit **(Win) or** Dreamweaver **(Mac) on the menu bar, click** Preferences**, click** Accessibility **in the Category list, if necessary, click the** the four options shown **to select them if necessary, as shown in Figure E-12, then click** OK

   Dreamweaver will now prompt you to enter alternate text for new objects you add to the Web site, including images.

9. **Save your work, preview the page in your browser, then place your pointer over each image on the page**

   Each image now displays alternate text.

10. **Close your browser to return to the Dreamweaver window**

FIGURE E-10: Alternate text setting on the Property inspector

Alternate text for the club house image

FIGURE E-11: Alternate text appears in browser

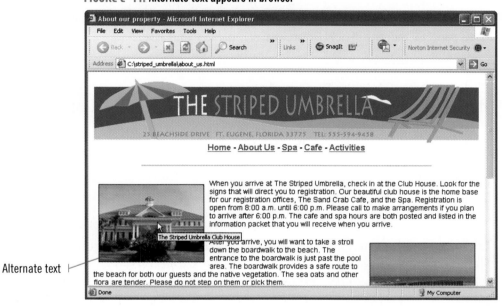

Alternate text

FIGURE E-12: Accessibility preferences

Accessibility preferences

Show attributes when inserting: options

Macintosh users may not see these options

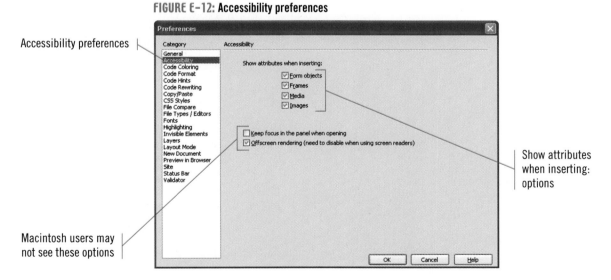

Clues to Use

Alternate text limits

The alternate text for a graphic stays on the screen for a limited time, so you should consider the text length. A general rule is to avoid using over 50 characters. If you need to enter more than 50 characters, create a separate file with the information you want to convey. Enter the location of the file in the Long Description text box that appears under the Alternate Text text box in the Image Tag Accessibility Attributes dialog box. This information will appear in the browser when the viewer clicks the image.

Viewing the Assets Panel

The **Assets panel** contains all of the assets in a Web site. There are nine categories of assets, represented by buttons, on the Assets panel. These include Images, Colors, URLs, Flash, Shockwave, Movies, Scripts, Templates, and Library. There are two options for viewing the assets in each category. You can click the Site option button to view all the assets in a Web site, or the Favorites option button to view those assets that you have designated as **favorites**—assets that you expect to use repeatedly while you work on the site. So far, your Web site includes several images, several colors, and a Flash text button. You explore the Assets panel to understand how Dreamweaver organizes your assets.

STEPS

1. **Click the Assets tab in the Files panel group, if necessary**

   The first time you use the Assets panel, it displays the Images category; after that, it displays the category that was selected in the last Dreamweaver working session.

2. **Click each category button on the Assets panel**

   Each time you click a button, the contents in the Assets panel window change. Figure E-13 displays the Images category, and lists the seven images in the Web site.

3. **Click the Colors button ▦ to display the Colors category**

   There are two colors listed in the Web site, and both colors are Websafe, as shown in Figure E-14.

4. **Click the Flash button ◉ on the Assets panel, then click the Play button ▶ to see the Flash text preview**

   When you place your mouse over the Flash text, you see it change to the rollover color.

5. **Click the Stop button ▦**

FIGURE E-13: Assets panel

Images button selected

Assets categories

Favorites option

Site option

Click the column headings to sort the items by name, size, or type

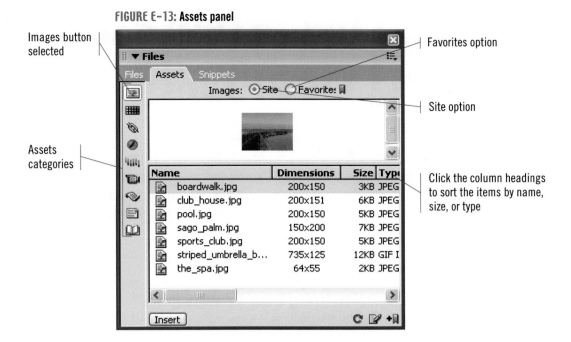

FIGURE E-14: Assets panel showing Colors category

Colors button

All colors are Websafe

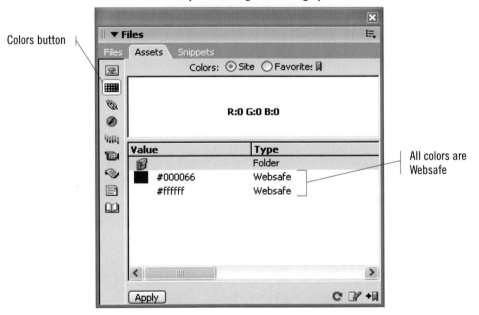

Clues to Use

Using Favorites in the Assets panel

For assets such as images that you plan to use repeatedly, you can place them in the Favorites list in the Assets panel to make them readily available. There are a few ways to add favorites to the Favorites list in the Assets panel. You can right-click (Win) or [ctrl]-click (Mac) an image on a Web page, then click Add to Image Favorites. When you click the Favorites option in the Assets panel, you will see the image in the list. You can also right-click (Win) or [ctrl]-click (Mac) the name of an image in the Site list (when the Site option is selected in the Assets panel), then click

Add to Favorites. In addition, you can create a folder for storing assets by category by clicking the Favorites option in the Assets panel, clicking the Files panel group list arrow, then clicking New Favorites Folder. You can give the folder a descriptive name, then drag assets in the Favorites list on top of the folder to place them in the folder. You can create nicknames for assets in the Favorites list by right-clicking (Win) or [ctrl]-clicking (Mac) the asset in the Favorites list, then clicking Edit Nickname.

Using the Assets Panel to Insert Flash Text

So far you have used the Insert bar to insert new elements, such as images and horizontal rules, onto Web pages. You can also insert elements that are currently in your Assets panel onto Web pages. This feature is especially handy with the Colors category. You can highlight text, and then apply a color in the Colors list of the Assets panel so you can be sure you are using colors consistently. You can insert page elements easily by clicking the asset, then clicking the Insert button or dragging the asset's icon onto the Web page. ▰▰▰▰ You would like to place the home page button you created with Flash onto the about us page. You use the Assets panel to insert the Flash text at the bottom of the about us page.

STEP

1. **With the about us page open in Design View, place the insertion point at the bottom of the page, then press [Enter] (Win) or [return] (Mac)**

   You have positioned the insertion point below the last line of text on the page.

2. **Click the Assets tab, if necessary, then click the Flash button ⊘ to view the Flash category in the Assets panel**

   The home.swf file (which is a Flash movie) appears in the list of Flash assets, as shown in Figure E-15. This is the home page button you created for the spa page. Before you insert it at the bottom of the about us page, you play the movie in the Assets panel preview window.

3. **Click the Play button ▶ in the upper-right corner of the Assets preview window, shown in Figure E-15, then move the pointer over the word Home**

   The Play button changes to a Stop button. As the pointer moves over the text, the text turns light blue.

4. **Click the Stop button ▦ to stop the movie**

   The movie stops, and the Stop button becomes the Play button again.

5. **Click home.swf in the Assets panel to select it if necessary, click Insert at the bottom of the Assets panel, then type Flash text link to home page in the Object Tag Accessibility Attributes dialog box, then click OK**

   The icon for the Flash text is inserted at the bottom of the page. You decide to preview the page in your browser to test the Flash text.

6. **Save your work, then preview the page in your browser**

7. **Scroll to the bottom of the page, then click Home**

   Clicking the Home button displays The Striped Umbrella home page.

8. **Close your browser window**

   You return to the Dreamweaver window and decide to examine the source code for the Flash text.

9. **Click the Show Code View button ⟨⟩ Code, scroll to view the Flash text code, as shown in Figure E-16, click on the page to deselect the code, then examine the code**

   In Code View, the code for the Flash object appears, beginning and ending with object tags. The object tag will automatically install or update the Flash Player in Internet Explorer, and the embed tag will prompt users to install or update the player/plugin in non-object friendly browsers. **Flash Player** is a software extension that is added to a Web browser to display animation, video, or sound. Notice the Coding toolbar to the left of the code. This toolbar is used when you are editing the code and is only displayed in Code View.

10. **Click the Show Design View button 🖥 Design**

FIGURE E-15: Flash category in the Assets panel

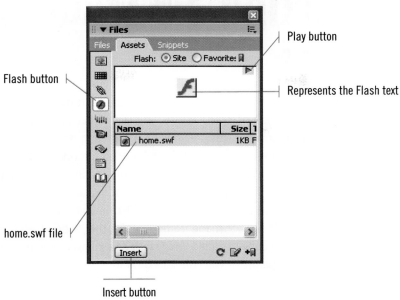

Play button

Flash button

Represents the Flash text

home.swf file

Insert button

FIGURE E-16: Code View for Flash text

Object tags

Coding toolbar

Embed tags

Macromedia
URL for
Flash
download

Inserting a Background Image

Some Web pages have a background image in order to provide depth and visual interest to the page. **Background images** are graphic files used in place of background colors. Background images may create a dramatic effect; however, they may be too distracting on Web pages that have lots of text and other elements. Although some may consider them too plain, standard white backgrounds are usually the best choice for Web pages. If you choose to use a background image on a Web page, it should be small in file size. A **tiled image** is a small graphic that repeats across and down a Web page, appearing as individual squares or rectangles. A **seamless image** is a tiled image that is either blurred at the edges so that it appears to be all one image, or made from a pattern that, when tiled, appears to be one image, such as vertical stripes. You can convert a tiled image into a seamless image by using an image editor to blend the edges. ▰▰▰ You experiment with the background of the about us page by choosing two tiled images: one with a stripe that repeats across the page and one with an umbrella image.

STEPS

1. **Click** Modify **on the menu bar, then click** Page Properties

2. **Click** Browse **next to the Background image text box, click the drive and folder where your Unit E Data Files are stored, double-click the** assets **folder if necessary, double-click** umbrella_back.gif, **then click** OK

   The file is copied to the assets folder for the The Striped Umbrella Web site. Small umbrella images replace the white background on the about us page. Notice that the background is made up of individual umbrellas, as shown in Figure E-17. You realize that the images do not display well against this busy background.

3. **Click** Modify **on the menu bar, click** Page Properties, **click** Browse **next to the Background image text box, click the drive and folder where your Unit E Data Files are stored, double-click the** assets **folder, double-click** stripes_back.gif, **then click** OK

   The file is copied to the assets folder for The Striped Umbrella Web site. The umbrellas have been replaced with multi-colored stripes. Notice that, because of the pattern, it is now harder to tell where one square stops and the other begins, as shown in Figure E-18. The page is still too busy, however.

4. **Click** Modify **on the Document window menu bar, then click** Page Properties

   You can remove a background image from a Web page by removing the background image filename in the Page Properties dialog box.

5. **Highlight the information in the Background image text box, press** [Delete], **then click** OK **to close the Page Properties dialog box**

   Much better! The background returns to white.

6. **Save your work**

FIGURE E-17: About us page with a tiled background

Individual
squares make a
tiled background

FIGURE E-18: About us page with a seamless background

Stripes make a
seamless
background

Deleting Image Files from a Web Site

As you work on a Web site, it is very common to accumulate files that are never used on any page in the site. One way to avoid this is to look at an image on a page first, before you copy it to the root folder. If the file has been copied to the root folder, however, you should delete it or at least move it to another location to ensure that the Assets panel only lists the assets actually used in the Web site. This practice is considered good Web site management. You delete the two background images from the Assets panel since you decided not to use them on the about us page.

STEPS

QUICK TIP

The Refresh button does not appear when the Favorites option is selected.

1. **Display the Assets panel, if necessary; click the Images button on the Assets panel, verify that the Site option is selected, then click the Refresh Site List button to refresh the list of images**

   The two background files are listed in the Images list, even though you have deleted them from the page. You navigate to the location of the images in the Web site folder structure.

2. **Right-click (Win) or [ctrl]-click (Mac) stripes_back.gif in the Assets panel, then click Locate in Site, as shown in Figure E-19**

   The Files panel appears, and the stripes_bak.gif file is highlighted.

3. **Press [Delete] to delete the file, click Yes in the dialog box asking if you really want to delete the file, display the Assets panel, then click on the Assets panel to refresh the list of images**

   The file is no longer listed in the Assets panel because it has been deleted from the Web site.

4. **Right-click (Win) or [ctrl]-click (Mac) umbrella_back.gif in the Assets panel, then click Locate in Site**

   The Site panel appears, and the umbrella_back.gif is highlighted.

5. **Press [Delete] to delete the file, click Yes in the dialog box asking if you really want to delete the file, display the Assets panel, then click to refresh the list of images**

   Because you deleted the file from the Web site, it no longer appears in the site. You have cleaned up the list of images in the Assets panel and in the Web site.

6. **Save your work, then preview your file in your browser.**

   Your about us page is finished for now and should resemble Figure E-20.

7. **Close the page, then Exit (Win) or Quit (Mac) Dreamweaver**

FIGURE E-19: Locate in Site option in Assets panel

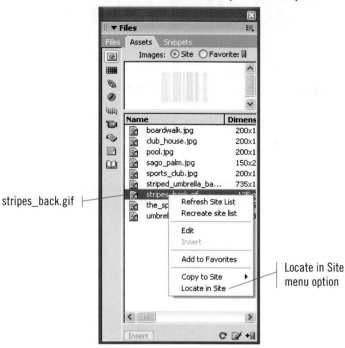

stripes_back.gif

Locate in Site menu option

FIGURE E-20: The finished page

Design Matters

Image file management

It is a good idea to have an additional storage space for your Web site image files, besides the assets folder in the Web site. Keep all original image files outside the Web site and save them once with their original settings. As you edit them, save them using a different name. This way, you will always be able to find the original file before it is resized or edited. You may also have files you don't want to use now but may need later. Store them outside your Web site to keep from cluttering up the assets folder.

Creating and Finding Images for a Web Site

There are several resources for locating high-quality images for a Web site. You can create images "from scratch" using an image-editing or drawing program, such as Macromedia Fireworks, Adobe Illustrator, or Adobe Photoshop. Original photography is another option for colorful, rich images. You can also purchase images as clip art collections. **Clip art collections** are groups of image files collected on CDs and sold with an **index**, or directory of the files. The Internet, of course, is another source for finding images. Table E-2 describes three image types frequently used on Web pages. Now that you understand how to incorporate images into The Striped Umbrella Web site, you explore the advantages and disadvantages of the different ways to accumulate images.

DETAILS

- **Original images**

  Programs such as Macromedia Fireworks, Adobe Illustrator, and Adobe Photoshop, give you the ability to create and modify original artwork. These image editing programs have numerous features for manipulating images. For example, you can adjust the color, brightness, or size of an image. Plus you can set a transparent background for an image. **Transparent backgrounds** have transparent pixels, rather than pixels of another color, resulting in images that blend easily on a Web page background. Figure E-21 shows an example of an image with a colored background, while Figure E-22 has a transparent background.

- **Original photography**

  High-quality photographs can greatly enhance a Web site. Fortunately, digital cameras and scanners have made this venture much easier than in the past. Once you scan a photograph or shoot it with a digital camera, you can further enhance your images using an image editing software program. Photographs taken with digital cameras are very large images. Resize them using an image editing program before placing them on Web pages. Many digital cameras come with software programs that you can use to resize and enhance digital photographs.

- **Clip art collections**

  Clip art collections are available in computer software stores, office supply stores, and over the Internet. When using clip art collections, you should read the terms of the copyright statement in the user's manual. The publisher may have placed limitations on the use of the clip art. Not all clip art is **royalty-free**, that is, free for the purchaser to copy and publish without having to pay a royalty to the company that made the clip art.

- **The Internet**

  There are many Web sites that allow you to copy their graphics, but, again, look carefully for copyright statements regarding the use of the graphics. There are many collections of clip art online that are free for you to use, but some sites ask that you give them credit on your Web site with either a simple statement or a link to their Web site. Images that are labeled as **public domain** are free to use without restrictions. *If you copy and paste images you find while accessing other Web sites and use them for your own purposes, you may be violating copyright laws.*

TABLE E-2: Common graphic file formats for Web page images

format (file extension)	stands for	details
.jpg	Joint Photographic Experts Group	Pixel-based; a Web standard. Can set image quality in dots per inch (dpi), which affects file size. Supports millions of colors. Use for full-color images, such as photographs or those with lifelike artwork.
.png	Portable Network Graphics	Can be compressed for storage and quicker download, without loss of picture quality. Supports variable levels of transparency and control of image brightness on different computers. Used for small graphics, such as bullets and banners, as well as for complex photographic images.
.gif	Graphics Interchange Format	Most popular Web graphics format, but limited to 256 colors. Low color quality and limited detail make them unsuited for printing. Small file size means faster transmission. Use for images with only a few colors, such as cartoons, simple illustrations, icons, buttons, and horizontal rules. This format is used for transparent images.

FIGURE E-21: Graphic with colored background

FIGURE E-22: Graphic with transparent background

Alternating
squares indicate
transparent areas

Practice

▼ CONCEPTS REVIEW

Label each element shown in Figure E-23.

FIGURE E-23

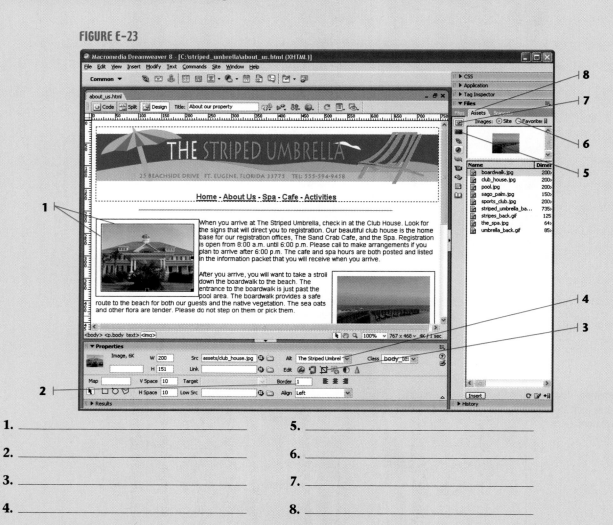

1. _____   5. _____

2. _____   6. _____

3. _____   7. _____

4. _____   8. _____

Match each of the following terms with the statement that best describes its function.

9. **Assets panel**   a. Positioning an image on a page
10. **JPEG**   b. Updates the current list of assets in the Assets panel
11. **Aligning an image**   c. Includes only those assets designated as Favorites
12. **Background image**   d. Small graphic that repeats across and down a Web page
13. **Favorites list**   e. Used in place of a background color
14. **Refresh Site List button** f. Describes an image on a Web page
15. **Tiled image**   g. A frame placed around an image
16. **Seamless image**   h. A graphic file format
17. **Alternate text**   i. Small background graphic that is tiled, but appears to be one image
18. **Border**   j. Lists all the assets of the Web site, including favorites

Select the best answer from the list of choices.

19. **The following category is not found on the Assets panel:**
    a. URLs.
    b. Colors.
    c. Tables.
    d. Movies.

20. **When you no longer need files in a Web site, you should:**
    a. Leave them in the Assets panel.
    b. Drag them off the Web page to the Recycle Bin (Win) or the Trash icon (Mac).
    c. Place them in the Site list.
    d. Delete them from the Web site.

21. **Background images:**
    a. Are never appropriate.
    b. Are always appropriate.
    c. Cannot be tiled.
    d. Can be seamless.

22. **Tiled background images generally:**
    a. Appear as one graphic on a Web page.
    b. Appear as many small squares on a Web page.
    c. Appear as many rows across a Web page.
    d. Appear as many columns down a Web page.

▼ SKILLS REVIEW

Important: *If you did not create this Web site in Unit B and maintain it during the preceding units, you will need to create a root folder for this Web site and define the Web site using files your instructor will provide. See the "Read This Before You Begin" section for more detailed instructions.*

1. **Insert an image.**
   a. Start Dreamweaver.
   b. Open the blooms & bulbs Web site.
   c. Open dwe_2.html from the drive and folder where your Unit E Data Files are stored, then save it as **plants.html** in the blooms & bulbs Web site, overwriting the existing plants.html file but not updating the links.
   d. Insert the petunias.jpg file from the assets folder in the drive and folder where your Unit E Data Files are stored, in front of the words Pretty petunias. (Enter alternate text, if prompted, as directed in Step 4a.)
   e. Insert the verbena.jpg file in front of the words Verbena is one. (Enter alternate text, if prompted, as directed in Step 4b.)
   f. Insert the lantana.jpg file in front of the words Dramatic masses. (Enter alternate text, if prompted, as directed in Step 4b.)
   g. Save your work.

2. **Align an image.**
   a. Select petunias.jpg and use the Property inspector to left-align the image.
   b. Right-align the verbena.jpg and left-align the lantana.jpg images.
   c. Save your work.

3. **Enhance an image.**
   a. Select petunias.jpg and apply a 2-point border to it.
   b. Add a 2-point border to the verbena.jpg and lantana.jpg images.
   c. Add horizontal spacing of 20 pixels around each image.
   d. Save your work.

4. Use alternate text.

   a. If you did not add alternate text in Step 1 above, select petunias.jpg, then use the Property inspector to enter **Petunias** as alternate text.

   b. If necessary, add the alternate text **Verbena** for verbena.jpg, and **Lantana** for lantana.jpg.

   c. If necessary, edit the Web site preferences to set the Accessibility prompt for graphics.

   d. Save your work.

5. View the Assets panel.

   a. Open the Assets panel, if necessary.

   b. View the Images list to verify that there are five images in the list. Refresh the Site list, if necessary.

   c. View the Colors list to verify that there are four Websafe colors.

   d. View the Flash list to verify that there is one Flash file.

6. Use the Assets panel to insert Flash text.

   a. Place a paragraph break after the last sentence on the page.

   b. Use the Assets panel to insert home.swf at the insertion point, adding **Link to home page** in the Object Tag Accessibility Attributes dialog box.

   c. Save your work.

   d. View and test the page with the Flash text in your browser, then close the browser window.

   e. View the Flash text code in Code View, then return to Design View.

7. Insert a background image.

   a. Use Page Properties to insert the daisies.jpg file as a background image and refresh the Assets panel. (This file is in the assets folder in the drive and folder where your Unit E Data Files are stored.)

   b. Save the page, then view it in your browser.

   c. Close the browser window.

   d. Remove the daisies.jpg image from the background.

8. Delete graphic files from a Web site.

   a. Delete the daisies.jpg file from the Files panel.

   b. Refresh the Files panel and verify that the daisies.jpg file has been removed from the Web site. (You may have to refresh the Site list first.)

   c. Preview the page in the browser, compare your screen with Figure E-24, and close the browser.

   d. Exit (Win) or Quit (Mac) Dreamweaver. (*Note*: Depending on your screen settings, your text wrapping may differ.)

Important: *If you did not create the following Web sites in Unit B and maintain them during the preceding units, you will need to create a root folder for the Web sites in the following exercises and define the Web sites using files your instructor will provide. See the "Read This Before You Begin" section for more detailed instructions.*

FIGURE E-24

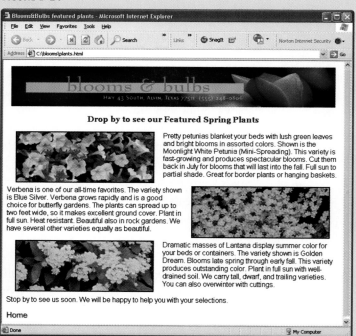

▼ INDEPENDENT CHALLENGE 1

You have been hired to create a Web site for a river expedition company named Rapids Transit, located on the Buffalo River in Arkansas. In addition to renting canoes, kayaks, and rafts, they have lodging for overnight stays. River guides are available, if requested, to accompany clients on float trips. The clients range from high school and college students to families to vacationing professionals. The owner's name is Mike Andrew. Mike has asked you to develop the page that introduces the Rapids Transit guides available for float trips. Refer to Figure E-25 as you work on this page.

a. Start Dreamweaver and open the Rapids Transit Web site.

b. Open dwe_3.html from the drive and folder where your Unit E Data Files are stored and save it in the Rapids Transit Web site as **guides.html**, overwriting the existing guides file but not updating links.

c. Check the path for the Rapids Transit banner and reset the path to the assets folder for the Web site, if necessary.

d. Verify that the Rapids Transit banner has alternate text. If it doesn't, add it.

e. Insert the image buster_tricks.jpg at an appropriate place on the page. (This file is in the assets folder in the drive and folder where your Unit E Data Files are stored.)

f. Create alternate text for the buster_tricks.jpg image, add a border to the image, then left-align it.

g. Crop the image as shown in Figure E-25 and add some horizontal and vertical space around the image.

FIGURE E-25

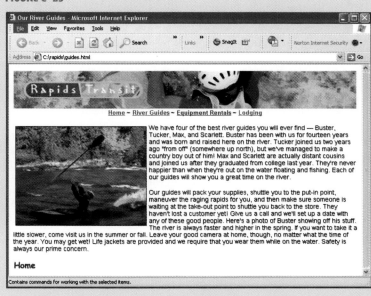

h. Use the Assets panel to insert the Flash text that links to the home page at the bottom of the page, then type **Link to home page** as the title in the Object Tag Accessibilities Attributes dialog box.

i. Format the text on the page appropriately by attaching the rapids_styles.css style sheet and applying the body_text style. Remember to remove any manual formatting first.

j. Save your work, preview the page in the browser, then compare your screen to Figure E-25 (your image location may differ).

k. Close the browser and Exit (Win) or Quit (Mac) Dreamweaver.

▼ INDEPENDENT CHALLENGE 2

Your company is designing a new Web site for TripSmart, a travel outfitter. TripSmart specializes in travel products and services. In addition to selling travel products, such as luggage and accessories, they sponsor trips and offer travel advice. Their clients range from college students to families to vacationing professionals. You are now ready to work on the destinations page. Refer to Figure E-26 as you work through the following steps.

a. Start Dreamweaver and open the TripSmart Web site.

b. Open dwe_4.html from the drive and folder where your Unit E Data Files are stored and save it in the TripSmart Web site as **destinations. html**, overwriting the existing destinations file but not updating links.

c. Check the path for the TripSmart banner and reset the path to the assets folder for the Web site, if necessary.

d. Apply the heading style to the Kenya heading and the body_text style to the rest of the text on the page.

FIGURE E-26

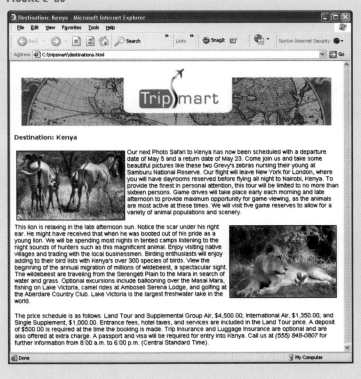

Dreamweaver 8

▼ INDEPENDENT CHALLENGE 2 (CONTINUED)

e. Change the Web site preferences to prompt you to add alternate text as you add new graphics to the Web site, if necessary.

f. Insert the images zebra_mothers.jpg and lion.jpg at the appropriate places on the page, adding alternate text for each image. (These files are in the assets folder in the drive and folder where your Unit E Data Files are stored.)

g. Add a border to each image, then choose an alignment setting for each one.

h. Add the page title **Destination: Kenya**, then add appropriate horizonal and vertical spacing around both graphcs.

i. Save your work, preview the page in the browser, then compare your page to Figure E-26 for one possible design solution.

j. Close the browser and Exit (Win) or Quit (Mac) Dreamweaver.

▼ INDEPENDENT CHALLENGE 3

Off Note is a music store specializing in classical, blues, rock, country, and jazz. Neil Gibson, the store manager, has asked you to find suitable graphics for their country music Web page in their Web site. You decide to look for some royalty-free images on the Internet.

a. Connect to the Internet and go to Alta Vista at www.altavista.com.

b. Click the Images tab.

c. Type **country music** in the Search text box.

d. Check the Photos and Graphics check boxes if they are not already selected. Make sure no other option buttons are checked.

e. Click the Find button to begin the search.

f. Choose one of the pictures found in your search, then click the more info link to see if you can locate copyright information on the page that opens.

g. Summarize the information that you found about the picture, including the copyright information if you were able to find it.

▼ INDEPENDENT CHALLENGE 4

Willie Whitescarver is a golf pro who tours nationally and offers private lessons at a resort golf course. He endorses a line of golf equipment and occasionally provides commentary at the Masters Tournament. He is learning Dreamweaver to be able to create a Web site for his company, Wesley Enterprises. He would like to look at some golf Web sites to get a feel for the types of graphics he may want to use in his Web site. Use a word processor or paper to answer the questions below.

a. Connect to the Internet and go to The English Golf Union at www.englishgolfunion.org as shown in Figure E-27.

b. What color is the background? Would you have selected a different one? Why, or why not?

c. Evaluate the graphics used in the Web site. Do they add interest to the pages, or are they distracting? Was alternate text used for any or all of the images?

d. How long did the home page take to download on your computer? In your opinion, was it too slow?

e. Are there too few graphics, too many, or just enough to add interest?

f. Go to Google at www.google.com or Yahoo! at www.yahoo.com to find another golf Web site.

g. Compare the site you found to The English Golf Union site by answering questions b through e above.

FIGURE E-27

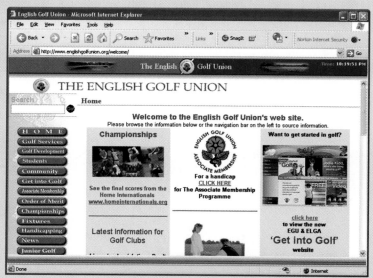

▼ INDEPENDENT CHALLENGE 5

This assignment will continue to build on the personal Web site that you created in Unit B. You have created and developed your index page. You have also added a page with either an ordered or an unordered list, a CSS Style Sheet with a minimum of two styles, and Flash text. In this lesson, you work with one of the other pages in your Web site.

    a. Consult your storyboard and decide which page you would like to develop in this lesson.

    b. Create content for this page and format the text attractively on the page using settings for font, size, text color, style, and alignment.

    c. Set the Accessibility option to prompt you for alternate text for new images added to the Web site, if necessary.

    d. Add at least two images with appropriate alternate text. Resize the images in an image-editing program if they are too large to place on the Web page.

    e. Align and enhance the images to place them attractively on the page.

    f. Document the source for the images and document that they are royalty free. Use your own photographs or drawings if you have difficulty obtaining royalty-free images.

    g. Document the estimated download time for the page and the setting you used to estimate download time.

    h. Save the file and preview the page in the browser.

After you are satisfied with your work, verify the following:

    a. Each completed page has a page title.

    b. All links work correctly.

    c. The completed pages view well using a screen resolution of 800 × 600.

    d. All images are properly set showing a path to the assets folder of the Web site.

    e. All images have alternate text and are royalty-free.

▼ VISUAL WORKSHOP

Your company has been selected to design a Web site for a bookstore named Emma's Book Bag, a small independent bookstore in rural Virginia. Open your Emma's Book Bag Web site. Emma has asked you to create a page that features the extensive children's section in the shop. This is where the weekly story hour and craft time is held. Open dwe_5.html from the drive and folder where your Unit E Data Files are stored. Save dwe_5.html as **corner.html**, in the Emma's Book Bag Web site, then add the reading.jpg image from the Unit E assets folder to create the page shown in Figure E-28. (*Hint*: You can copy the shop hours from the index page. Attach the Web site style sheet and use it to format all text on the page. Don't forget to add the page title shown in the figure.)

FIGURE E-28

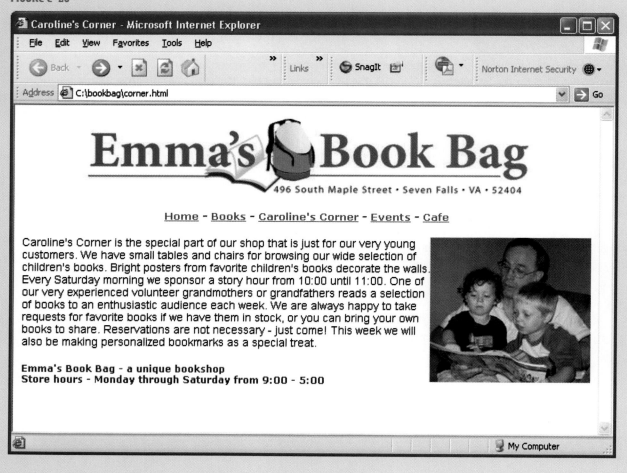

UNIT
F
Dreamweaver 8

Creating Links and Navigation Bars

OBJECTIVES

Understand links and paths
Create an external link
Create an internal link
Insert a named anchor
Create internal links to named anchors
Create a navigation bar with images
Modify a navigation bar
Copy a navigation bar to other pages in a Web site
Create an image map
Manage Web site links

As you learned in Unit C, links are the real strength of a Web site because they give viewers the freedom to open various Web pages as they choose. You created a navigation bar using a group of text links that help viewers navigate between pages of a Web site. In this unit, you will learn how to create links using button images with text and to create another form of link called an image map. An **image map** is a graphic that has clickable areas defined on it that, when clicked, serve as links to take the viewer to another location. You decide to start working on the link structure for The Striped Umbrella Web site. You also add links to the activities page and create a navigation bar and image map.

Understanding Links and Paths

You can use two types of links on Web pages. **Internal links** are links to Web pages within the same Web site, and **external links** are links that connect to pages in other Web sites or to e-mail addresses. Internal and external links both have two important parts that work together. The first part of a link is what the viewer actually sees and clicks, such as a word, an image, or an animated button. When the viewer places the mouse pointer over a link, the pointer's appearance changes to a pointing finger icon. The second part of a link is the **path**, which is the name and physical location of the Web page file that opens when the link is clicked. The information in a path depends on whether a link is internal or external. A link that returns an error message, or a **broken link**, occurs when files are renamed or deleted from a Web site, the filename is misspelled, or the Web site is experiencing technical problems. You spend some time studying the various types of paths used for internal and external links.

DETAILS

- **Absolute paths**

  Absolute paths are used with external links. They reference links on Web pages outside the current Web site, and include **"http"** (hypertext transfer protocol) and the **URL** (Uniform Resource Locator), or address, of the Web page. When necessary, the Web page filename and the folder hierarchy are also part of an absolute path. Figure F-1 shows an example of an absolute path.

- **Relative paths**

  Relative paths are used with internal links. They reference Web pages and graphic files within one Web site and include the filename and the folder hierarchy where the file resides. Figure F-1 also shows an example of a relative path. Relative paths are further classified as root-relative (relative to the root folder) and document-relative (relative to the current document).

  - **Root-relative paths**

    Root-relative paths are referenced from a Web site's root folder. As shown in Figure F-2, a root-relative path begins with a forward slash, which represents the Web site's root folder. This method is used when several Web sites are published to one server, or when a Web site is so large that it uses more than one server.

  - **Document-relative paths**

    Document-relative paths reference the path in relation to the Web page that appears. A document-relative path includes only a filename if the referenced file resides in the same folder as the current Web page. For example, index.html and spa.html both reside in the root folder for The Striped Umbrella. So you would simply type spa.html to link to the spa page from the index page. However, when an image is referenced in the assets folder, since the assets folder is a subfolder of the root folder, you must include the word assets/ (with the slash) in front of the filename, for example, assets/the_spa.jpg. See Figure F-2 for an example of a document-relative path.

  In the exercises in this book, you will use document-relative paths because it is assumed that you will not use more than one server to publish your Web sites. For this reason, it is very important to make sure that the Relative to text box in the Select File dialog box is set to Document, rather than Site Root, when creating links. This option can also be set in the Site Definition dialog box.

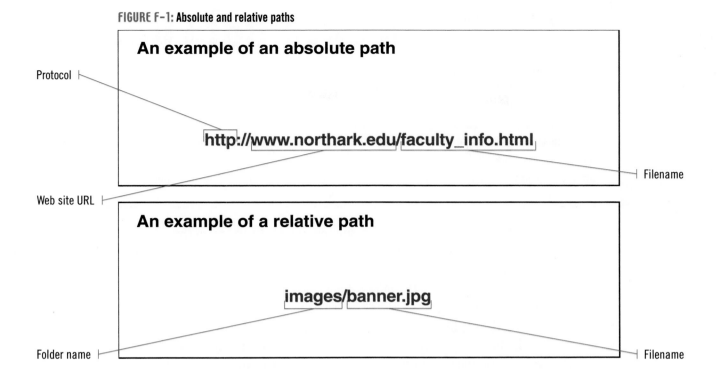

FIGURE F-1: Absolute and relative paths

An example of an absolute path

Protocol

http://www.northark.edu/faculty_info.html

Web site URL

Filename

An example of a relative path

images/banner.jpg

Folder name

Filename

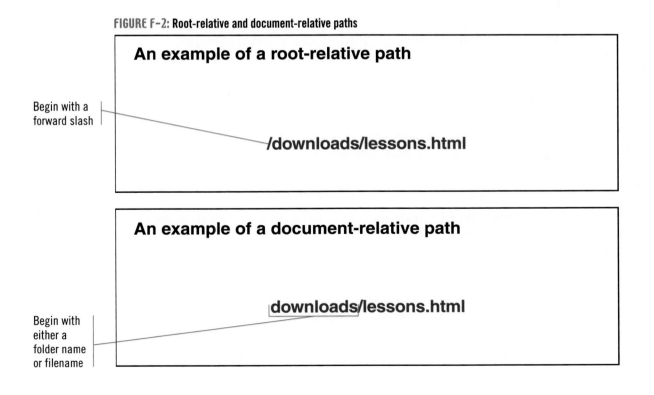

FIGURE F-2: Root-relative and document-relative paths

An example of a root-relative path

Begin with a forward slash

/downloads/lessons.html

An example of a document-relative path

downloads/lessons.html

Begin with either a folder name or filename

Creating an External Link

As you know, external links use absolute paths. Absolute paths must include the complete name and path of the Web address to link to the destination Web page successfully. Because the World Wide Web is a constantly changing environment, you should check external links frequently. Web sites may be up one day and down the next. If a Web site changes server locations or shuts down because of technical difficulties or a power failure, the links to it become broken. An external link can also become broken when an Internet connection is not working properly. Broken links, like misspelled words on a Web page, indicate that the Web site is not being maintained diligently. ▰▰▰▰ You create external links on the activities page.

STEPS

1. **Open the** The Striped Umbrella Web site, **open** dwf_1.html **from the drive and folder where your Unit F Data Files are stored, then save it as** activities.html **in the striped_umbrella root folder, overwriting the existing file but not updating links**

   The new activities page opens in Design View. The activities page lists two Web sites of possible interest to visitors to the resort. There are two broken image placeholders that represent images that must be copied to the Web site.

2. **Select the leftmost broken image, click the** Browse for File icon 🗀 **next to the Src text box on the Property inspector, select the heron_waiting.jpg in the Data Files assets folder to save the graphic in your assets folder, then click to the right of the placeholder**

   The image is copied to the Web site and now appears on the page.

3. **Repeat Step 2 for the second image,** two_dolphins.jpg

   The second image is displayed.

4. **Attach the** su_styles.css **file, then apply the** body_text **style to the paragraphs of text on the page (not to the navigation bar)**

5. **Scroll to the bottom of the page, then select the text** Blue Angels

   You are ready to make the Blue Angels text into an external link that will lead viewers to the Blue Angels Web site.

6. **Click the** Link text box **on the Property inspector, type** http://www.blueangels.navy.mil, **press [Tab], then compare your screen to Figure F-3**

   The link information is complete. You want to make sure the link works correctly.

TROUBLE

If your link does not work correctly, check for errors in the link path you typed. Be sure you type the letters exactly, including upper- and lowercase characters. If you have typed the link correctly and it still doesn't work, the site may be down.

7. **Click** File **on the menu bar, click** Save, **click the** Preview/Debug in Browser button 🌐, **click** Preview in [your browser], **click** Blue Angels **on the Web page, verify that the link works, then close your browser**

   You are ready to add the last external link on the activities page.

8. **Repeat Steps 5 and 6 to create the link for the** USS Alabama **text on the activities Web page:** http://www.ussalabama.com

9. **Save your work, click the** Expand to show local and remote sites button 🖿 **on the Files panel toolbar, click the** Site Map list arrow **on the toolbar, then click** Map and Files

   The activities page appears in the site map.

TROUBLE

If you want to view or hide page titles, click View on the menu bar, point to Site Map Options (Win) or View on the Files panel options menu (Mac) then click Show page titles.

10. **Click the** plus sign **to the left of the activities page icon**

   The links on the activities page appear. There are six links: the four internal links from the navigation bar and the two external links that you created. See Figure F-4.

FIGURE F-3: Creating an external link to the Blue Angels Web site

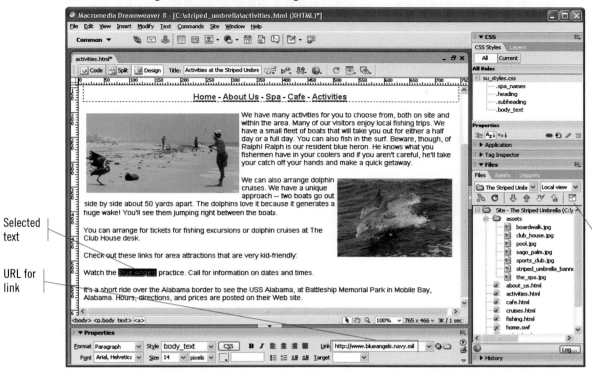

Selected text

URL for link

FIGURE F-4: Site Map displaying external links on the activities page

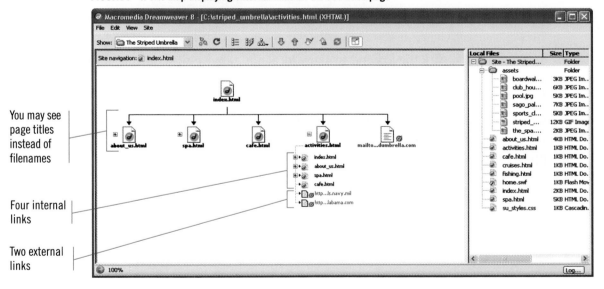

You may see page titles instead of filenames

Four internal links

Two external links

Ensuring error-free URLs

Typing URLs can be very tedious, and it is easy to make mistakes when you type long and complex URLs. URLs that contain mistakes cause broken links. Here is a way to minimize errors: If you know of a Web page that you would like to include as an external link in your Web site, open the Web page, then copy the link information in the Address text box (Internet Explorer) or the Location text box (Netscape Navigator and Communicator). Next, select the link text on your Web page and paste the link information in the Link text box in the Dreamweaver Property inspector. Copying and pasting a URL ensures that the URL is entered correctly.

Dreamweaver 8

Creating an Internal Link

As you know, internal links are used to link Web pages within the same Web site. A Web site usually contains individual pages for each category or major topic covered in the site. Within those pages, viewers may be able to link to other pages that relate to the particular topic. The home page should provide intuitive navigation to each category or major topic in a Web site. A good rule of thumb is to design your Web site so that viewers are never more than three clicks away from the page they are seeking. Refer to your storyboard frequently as you create pages, to help manage your site's navigation structure. ▰▰▰▰▰ You create internal links on the activities page that will link to other pages in the Striped Umbrella Web site.

STEPS

1. **Click the** Collapse to show only local or remote site button 🖻 **in the Site window (Win) or Files panel (Mac)**
   You are ready to create the internal links on the activities page.

2. **Using Figure F-5 as a reference, select** fishing excursions **in the third paragraph**
   The fishing excursions text will become an internal link to the fishing page.

QUICK TIP

You can also select the file to which you want to link in the Files panel and drag it to the Link text box or use the Point to File icon to create an internal link.

3. **Click the** Browse for File icon 📂 **next to the Link text box on the Property inspector, make sure the Relative To text box is set to Document, then double-click** fishing.html **in The Striped Umbrella Web site in the Select File dialog box**
   Figure F-5 shows fishing.html in the Link text box on the Property inspector. When viewers click the fishing excursions link, the fishing page will open.

4. **Select** dolphin cruises **in the same sentence**
   The dolphin cruises text will be an internal link to the cruises page.

5. **Click** 📂 **on the Property inspector, then double-click** cruises.html **in the Select File dialog box**
   The words dolphin cruises are now a link to the cruises page in The Striped Umbrella Web site.

TROUBLE

If you do not see the eight links, click the plus sign to the left of the activities page icon to expand the list. If they still don't appear, click the Refresh icon.

6. **Save your work, click the** Expand to show local and remote sites button 🖻 **on the Files panel, click the** Site Map list arrow, **then click** Map and Files, **if necessary**
   There are now eight links on the activities page: six internal links, and two external links, as shown in Figure F-6.

7. **Click the** Collapse to show only local or remote sites button **to collapse the Files panel**
   You have successfully created internal links for the activities page.

8. **Close the activities page**

Design Matters

Linking to the home page

It is very important to provide your viewers with instant access to the home page. Every page on your Web site should include a link to the home page so a viewer who has become "lost" in your Web site can quickly go back to the starting point without relying on the Back button. Also, and more important, if the page was opened as the result of a search, the Back button will take the viewer away from your Web site.

FIGURE F-5: Creating internal links on the activities page

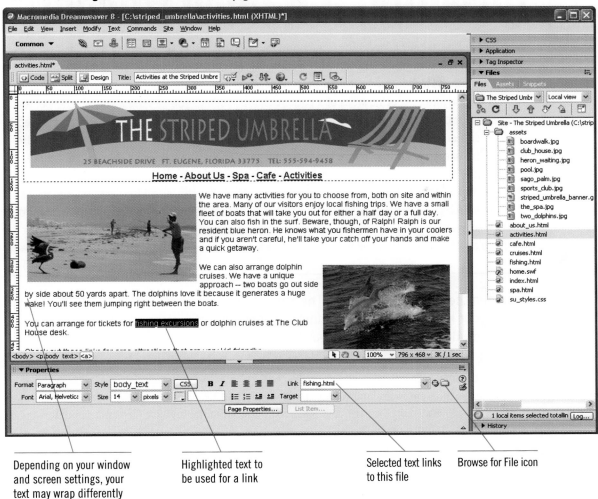

Depending on your window and screen settings, your text may wrap differently

Highlighted text to be used for a link

Selected text links to this file

Browse for File icon

FIGURE F-6: Site Map displaying internal and external links on the activities page

activities page icon

Six internal links, four from the navigation bar and two from text links

Two external links

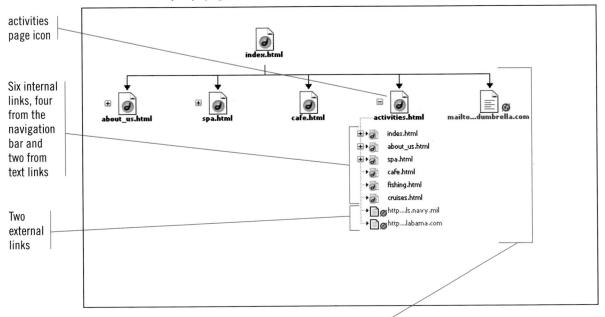

If your screen shows page titles, click View, Site Map options, then Show Page Titles to deselect it

Inserting a Named Anchor

While the links you have learned so far are good for linking to other site pages or to other Web sites, they are not useful to link to another location on the same page. Some Web pages have so much content that viewers must scroll repeatedly to get to the bottom of the page and then back to the top. To make it easier for viewers to navigate to specific areas of a page without scrolling, you can use a combination of internal links and named anchors. **Named anchors** are specific locations on a Web page that are represented by a special icon and are given descriptive names. You then create internal links on the page that the user clicks to jump to the named anchor location. For example, you can insert a named anchor called "top" at the top of a Web page, then create a link at the bottom of the page that, when clicked, will display the anchor location, the top of the Web page, in the browser window. You can also insert named anchors at strategic spots on a Web page, such as paragraph headings. You should create a named anchor before you create a link to it to avoid possible errors.  You insert five named anchors on the spa page: one for the top of the page and four more that will help viewers quickly access the Spa Services headings on the page.

1. **Open the** spa.html **page, click** The Striped Umbrella banner, **then press the** left arrow key **on your keyboard to place the insertion point directly before the banner**
   The insertion point is now at the top of the page. This will be the location for the first named anchor.

2. **Click** View **on the menu bar, point to** Visual Aids, **then click** Invisible Elements **to select it, if necessary**
   Named anchors are an example of Invisible Elements. Invisible Elements must be "on" to reveal where named anchors are located on the page. A check mark to the left of the Invisible Elements menu item indicates that the feature is turned on.

3. **Click the** Insert bar list arrow, **then click** Common, **if necessary**
   The Named Anchor button is in the Common group on the Insert bar.

4. **Click the** Named Anchor button 🔱 **on the Insert bar, type** top **in the Named Anchor text box of the Named Anchor dialog box, as shown in Figure F-7, then click** OK
   The named anchor icon appears before The Striped Umbrella banner. The name used for a named anchor should be short and should reflect its page location.

You should use only lowercase characters for named anchor names; do not use spaces or special characters, or begin an anchor name with a number.

5. **Click to place the insertion point to the left of the** Skin Care Treatments **heading, click** 🔱, **type** skin_care **in the Anchor name text box, then click** OK
   The second named anchor appears before the Skin Care Treatments heading.

6. **Insert named anchors in front of the** Body Treatments, Massages, **and** Spa Packages **headings, using the following names:** body_treatments, massages, **and** packages
   Your screen should resemble Figure F-8. Notice that the Property inspector shows the name of the selected anchor.

7. **Save your work**
   You are now ready to create internal links for the five named anchors.

FIGURE F-7: Named Anchor dialog box

Named Anchor button

Anchor name text box

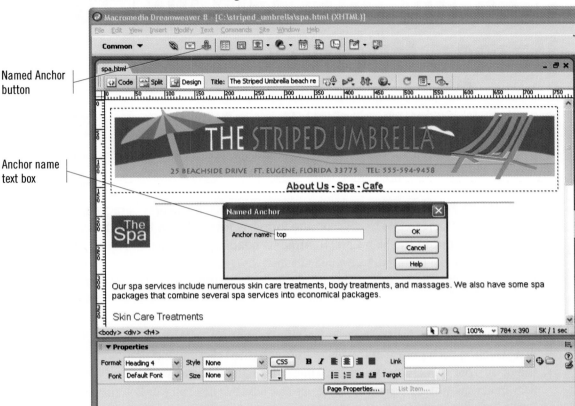

FIGURE F-8: Named anchor icons

Named anchors appear blue when selected, yellow when not selected

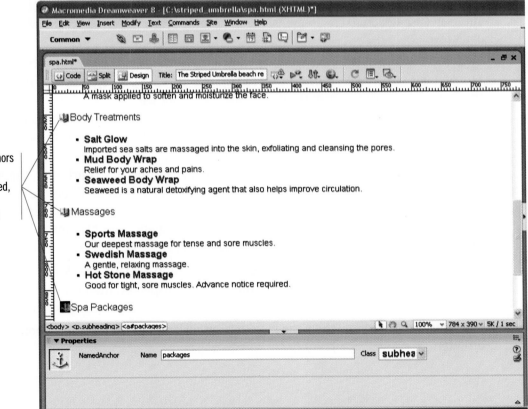

Dreamweaver 8

Creating Internal Links to Named Anchors

Named anchors act as targets for internal links. A **target** is the location on a Web page that the browser will display when a link is clicked. You use the Point to File icon on the Property inspector to connect an internal link to a named anchor. You create internal links and link them to each named anchor on the activities page. You also create a link at the bottom of the page that viewers can use to return to the top of the page.

STEPS

1. **Using Figure F-9 as a guide, select** skin care treatments **in the first paragraph, then click and drag the** Point to File icon ⊕ **on the Property inspector on top of the anchor named** skin_care **in front of the Skin Care Treatments heading, as shown in Figure F-9**

   The words "skin care treatments" are now a link that, when clicked, will display the Skin Care Treatments heading at the top of the browser window because the skin_care named anchor is the target for the Skin Care Treatments link. The name of a named anchor is always preceded by a pound (#) sign in the Link text box on the Property inspector, as shown in Figure F-9.

   > **QUICK TIP**
   > After you select the text you are going to use for a link, you can scroll the text off the screen and still be able to use ⊕ to create a link.

2. **Create internal links for the headings** Body Treatments, Massages, **and** Spa Packages **by first selecting each phrase in the first paragraph, then clicking and dragging** ⊕ **on top of the** body_treatments, massages, **and** packages **named anchors**

   Body treatments, massages, and spa packages are now links that link to the Body Treatments, Massages, and Spa Packages headings. You are ready to create a Flash button called Top at the bottom of the spa page that, when clicked, will bring viewers to the top of the page.

3. **Click at the end of the last item in the Spa Packages section, click the** Media list arrow **in the Common group on the Insert bar, if necessary, then click the** Flash Text 🅐

   The Insert Flash Text dialog box opens. You will now create a different Flash text link that will link to the top of the page.

   > **QUICK TIP**
   > As shown in Figure F-10, spa.html is entered in front of #top in the Link text box.

4. **Type** Top of page **in the Text text box, match the settings in the Insert Flash Text dialog box on your screen with those shown in Figure F-10, click** OK , **type** Link to top of page **in the Flash Accessibility Attributes dialog box, then click** OK

   The Top of page Flash text appears beside the last item in the group. When the Top of page Flash text is clicked, the top of the page will appear in the browser window. You think the Top of page Flash text would also be useful for viewers at the end of each of the other spa services groups.

5. **Click the** Assets tab **in the Files panel group (Win), click the** Flash button **on the Assets panel (Win) or Files panel (Mac), click the** Refresh Site List button 🔄 **on the Assets panel to display top.swf, then drag** top.swf **to the end of each of the other spa services groups, entering** Link to top of page **in the Object Tag Accessiblity Attributes text box**

   You decide to change the alignment of the Top of page button so that it aligns better with the text.

6. **Click the** Top of page button **at the end of each section, expand the Property inspector if necessary, click the** Align list arrow **on the Property inspector, then click** Top

   The new alignment of the Top of page buttons no longer distorts the vertical spacing, as shown in Figure F-11.

7. **Save your work, preview the page in your browser and test each button, then close your browser**

FIGURE F-9: Using the Point to File icon

Selected text

Drag Point to File icon to skin_care named anchor

sign in anchor name

Link text box

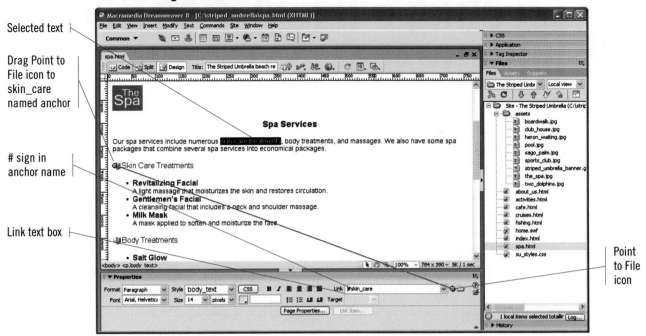

Point to File icon

FIGURE F-10: Insert Flash Text dialog box

Arial font

14-point text

Choose color #66CCFF for the Rollover color

Choose color #000066

Text text box

Target text box

Type top.swf in the save as text box

Type spa.html#top in the Link text box

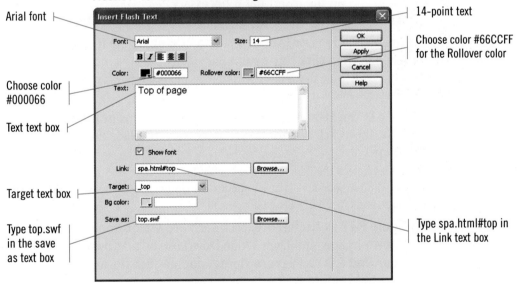

FIGURE F-11: Flash text links to top of page

Flash text linking to top of the page

Top alignment makes paragraph spacing consistent

Existing Flash text linking to the home page

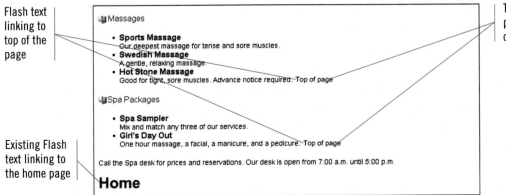

Dreamweaver 8

Creating a Navigation Bar with Images

Recall from Unit C that a **navigation bar** is a set of text or image links that viewers can use to navigate between pages of a Web site. When you create a navigation bar with images rather than text, you use images created in a graphics program. All image links created for a navigation bar must be exactly the same size to be displayed correctly in a browser. The Insert Navigation Bar dialog box refers to each link as an **element**. Each element can have four possible **states**, or appearances, based on the location of the mouse pointer. These states include **Up Image** (when the mouse pointer is not on the element), **Over Image** (when the mouse pointer is over the element), **Down Image** (when you click the element with the mouse pointer), and **Over While Down Image** (when you click the element and continue holding with the mouse pointer). You can create a rollover by using different images to represent each button state. When the mouse rolls over the button or link, the button's appearance changes. ▄▄▄▄ You begin creating a navigation bar that will have five navigation elements: home, about us, cafe, spa, and activities.

1. **Make sure the spa page is open in Design View, click** View **on the menu bar, point to** Visual Aids, **click** Invisible Elements **to uncheck Invisible Elements, then change to the** Common group **on the Insert bar if necessary**

    You want to replace the current navigation bar right below The Striped Umbrella banner.

    QUICK TIP
    You can also insert a navigation bar by clicking Insert on the menu bar, pointing to Image Objects, then clicking Navigation Bar.

2. **Select the navigation bar (About Us - Spa - Cafe), delete it, click the** Images list arrow **on the Insert bar, then click** Navigation Bar

    The Insert Navigation Bar dialog box opens. You use this dialog box to name each element and assign graphics for each element's four states.

3. **Type** home **in the Element name text box, click the** Insert list arrow **at the bottom of the dialog box, then click** Horizontally, **if necessary, to place the navigation bar horizontally on the page**

    The Element Name is the name that you choose for the image that will appear on the navigation bar. The home link will have two appearances: one for the Up Image state, and a different one for the Over Image, Down Image, and Over While Down Image states.

    TROUBLE
    Click Yes when you are asked if you want to replace the existing Down Image files in the Macromedia Dreamweaver dialog box.

4. **Using Figure F-12 as a reference, click each** Browse button **next to the Up Image, Over Image, Down Image, and Over While Down Image text boxes, click the drive and folder where your Unit F Data Files are stored, double-click the** assets **folder, then click the filenames shown in Figure F-12**

    These images were created in Adobe Photoshop. To insert a navigation bar in Dreamweaver, you must create your own images before you can begin. Next, you need to link the home element to The Striped Umbrella home page, which is named index.html.

5. **Enter** Link to home page **as the alternate text, as shown in Figure F-12**

6. **Type** index.html **in the When clicked, Go to URL text box, as shown in Figure F-12, make sure the Use tables option is not checked, click** OK, **then save your work**

    The home element, which is the first element in your navigation bar, appears on the spa page.

    TROUBLE
    You may have to click the plus sign next to the assets folder to display its contents.

7. **Click the** Files panel tab **to display the two image files added to the assets folder**

    The two files, home_down.gif and home_up.gif, are listed in the assets folder, as shown in Figure F-13.

Element name
text box

When clicked,
Go to URL text box

Preload Images
option

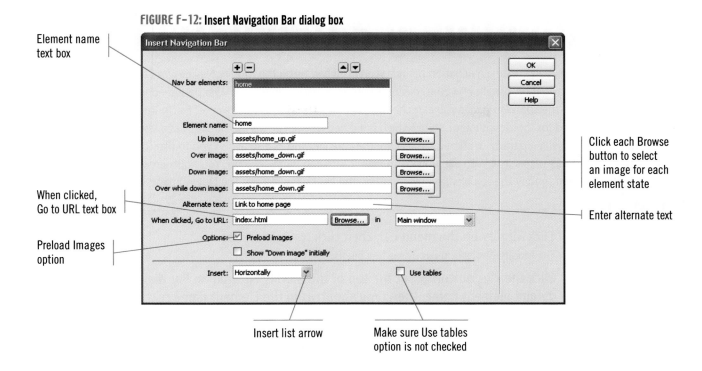

Click each Browse
button to select
an image for each
element state

Enter alternate text

Insert list arrow

Make sure Use tables
option is not checked

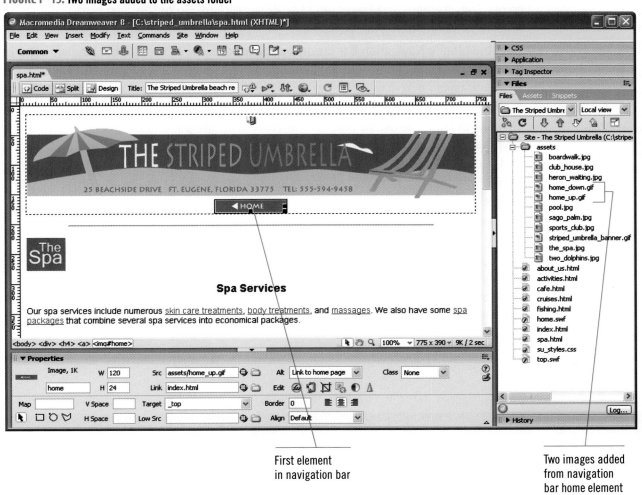

First element
in navigation bar

Two images added
from navigation
bar home element

Dreamweaver 8

Modifying a Navigation Bar

After you create a navigation bar, you can modify it using the Modify Navigation Bar dialog box. Modifying a navigation bar allows you to customize its appearance on various Web pages. For example, if you are editing the spa Web page, you can change the image for the services element's Up Image state to the graphic used for the Down Image state (which is a different color). This method acts as a visual clue to remind viewers which page or section of a Web site they are viewing. It also allows you to place the same navigation bar on all pages in a Web site and customize it for each page. ▰▰▰▰ You finish creating the navigation bar, then modify the spa element by changing the Up Image state to the Down Image state.

STEPS

QUICK TIP
You don't have to select the navigation bar to modify it.

1. **Click Modify on the menu bar, then click Navigation Bar**

   The Modify Navigation Bar dialog box opens.

2. **Click the Plus button ➕ at the top of the Modify Navigation Bar dialog box, select the default element name, then type about_us in the Element name text box, as shown in the About Us section of Figure F-14**

   You click ➕ to add a new navigation element to the navigation bar, and click ➖ to delete a navigation element from the navigation bar. If a dialog box asks if you want to overwrite a selected file, click Yes.

QUICK TIP
If you want to rearrange the order of the elements while the Modify Navigation Bar dialog box is open, select the element you want to move, then click the up ▲ or down ▼ arrow in the Modify Navigation Bar dialog box to move the element backward or forward in the order of elements. If the dialog box is closed, you can drag any of the navigation bar images in Design View to rearrange them.

3. **Using the four sections in Figure F-14 as a guide, finish the about_us element and create three more elements called cafe, spa, and activities by filling in the four image state text boxes, the alternate text boxes, and the When clicked, Go to URL text boxes**

   You are now ready to modify the spa element.

4. **With the Modify Navigation Bar dialog box open, click spa in the Nav bar elements text box, then click the Show "Down image" initially check box to select it, as shown in Figure F-15**

   An asterisk appears next to spa in the Nav Bar Elements text box, indicating that this element will initially appear in the Down Image state.

5. **Click OK to close the dialog box, click anywhere on the page to deselect the text, then save the file**

   The Up Image state of the spa element displays the pink graphic normally used for the Down Image state of the navigation bar elements. This "trick" reminds viewers which page of a Web site they are currently viewing.

6. **Preview the page in your browser**

   If you see spaces between each navigation bar element when you preview the page in your browser, try recreating your navigation bar with the "Use Tables" option selected.

7. **Click each button in the navigation bar, then click the Back button to return to the spa page**

   When you return to the spa page, it loads with the spa element in the Down image state. As you place your mouse over each of the other elements, they go to their down state.

8. **Close the browser**

Design Matters

Creating navigation bars

Using the Dreamweaver Insert Navigation Bar program feature is only one way to create a navigation bar. Other ways include creating image maps, which you will learn about later in this unit; creating simple tables with either text, images, or a combination of the two placed in the table cells. interactive navigation bars using the Macromedia Flash program; or creating simple tables with either text, images, or a combination of the two placed in the table cells.

FIGURE F-14: **Creating four navigation elements**

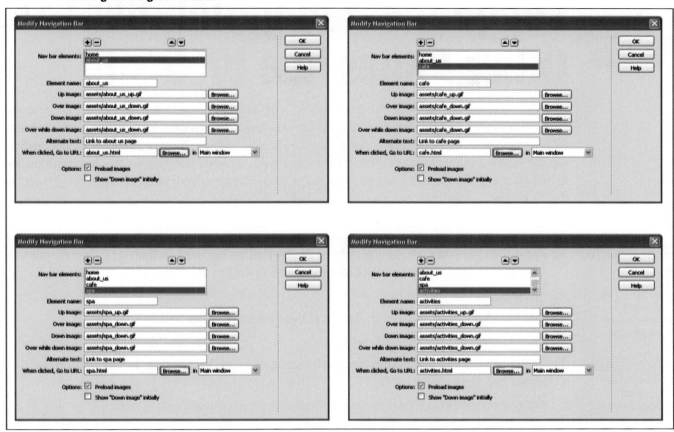

FIGURE F-15: **Modify Navigation Bar dialog box**

Asterisk indicates element is shown in "Down image" initially

Show "Down image" initially selected

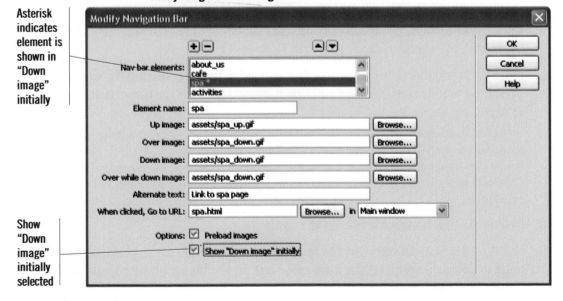

Copying a Navigation Bar to Other Pages in a Web Site

When you create a navigation bar for one page in a Web site, you should copy and paste it on all of the other main pages in the site. This practice provides continuity in the navigation structure and makes it easy for viewers to navigate comfortably to pages in your site. After copying the navigation bar to other pages, you can modify it further to reflect the content of the individual pages. ▰▰▰ You copy the navigation bar to the about us, cafe, spa, and activities pages in The Striped Umbrella Web site, and modify it by changing the navigation bar elements from the Up Image state to the Down Image state for the appropriate pages.

STEPS

QUICK TIP

You can also use the [Shift]-click method to select the navigation bar, but be careful to select only the navigation bar.

1. **Place the insertion point to the right of the navigation bar, click-and-drag the mouse pointer over the navigation bar to select all of it, click Edit on the menu bar, then click Copy**

   The navigation bar can now be pasted on other pages in the Web site.

2. **Double-click about_us.html in the Local View list of the Files panel**

   The about us page opens in Design View.

TROUBLE

If the navigation bar is not centered on the page, center it to match the navigation bar alignment on the spa page.

3. **Select the current navigation bar by the same method used in step 1, click Edit on the menu bar, then click Paste**

   The new navigation bar appears on the page in place of the previous one.

4. **Click Modify on the menu bar, then click Navigation Bar**

   The Modify Navigation Bar dialog box opens. You need to set the Down image state to show initially when the page opens.

5. **Click about_us in the Nav bar elements box, then click the Show "Down image" initially check box, as shown in Figure F-16**

   Now you are ready to modify the spa element so it appears in the Up image state.

6. **Click spa in the Nav bar elements box, click the Show "Down image" initially check box to remove the check mark, as shown in Figure F-17, then click OK**

QUICK TIP

When you work on multiple open pages using a Windows computer, use the filename tabs at the top of the Document toolbar to move quickly between pages.

7. **Paste the navigation bar on the activities and index pages, replacing the existing navigation bars, then modify the Up image and Down image states for the navigation bar elements, as necessary**

   For example, the home element on the navigation bar should show the Down image state initially on the index page, as a visual clue that the viewer is looking at the index page. The spa element on the index page should not have the Down image state initially checked. A copy of the navigation bar remains on the Clipboard, meaning that you can continue pasting it without copying it each time you want to paste it onto a new page.

8. **Delete the first horizontal rule on the index page**

QUICK TIP

If possible, view the page at a high resolution to make sure that the navigation bar does not start at the right side of the banner, rather than under it. If it does, enter a line break to force it under the banner.

9. **Use the File, Save All command to save your work on each page, preview the current page in your browser, test the navigation bar on the home, about us, spa, and activities pages, then close your browser**

   The navigation bar appears on the home, about us, spa, and activities pages of The Striped Umbrella Web site. Feel free to adjust the page elements as necessary so no page appears to "jump" when you link to it. Although the cafe page is not designed yet, you see that the link to the cafe page works correctly.

FIGURE F-16: Changing settings for the about_us element

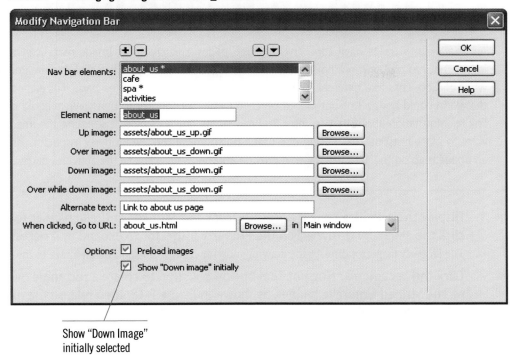

Show "Down Image"
initially selected

FIGURE F-17: Changing settings for the spa element

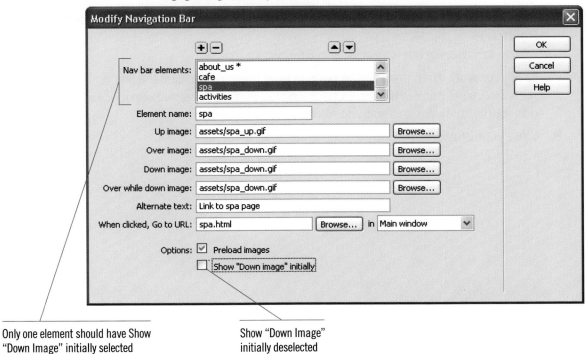

Only one element should have Show
"Down Image" initially selected

Show "Down Image"
initially deselected

Dreamweaver 8

Creating an Image Map

Another way to create navigation links for Web pages is to create an image map. An **image map** is an image that has one or more hotspots placed on top of it. A **hotspot** is a clickable area on an image that, when clicked, links to a different location on the page or to another Web page. For example, a map of the the world could have a hotspot placed on each individual country so that viewers could click a country to link to information about that country. You can create hotspots by first selecting the image on which you want to place hotspots, then using one of the hotspot tools on the Property inspector. ◼◼◼◼◼ You create an image map on the activities page to provide another way to link to the activities page.

STEPS

1. **Display the activities page if necessary, click The Striped Umbrella banner to select it, then click the expander arrow ▾ on the Property inspector to expand it, if necessary**
   The Property inspector displays the drawing tools for creating hotspots on an image in the lower-left corner.

TROUBLE

If you don't see the blue box, click View, point to Visual Aids, then click Image Maps to select it.

2. **Click the Rectangular Hotspot Tool button ▣, drag to create a rectangle over the left side of The Striped Umbrella banner, as shown in Figure F-18, then release the mouse button**
   A shaded blue box appears over the area that you outlined. This blue box is the hotspot.

3. **Drag the Point to File icon ⊕ on the Property inspector to index.html in the Files panel**
   This links the hotspot to the index.html file. When the hotspot is clicked, the index file opens.

4. **Type home in the Map text box on the Property inspector to give the image map a unique name**
   Each image map should have a unique name, especially if a page contains more than one image map.

5. **Click the Target list arrow on the Property inspector, then click _self**
   When the hotspot is clicked, the home page opens in the same window.

6. **Type Link to home page in the Alt text box on the Property inspector, as shown in Figure F-19**
   This gives the viewer a clue to what happens if the hotspot is clicked.

TROUBLE

Macintosh users may not see alternate text.

7. **Save your work, then preview the page in your browser and test the link on the image map**
   The hotspot is not visible in the browser, but if you place the mouse over the hotspot, you will see the pointer change to indicate a link is present, and you will see the alternate text.

8. **Close your browser**

FIGURE F-18: Drawing a rectangular hotspot on The Striped Umbrella banner

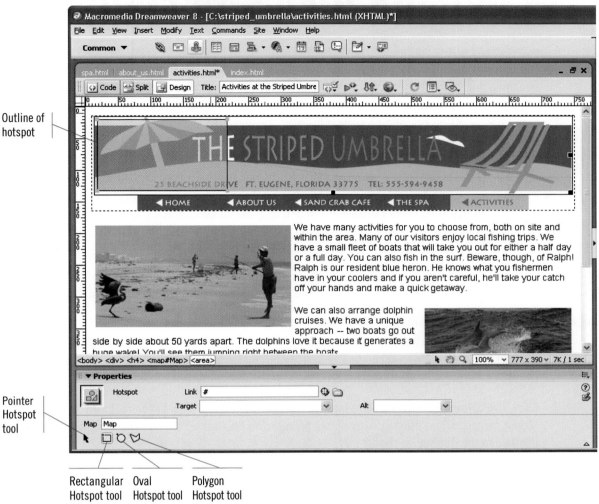

Outline of hotspot

Pointer Hotspot tool

Rectangular Hotspot tool   Oval Hotspot tool   Polygon Hotspot tool

FIGURE F-19: Adding a link, a target, and alternate text to a hotspot

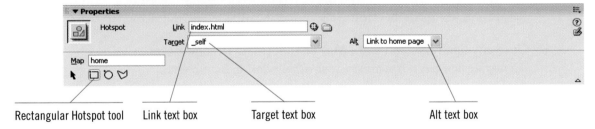

Rectangular Hotspot tool   Link text box   Target text box   Alt text box

Design Matters

Creating and modifying hotspots

The hotspot tools in Dreamweaver make creating image maps a snap. In addition to the Rectangular Hotspot tool, there is an oval tool and a polygon tool. These tools can be used to create any shape hotspot that you need. For instance, on a map of the United States, you can draw an outline around each state with the polygon tool. You can then make each state "clickable." Hotspots can be easily changed and rearranged on the image. Use the Pointer Hotspot tool ▶ to select the hotspot you would like to edit. You can drag one of the hotspot selector handles to change the size or shape of a hotspot. You can also move the hotspot by dragging it to a new position on the image. It is a good idea to limit the number of complex hotspots in an image because the code can become too lengthy for the page to download in a reasonable amount of time. You should also make the hotspot boundaries a little larger than they need to be to cover the area you want to set as a link. This allows viewers a little leeway when they place their mouse over the hotspot by creating a larger target area for them.

Dreamweaver 8

Managing Web Site Links

As your Web site grows, so will the number of links in it. Checking links to make sure they work is a crucial and ongoing task that must be performed regularly. The Check Links Sitewide feature is a helpful tool for managing your links. It checks your entire Web site for the total number of links and for the number of links that are OK, external, or broken, and then displays the information in the Link Checker dialog box. The Link Checker dialog box also provides a list of all the files used in a Web site, including those that are **orphaned files**, files that are not linked to any pages in the Web site. **Broken links** are links that cannot find their destination. When you find broken internal links (linking to files within the Web site), you should carefully check the code entered in the Link text box for errors. You can either use the Browse for File icon in the Link Checker dialog box to correct the link, or type the correction in the Link text box on the Property inspector. You check broken external links (links to files outside the Web site) by testing the links in your browser. Due to the volatility of the Web, it is important to check external links routinely, as Web sites go up, go down, and change addresses.  You check The Striped Umbrella Web site for any broken links or orphaned files.

STEPS

TROUBLE
If you show broken links, click Site, point to Advanced, then click Recreate Site Cache.

1. **Click** Site **on the menu bar, then click** Check Links Sitewide

   The Link Checker panel in the Results panel group opens. By default, the Link Checker panel initially displays any broken internal links found in the Web site. The Striped Umbrella Web site has no broken links, as shown in Figure F-20.

QUICK TIP
If you show orphaned files, click Site, point to Advanced, click Recreate Site Cache, then run the report again.

2. **Click the** Show list arrow **in the Link Checker panel, then click** External Links

   Some external links are listed more than once because the Link Checker displays each external link each time it is used in the Web site. See Figure F-21.

3. **Click the** Show list arrow, **then click** Orphaned Files

   The Link Checker shows no orphaned files for the Web site. See Figure F-22.

TROUBLE
The number of files in your window may differ from those shown in Figure F-23.

4. **Close the Results panel group, click the** Assets tab **on the Files panel group if necessary, then click the** URLs button ⬛ **on the Assets panel to display the list of links in the Web site**

   The Assets panel displays the external links used in the Web site. See Figure F-23.

5. **Close any open files and** Exit **(Win) or** Quit **(Mac)** Dreamweaver

   You now see how easy it is to manage your Web site links in Dreamweaver.

FIGURE F-20: **Link Checker displaying no broken internal links**

Show list arrow

No broken links

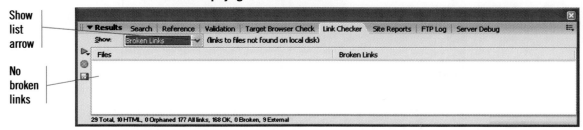

FIGURE F-21: **Link Checker displaying external links**

External links listed

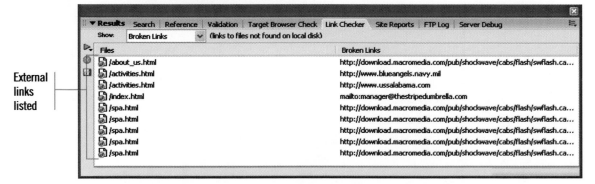

FIGURE F-22: **Link Checker displaying no orphaned files**

No orphaned files listed

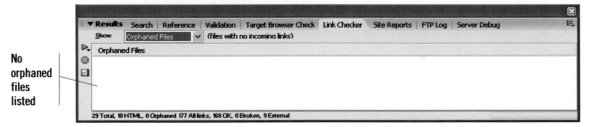

FIGURE F-23 **Assets panel displaying links**

List of Web site links

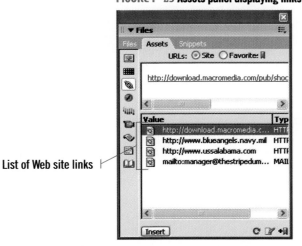

Designing for easy navigation

As you work on the navigation structure for a Web site, you should try to limit the number of links on each page. Too many links may confuse visitors to your Web site. Another consideration is to design links so that viewers can reach the information they seek within three or four clicks. Otherwise viewers may become discouraged or lost in the site. You should also provide visual clues on each page to let viewers know where they are, much like a "You are here" marker on a store directory at the mall.

Dreamweaver 8

Practice

▼ CONCEPTS REVIEW

Label each element in the Dreamweaver window shown in Figure F-24.

FIGURE F-24

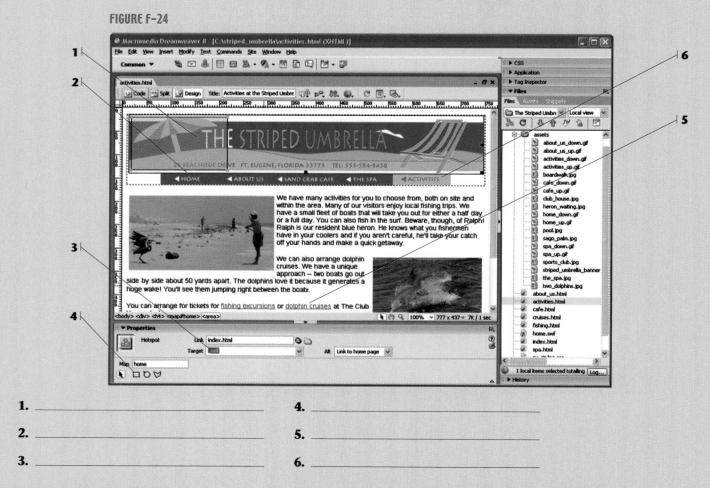

1. _____   4. _____

2. _____   5. _____

3. _____   6. _____

Match each of the following terms with the statement that best describes its function.

7. **Internal links**   a. Links that do not work correctly

8. **External links**   b. A set of text or image links used to navigate between pages of a Web site

9. **Broken links**   c. An image with hotspots on it

10. **Named anchor**   d. Links to pages within the Web site

11. **Navigation bar**   e. Clickable area on an image that serves as a link

12. **Rollover**   f. The effect of an image changing its appearance when the mouse pointer is
                                  positioned over it

13. **Image map**   g. A specific location on a Web page, represented by a special icon, that will fully

14. **Hotspot**   display in the browser window when a user clicks the link tagged to it

15. **Orphaned file**   h. A file that is not linked to any pages in a Web site

                               i. Links to pages outside the Web site

Select the best answer from the following list of choices.

16. **Which type of path begins with a forward slash?**
    a. Document-relative
    c. Absolute
    b. Root-relative
    d. Image-relative

17. **Which icon on the Property inspector do you use to connect an internal link to a named anchor?**
    a. Point to File
    c. Anchor to File
    b. Point to Anchor
    d. Point to Named Anchor

18. **The four possible states of an element in a navigation bar are:**
    a. Up image, Over image, Down image, Under image.
    b. Up image, Over image, Down image, Over While Down image.
    c. Up image, Over image, Down image, Up While Down image.
    d. Up image, Over image, Down image, Up While Under image.

19. **To see all links in a Web site, you click which icon on the Assets panel?**
    a. Links
    c. URLs
    b. Paths
    d. Anchors

20. **Which dialog box shows you a list of orphaned files?**
    a. Orphaned Files
    c. Check Links Sitewide
    b. Link Checker
    d. Assets

▼ SKILLS REVIEW

Important: If you did not create this Web site in Unit B and maintain it during the preceding units, you will need to create a root folder for this Web site and define the Web site using files your instructor will provide. See the "Read This Before You Begin" section for more detailed instructions.

1. **Create an external link.**
    a. Start Dreamweaver and open the blooms & bulbs Web site.
    b. Open dwf_2.html from the drive and folder where your Unit F Data Files are stored, then save it as newsletter.html in the blooms root folder, replacing the existing file and not updating links.
    c. Apply the headings style to the heading "Gardening Matters", the seasons style to the five subheadings on the page, and the body_text style to the rest of the text on the page.
    d. Scroll to the bottom of the page and link the National Gardening Association text to http://www.garden.org.
    e. Link the *Better Homes and Gardens* Gardening Home Page text to http://bhg.com/gardening.
    f. Link the *Southern Living* text to http://www.southernliving.com/southern.
    g. Save the file and preview it in your browser.
    h. Test the links to make sure they all work correctly.

2. **Create an internal link.**
    a. Select the text "gardening tips" in the last sentence in the Gardening Issues paragraph.
    b. Use the Point to File icon to link the text to the tips.html page.
    c. Save the file and test the link in your browser.

3. **Insert a named anchor.**
    a. Show Invisible Elements, if necessary.
    b. Insert a named anchor in front of the Grass subheading, then name it grass.
    c. Insert a named anchor in front of the Plants subheading, then name it plants.
    d. Insert a named anchor in front of the Trees subheading, then name it trees.
    e. Save the file.

4. Create an internal link to a named anchor.

   a. Using the Point to File icon on the Property inspector, create a link from the word grass in the Gardening Issues paragraph to the grass named anchor.

   b. Create a link from the word trees in the Gardening Issues paragraph to the trees named anchor.

   c. Create a link from the word plants in the Gardening Issues paragraph to the plants named anchor.

   d. Save the file and test the links in your browser.

5. Create a navigation bar with images.

   a. Using the Insert bar, create a navigation bar at the top of the newsletter page under the banner.

   b. Type **home** as the first element name, and use the b_home_up.jpg file for the Up Image state and the b_home_down.jpg file for the three remaining states. These files are in the drive and folder where your Unit F Data Files are stored.

   c. Add the alternate text **Link to home page**.

   d. Set the index.html file as the link for the home element.

   e. Create a new element named **plants**, and use the b_plants_up.jpg file for the Up image state and the b_plants_down.jpg file for the remaining three states from your Unit F Data Files folder.

   f. Add the alternate text **Link to plants page**.

   g. Set the plants.html file as the link for the plants element.

   h. Create a new element named **tips**, and use the b_tips_up.jpg file for the Up image state and the b_tips_down.jpg file from your Unit F Data Files folder for the remaining three states.

   i. Add the alternate text **Link to tips page**.

   j. Set the tips.html file as the link for the tips element.

   k. Create a new element named **classes**, and use the b_classess_up.jpg file for the Up image state and the b_classes_down.jpg file from your Unit F Data Files folder for the remaining three states.

   l. Add the alternate text **Link to classes page**.

   m. Set the classes.html file as the link for the classes element.

   n. Create a new element named **newsletter**, and use the b_newsletter_up.jpg file for the Up image state and the b_newsletter_down.jpg file (both from your Unit F Data files folder) for the remaining three states.

   o. Add the alternate text **Link to newsletter page**.

   p. Set the newsletter.html file as the link for the newsletter element, then close the Insert Navigation Bar dialog box.

   q. Save the page and test the links in your browser.

6. Modify a navigation bar.

   a. Modify the navigation bar to Show "Down image" initially for the newsletter element in the Modify Navigation Bar dialog box.

   b. Save the page and test the links in your browser.

7. Copy a navigation bar to other pages in a Web site.

   a. Select and copy the navigation bar.

   b. Open the home page.

   c. Delete the current navigation bar and paste the new navigation bar on the home page under the banner.

   d. Modify the newsletter element on the navigation bar so it does not show the Down image state initially.

   e. Modify the home element on the navigation bar so that it shows the Down image state initially.

FIGURE F-25

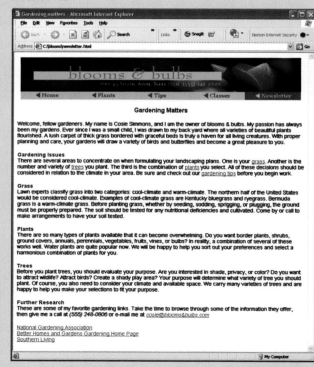

   f. Save the page and test the links in your browser.

   g. Copy the navigation bar to the plants page and the tips page, making the necessary modifications.

8. Create an image map.

   a. On the newsletter page, create a rectangular hotspot over the words "blooms & bulbs" on the the blooms & bulbs banner.

   b. Name the image map **home** and link it to the home page.

   c. Set the target as _top.

   d. Enter the alternate text **Link to home page**.

   e. Save all pages, then preview the newsletter page in the browser, testing all links. Refer to Figure F-25 to check your work.

9. Manage Web site links.

   a. Use the Check Links Sitewide command to view broken links, external links, and orphaned files.

   b. Refresh the Site list in the Files panel if you see broken links or orphaned files. If you see any, locate them and analyze the problem.

   c. View the external links in the Assets panel.

   d. Exit (Win) or Quit (Mac) Dreamweaver.

Important: *If you did not create the following Web sites in Unit B and maintain them during the preceding units, you must create a root folder for the Web sites in the following exercises and define the Web sites using files your instructor will provide. See the "Read This Before You Begin" section for more detailed instructions.*

▼ INDEPENDENT CHALLENGE 1

You have been hired to create a Web site for a river expedition company named Rapids Transit, located on the Buffalo River in Gilbert, Arkansas. In addition to renting canoes, kayaks, and rafts, they have lodging available for overnight stays. River guides are available to accompany clients on float trips. The clients range from high school and college students to families to vacationing professionals. The owner's name is Mike Andrew. Mike asked you to create a new Web site page that lists helpful links for his customers. Refer to Figure F-26 as you work on this page.

FIGURE F-26

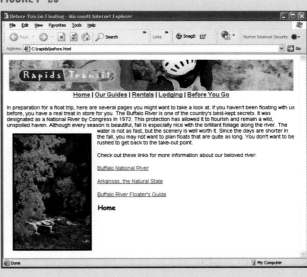

   a. Start Dreamweaver and open the Rapids Transit Web site.

   b. Open dwf_3.html in the drive and folder where your Unit F Data Files are stored, then save it as **before.html**, replacing the existing file and without updating the links. You need to save the buffalo_fall.gif file (the photo) in the assets folder of the Rapids Transit Web site and correct the path for the banner, if necessary.

   c. Create the following links:

Buffalo National River	http://www.nps.gov/buff/
Arkansas, the Natural State	http://www.arkansas.com/
Buffalo River Floater's Guide	http://www.ozarkmtns.com/buffalo/bfg.html

   d. Drag the home.swf button from the Assets panel to the area below the list of links and enter an appropriate title.

   e. Design a navigation bar on the before.html page, using either text or images, and copy it to the guides, index, and lodging pages. The navigation bar should include the following text: Home, Our Guides, Rentals, Lodging, and Before You Go. Link the text to the appropriate files in your Rapids Transit site. If you decide to use images for the navigation bar, you must create your own files. Preview each page to make sure the navigation bar doesn't appear to "jump," or shift position, when you move from page to page.

   f. Attach the style sheet for the Web site and apply a style to all text on the page. You may want to create a new style for the navigation bar.

   g. Save the file and test all links in your browser.

   h. Exit your browser, then close all files and Dreamweaver.

▼ INDEPENDENT CHALLENGE 2

Your company is designing a new Web site for TripSmart, a travel outfitter. TripSmart specializes in travel products and services. In addition to selling travel products, such as luggage and accessories, they sponsor trips and offer travel advice. Their clients range from college students to families to vacationing professionals. You are now ready to work on the services page. The services will include several helpful links for their clients to use in planning trips.

a. Start Dreamweaver and open the TripSmart site.

b. Open the file dwf_4.html from the drive and folder where your Unit F Data Files are stored and save it as **services.html** in the tripsmart root folder, replacing the existing file but not updating the links.

FIGURE F-27

c. Apply the heading style from the attached style sheet to the four paragraph headings and apply the body_text style to the rest of the text on the page.

d. Create the following links:
CNN Travel Channel: http://www.cnn.com/TRAVEL
US Department of State: http://travel.state.gov
MapQuest: http://www.mapquest.com
Rand McNally: http://www.randmcnally.com
AccuWeather: http://www.accuweather.com
The Weather Channel: http://www.weather.com

e. Create named anchors called **reservations**, **outfitters**, **tours**, and **links** in front of the respective headings on the page, then link each named anchor to "Reservations", "Travel Outfitters", "Escorted Tours", and "Helpful Links in Travel Planning" in the first paragraph.

f. Create a navigation bar with either text or images that links to the home, destinations, newsletter, services, and catalog pages, replacing any existing navigation bars. If you decide to use image links you must create the supporting files. If you use text links, create a new style and apply it to the navigation bar.

g. Copy the navigation bar to the other completed pages in the Web site: index, newsletter, and destinations pages, replacing any existing navigation bars.

h. Save any unsaved changes, then preview the services page in the browser, as shown in Figure F-27, and test all links.

i. Use the Link Checker to check for broken links and orphaned files.

j. Exit your browser, then close all files and exit Dreamweaver.

▼ INDEPENDENT CHALLENGE 3

FIGURE F-28

Dr. Joan Sullivent's patients often ask her questions about the current treatment protocol for Parkinson's disease, a debilitating neurological disease. She would like to post some helpful links in her clinic Web site to provide information for her patients.

a. Connect to the Internet and go to your favorite search engine, for example, Google at www.google.com.

b. Type keywords that would help you find Web sites that have helpful medical information about Parkinson's disease.

c. Note the placement and appearance of the navigation bars used in each site. Do they use text, images, or a combination of the two to form the links?

d. List at least five helpful links that Dr. Sullivent should consider for her site, including the National Parkinson Foundation pictured in Figure F-28. Use paper or your word processor to record your links.

▼ INDEPENDENT CHALLENGE 4

Barb Holmes, the dive master at the Over Under Dive Shop in Nevis, West Indies, would like you to create a navigation bar for her Web site that includes both images and text. She asks you to look at navigation links she saw in another Web site, shown in Figure F-29. She likes the look of it and wants something similar but warns you not to violate copyright laws by copying it. Use paper or your word processor to record your answers to the questions below.

FIGURE F-29

a. Connect to the Internet and go to the Maui Dive Shop at www.mauidiveshop.com to view the navigation links.

b. What do you like about the navigation links?

c. What do you dislike about the navigation links?

d. How would you describe the quality of the site? Excellent? Good? Fair? Poor? Defend your answer.

e. Why do you think some of the links are listed with images and text?

f. Do you see any copyright information on the page?

▼ INDEPENDENT CHALLENGE 5

This assignment will continue to build on the personal Web site that you created in Unit B. In Unit C you created and developed your index page. In Unit D you added a page with either an ordered or an unordered list, a CSS Style Sheet with a minimum of two styles, and Flash text. In Unit E you added a page that included at least two graphics. In this lesson, you work with one of the other pages in your Web site.

a. Consult your storyboard and decide which page you would like to develop in this lesson.

b. Create content for this page and format the text attractively on the page using styles.

c. Add at least three external links to this page.

d. Think about a creative use for an image map, and add it to the page.

e. Add a named anchor and link to it.

f. Design a navigation bar linking to the main pages of your Web site and copy it to all of the main pages.

g. Save the file and preview the page in the browser.

After you are satisfied with your work, verify the following:

a. Each completed page has a page title.

b. All links work correctly.

c. The completed pages view well using a screen resolution of 800 × 600.

d. All graphics are properly set showing a path to the Web site assets folder.

e. All graphics have alternate text and are royalty-free.

f. The Link Checker shows no broken links or orphaned files. If there are orphaned files, note your plan to link them.

Use Figure F-30 as a guide to continue your work on the Emma's Book Bag Web site. Emma Claire has asked you to create a page describing the upcoming book sale and a book signing event. Open the file dwf_5.html and save it as **events.html**, over-writing the existing file, and not updating links. Be sure to include the use of styles, an appropriate page title, and a consistent navigation bar across the Web site. The image on the page, grif_stockley.jpg is in the unit_f data files assets folder.

FIGURE F-30

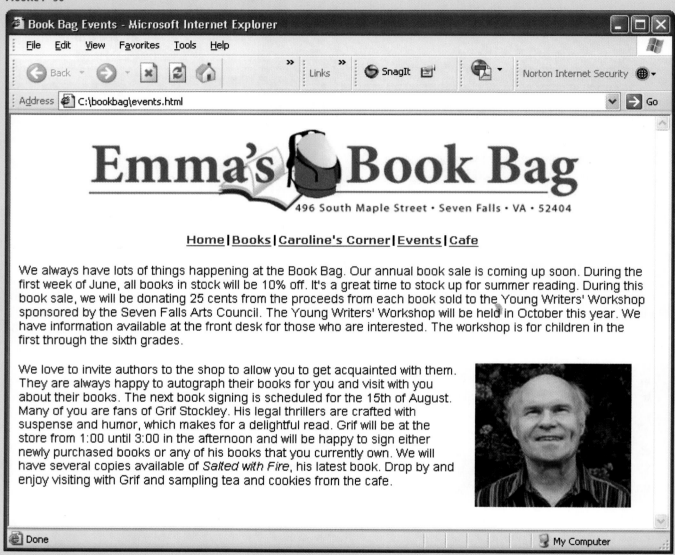

UNIT
G
Dreamweaver 8

Working with Tables and Layers

OBJECTIVES

| Understand table modes |
| Create a table |
| Resize tables, rows, and columns |
| Merge and split cells |
| Insert and align images in table cells |
| Insert text |
| Format and modify cell content |
| Format cells |
| Add multimedia content |
| Add a layer |
| Position and format a layer |

You have learned how to place elements on a page, align them, and enhance them through various formatting options. Another way to position page elements is by using tables. **Tables** are placeholders made up of small boxes called **cells**, where you can insert text and graphics. Cells are arranged horizontally in rows and vertically in columns. Using tables on a Web page gives you total control over the placement of each object on the page. In this unit you learn how to create and format tables, work with table rows and columns, and format the contents of table cells. You enter multimedia content, and also learn the benefits of using layers to add page content. A **layer** is an HTML page element that can contain any other type of page element, such as text and graphics. After you create a layer, you can then position it anywhere on the page. It is time to work on the cafe page. You have been given two graphics and a Flash animation to position attractively with the text on the page. You have decided to use a table to position each page element.

Understanding Table Modes

There are two ways to create a table in Dreamweaver. You can use the Table button in the Common or Layout groups on the Insert bar, or draw your own table using tools in the Layout group on the Insert bar. Each method for creating a table requires a specific mode. You use **Standard mode** to insert a table using the Table button, or **Layout mode** to draw your own table. Layout mode shows only the cells you create, then uses them to generate a table on the page. **Expanded Tables mode** is similar to Standard mode with expanded table borders and temporary space between the cells to make it easier to work with individual cells. You can choose the mode that you want by clicking the Standard mode button, the Layout mode button, or the Expanded Tables mode button in the Layout group on the Insert bar. It is common to switch among modes as you work with tables in Dreamweaver. You can also use the Import Tabular Data command on the Insert/Table Objects menu to place an existing table on a Web page. ▰▰▰▰ You review the three methods for creating tables using the Standard, Layout, and Expanded Tables modes so that you can pick the most appropriate method for creating and editing your table.

DETAILS

- ### Creating a table in Standard mode
  Standard mode is the mode you have used for page layout up to this point. Creating a table in Standard mode is useful when you have a specific number of columns and rows in mind. To create a table in Standard mode, you click the Table button in the Common or Layout group on the Insert bar. The Table dialog box opens and allows you to enter values for the number of rows and columns, the border size, table width, cell padding, and cell spacing. The **border** is the outline or frame around the table and the individual cells. It is expressed in pixels. The **width** refers to the width of the table. The width is expressed either in pixels or as a percentage of page width. When expressed as a percentage, the table width adjusts to the width of the page in the browser window. When expressed in pixels, the table width does not change, regardless of the size of the browser window. **Cell padding** is the distance between the cell content and the **cell walls**, the lines inside the cell borders. **Cell spacing** is the distance between cells. Figure G-1 shows an example of a table created in Standard mode.

- ### Editing a table in Expanded Tables mode
  Expanded tables mode lets you view a table with expanded table borders and temporary cell padding and cell spacing. This mode makes it easier to see how many rows and columns you have in your table. Often, especially after splitting empty cells, it is difficult to place the insertion point precisely in a table cell. The Expanded Tables mode lets you see each cell clearly. After you select a table item or place the insertion point, it's best to return to Standard mode to maintain the WYSIWYG environment. **WYSIWYG** is the acronym for What You See Is What You Get. This means that your Web page should look the same in the browser as it does in the Web editor. You can toggle between the Expanded Tables mode and Standard mode by pressing [F6]. Figure G-2 shows an example of a table in Expanded Tables mode.

- ### Drawing a table in Layout mode
  Layout mode is the view that you use when you want to draw your own table. Layout mode is a good choice when you know where you want to place elements on a page and do not need a specific number of rows and columns. You can use the Draw Layout Cell or the Layout Table buttons in the Layout group on the Insert bar to draw a cell or a table. You do not have to draw a table before you draw an individual cell because Dreamweaver plots a table for you automatically after you draw your first cell. Note, though, that a large number of cells drawn on a page may slow your computer's processing speed. Figure G-3 shows an example of a table created in Layout mode.

FIGURE G-1: **Table created in Standard mode**

Common group

Table button

Selected table

Tag selector

Property inspector expanded to access table properties

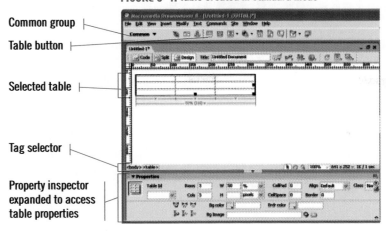

FIGURE G-2: **Same table shown in Expanded Tables mode**

Layout group

Expanded Tables mode button

More space between table cells

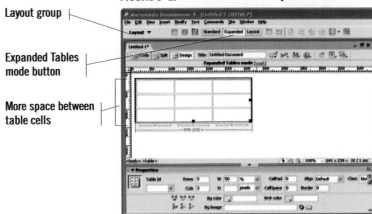

FIGURE G-3: **Table created in Layout mode**

Layout group

Layout mode

Draw Layout Cell button

Layout Table button

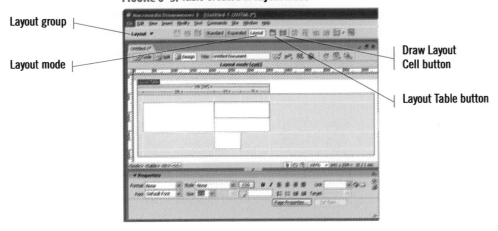

Clues to Use

HTML table tags

When formatting a table, it is important to understand the basic HTML table tags. The tags that represent a table are **<table></table>**. The tags that represent table rows are **<tr></tr>**. The tags that represent table data cells are **<td></td>**. Dreamweaver places the   code into each empty table cell at the time it is created. The ** ** code represents a nonbreaking space. A **nonbreaking space** is a space that appears on the page in a browser. Some browsers collapse an empty cell, which can ruin the look of a table. The nonbreaking space displays the cell until you place content in it. Then Dreamweaver automatically removes the nonbreaking space.

Dreamweaver 8

Creating a Table

Before you begin creating a table in any mode, it is imperative that you plan in advance where you want to place the table and how you want it to look. If you plan to insert images into a table, you should know exactly where you want them to appear on the page. Having an overall plan before you begin saves you a lot of time. You should also consider whether you want the table borders and the cell walls to appear in the browser window. You can make a table "invisible" by setting the border value to zero. Then the viewer will not be aware that you used a table to arrange the text or images on the page. You can also create a table inside a cell of another table. This is called a **nested table**. After consulting with the restaurant manager, you sketch your ideas for the new cafe page in The Striped Umbrella Web site, as shown in Figure G-4. You then insert a table using Standard mode.

STEPS

1. **Open The Striped Umbrella Web site, then double-click cafe.html in the Files panel to open the cafe page in Design View**
    The cafe page needs a descriptive title.

2. **Type The Sand Crab Cafe in the Title text box on the Document toolbar, replacing Untitled Document, then press [Enter] (Win) or [Return] (Mac)**

> **TROUBLE**
> You cannot use the Table button in Layout mode.

3. **Click the Standard mode button Standard in the Layout group on the Insert bar if necessary, then click the Table button**
    The Table dialog box opens.

4. **If necessary, type 7 in the Rows text box, 3 in the Columns text box, and 750 in the Table width text box, click the Table Width list arrow, click pixels if necessary, type 0 in the Border thickness text box, (leave the cell padding and spacing options blank), type This table is used for page layout in the Summary text box, as shown in Figure G-5, then click OK**
    You can leave the cell padding and cell spacing blank or with a value of 0 to not include padding or spacing. A value of 0 will make the table a little tighter. A table with seven rows and three columns appears on the page. Because the table is selected, the Property inspector displays the table settings that you entered in the Insert Table dialog box. You can modify the table by changing its values on the Property inspector.

> **TROUBLE**
> To select a table, move the pointer slowly to the top or bottom edge of the table until you see the pointer change to, then click the table border.

5. **With the table still selected, expand the Property inspector if necessary, click the Align list arrow on the Property inspector, then click Center to center-align the table on the page**
    Because you chose to measure table width using pixels rather than percent and because the table has been center aligned, it will appear in the same position and size in all browser window sizes. This will look nice with an 800 × 600 resolution. With larger sized windows, the table will remain the same size and appear centered in the window. Viewers using a 640 × 480 resolution will be forced to scroll to view the table, but they would have to anyway due to the width of the banner.

> **QUICK TIP**
> If the Getting Started in Layout Mode window opens, click OK to close it.

6. **Click the Layout mode button on the Insert bar**
    The table appears in Layout Mode, as shown in Figure G-6. The Property inspector now displays the properties for tables shown in Layout Mode.

7. **Click the Standard mode button on the Insert bar, then save your work**
    The table again appears in Standard Mode. As you place content into the table cells, the table will lengthen.

Clues to Use

Selecting a table

There are several ways to select a table in Dreamweaver. First, you can click the insertion point in the table, click Modify on the menu bar, point to Table, then click Select Table. Second, you can select a table by double-clicking the table border when the pointer changes to. Finally, you can click the table tag icon **<table>** on the tag selector on the Status Bar.

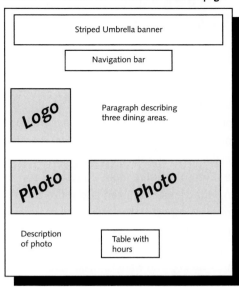

Rows text box

Table width text box

Border thickness text box

Columns text box

Width list arrow

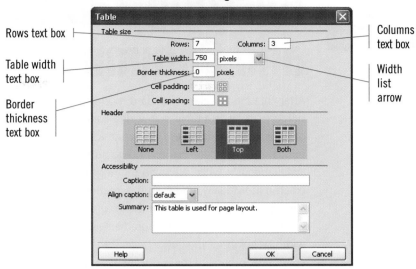

FIGURE G-6: Table in Layout Mode

Property inspector shows Layout Table options in Layout mode

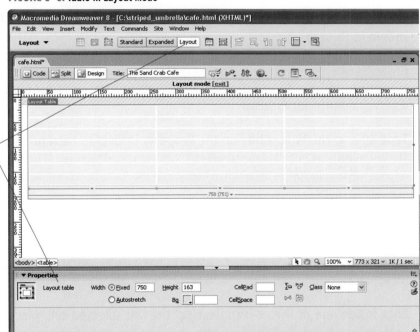

Design Matters

Setting table and cell widths for page layout

If you use a table to position text and graphics on an entire Web page, it is wise to set the width of the table in pixels. This way, the table does not resize itself proportionally if the browser window size is changed. If you set the width of a table using pixels, the table remains one size, regardless of the browser window size. Most designers today design to a setting of 800 × 600. By using a table width of slightly under 800, the table will cover the width of the window. Those viewers using a higher resolution, such as 1024 × 768, then can view the table without having it spread out across the screen and altering your intended formatting, as would happen if the width were set using a percent. You can also set each cell width as either a percent of the table or as pixels. If you expect your users to print the page, consider making the table narrower so it will fit on a printed page.

Resizing Tables, Rows, and Columns

After creating a table in Standard mode, you can resize the table and its rows or columns by adjusting the borders. To resize a table, a row, or a column proportionately, you must first select the table, then drag one of three selection handles. To change all of the columns in a table so that they are the same size, drag the middle-right selection handle; dragging the middle-bottom selection handle resizes the height of all rows simultaneously, while dragging the right-corner selection handle resizes the entire table. To resize a row or column individually, you drag the interior cell borders up, down, left, or right. You can also resize column widths and row heights using the W and H text boxes on the Property inspector. You can resize cells using pixels or a percent as a measurement. Cells resized as a percent maintain that percent in relation to the width or height of the entire table, if the table is resized. It is a good idea to set the cell widths before you enter data; otherwise the widths tend to shift as you enter the data. ▓▓▓▓ You want to make sure that the contents of the three cells in the last row will be distributed according to your plan. You set the width of each by entering width values using percentages. You also experiment with resizing a row height.

STEPS

QUICK TIP
You do not actually have to select the cell to see or edit cell properties; you can place the insertion point inside the cell instead.

1. **Click inside the bottom-left cell, then click the cell tag icon <td> on the tag selector, as shown in Figure G-7**

   The **tag selector**, located on the Status bar, displays HTML tags for the various page components, including tables and cells. Clicking a table tag selects the table associated with that tag. Clicking a cell tag selects the corresponding table cell. The cell is now selected with a dark border surrounding it. The Property inspector displays properties of the selected cell.

QUICK TIP
Type the % sign next to a number you want expressed as a percent. Otherwise, it will be expressed in pixels.

2. **Type 30% in the W text box on the Property inspector, then press [Tab]**

   The cell width is set to 30% of the table width. Now, as you add content to the table, you can be sure that this column will remain 30% of the width of the table. Notice that the cell width, 30%, is displayed under the cell, as shown in Figure G-7.

3. **Repeat Steps 1 and 2 for the next two cells in the last row, using 30% for the middle cell and 40% for the last cell**

   The combined widths of the three cells add up to 100%. If your widths do not add up to 100%, the table may not appear as you intended. Now you experiment with changing the height of the first row.

QUICK TIP
The height of a row also automatically increases to accommodate the height of its contents.

4. **Click inside one of the cells to deselect the last selected cell, place the pointer over the bottom row border of the first row until the pointer changes to a resizing pointer ⬍, as shown in Figure G-8, then click and drag downward to increase the height of the row slightly**

   The color of the border becomes darker once you drag it.

5. **Click Window on the menu bar, click History to open the History panel, if necessary, then drag the slider in the History panel up until Set Height is dimmed, to undo the Set Height command**

   The row returns to the original height.

6. **Save the file**

FIGURE G-7: Selecting a cell

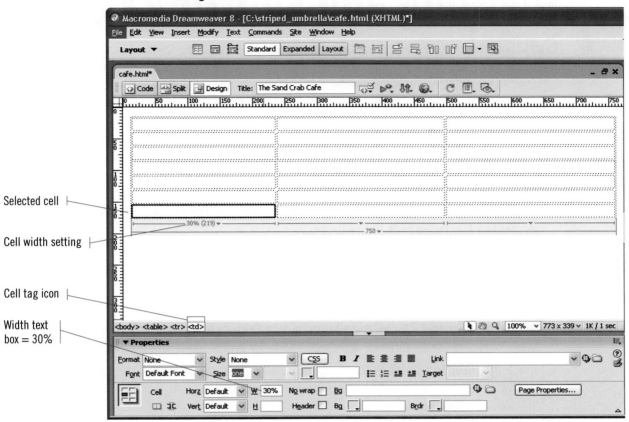

Selected cell

Cell width setting

Cell tag icon

Width text
box = 30%

FIGURE G-8: Resizing the height of a row

Heavy line shows
that row border
is selected

Resizing pointer

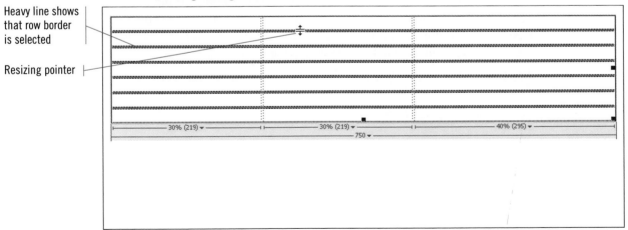

Clues to Use

Resetting table widths and heights

After resizing columns and rows in a table, you may want to return your table to the default column widths and row heights. To do so, select the table, click Modify on the menu bar, point to Table, then click Clear Cell Heights or Clear Cell Widths. You can also use these commands to tighten up any extra white space in a cell. Using the Clear Cell Heights command forces a cell border to align with the bottom of an inserted graphic.

Merging and Splitting Cells

In addition to resizing the columns and rows of a table you create using Standard mode, you may need to adjust the table cells by splitting or merging them. To **split** a cell means to divide it into multiple rows or columns. To **merge** cells means to combine multiple cells into one cell. Splitting and merging cells gives you more flexibility for inserting images or text into your table. When cells are merged, the HTML tag used to describe them changes from a width size tag to a column span or row span tag. You can split merged cells and merge split cells. ████ You merge some cells to make room for the banner and navigation bar at the top of the page. You then split one cell that will be used to place a graphic with descriptive text under it.

STEPS

1. **Click to place the insertion point in the upper-left cell, then click and drag the pointer across the top three cells in the first row**

   A black border surrounds the cells, indicating that they are selected.

QUICK TIP

You can only merge cells that, together, form a rectangle.

2. **Click the** Merges selected cells using spans button 🔲 **on the Property inspector**

   The three cells are merged into one cell, as shown in Figure G-9. This row will contain the banner and navigation bar.

3. **Repeat Steps 1 and 2 to merge the second and third cells in the fifth row**

   This row will contain a wide image of the cafe. You decide to experiment with splitting cells.

4. **Place the insertion point in the first cell in the fifth row, then click the** Splits cell into rows or columns button 🔳 **on the Property inspector**

   The Split Cell dialog box opens.

5. **Click the** Split cell into Rows option **to select it if necessary, type** 2 **in the Number of Rows text box if necessary, as shown in Figure G-10, then click** OK

   The dialog box closes, and the cell is split into two rows.

6. **Click the** Show Code View button 🔳 Code **on the Document toolbar**

   The code for the split and merged cells appears. Notice the table tags denoting the column span and the non-breaking spaces ( ) inserted in the empty cells. The tag <td colspan="3"> refers to the three cells that have been merged into one cell that spans three columns.

7. **Click the** Show Design View button 🔳 Design, **then save your work**

Clues to Use

Adding and deleting rows and columns

As you add new content to your table, you may find that you have too many rows or columns, or not enough rows or columns. You can add or delete one row or column at a time or add several at once, using commands on the Modify menu to add and delete table rows and columns. When you add a new column or row, you must first select an existing column or row to which the new column or row will be adjacent. The Insert Rows or Columns dialog box lets you choose how many rows or columns you want to insert and where you want them placed, relative to the selected row or column. To add a new row to the end of a table, simply press [Tab].

FIGURE G-9: Merging selected cells into one cell

Resulting merged cells

Merges selected cells using spans button

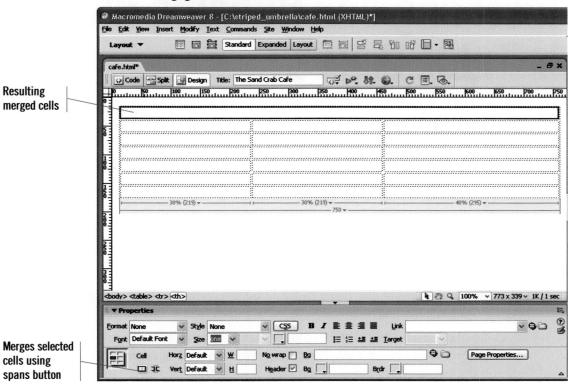

FIGURE G-10: Splitting a cell into two rows

Rows option button

Number of rows text box

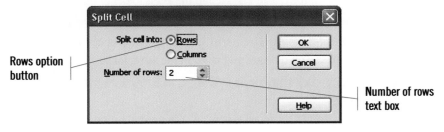

Clues to Use

Merging and splitting cells in Layout Mode

As you draw cells of different sizes in Layout Mode, you are creating a layout that looks similar to merged and split cells. However, drawing cells of different sizes and shapes in Layout Mode generates different HTML code from splitting or merging cells. This is important to keep in mind if you are trying to resize cells in Standard Mode that were originally drawn in Layout Mode. If you are having problems formatting a table created in Layout Mode, check the HTML code to try to determine how the original layout was converted into HTML code. Then you can attempt to make the corrections directly into the code. If this doesn't work, try deleting the troublesome cells and creating them in Standard Mode.

Dreamweaver 8

Inserting and Aligning Images in Table Cells

Designers use tables for page layout because by placing text and images in table cells, they can control the exact location of text and images on a page. You can type or paste text into table cells. You can insert images into cells just as you would place them on a page, using the Insert bar. As you add content to cells, the cells expand in height to make room for the content. ▆▆▆▆ You insert The Striped Umbrella banner, the navigation bar, and two images into the table on the cafe page, then center each within its cell.

STEPS

TROUBLE

If you do not see a dialog box prompting you to insert alternate text, type the text in the Alt text box on the Property inspector.

1. **Open the index page, click the** banner **to select it, press and hold** [Shift], **then click to the right of the navigation bar to select both the banner and the navigation bar**

2. **Click** Edit **on the menu bar, click** Copy, **then close the index page**

3. **Click in the top cell on the cafe page, click** Edit **on the menu bar, then click** Paste
   The Image Description (Alt Text) dialog box opens, showing that alt text is missing from the banner graphic.

4. **Click in the blank space under the Description heading, as shown in Figure G-11, type** The Striped Umbrella banner, **click** OK, **then center the banner if necessary**
   The banner and navigation bar appear in the top row of the table. Notice how the cell expands to adjust to the height of the contents.

5. **Click to place the insertion point in the first cell in the fifth row (the top row in the set of split cells), click the** Image button ▣ **in the** Common **group on the Insert bar, navigate to the drive and folder where your Unit G Data Files are stored, double-click the** assets folder, **double-click** cheesecake.jpg, **inserting the alternate text** Banana Chocolate Cheesecake **when prompted, click** OK, **then refresh the Files panel**
   The image appears in the cell and is saved in the assets folder of the Web site.

QUICK TIP

You can press [Tab] to move your insertion point to the next cell in a row, and press [Shift] [Tab] to move your insertion point to the previous cell.

6. **Repeat Step 5 to insert the** cafe_photo.jpg **in the merged cells to the right of the cheesecake image, using** The Sand Crab Cafe **as the alternate text**
   The images are placed on the page and saved in the assets folder.

7. **Save your work, click the** Preview/Debug in Browser button ▣, **then click** Preview in [your browser name]
   The cafe page appears in the browser window. You need to improve the alignment of the two images.

8. **Close your browser, click the** cheesecake image, **then click the** Align Center button ▣ **on the Property inspector**
   The image is horizontally centered in its cell.

9. **Repeat Step 8 to center the cafe image**
   Compare your screen to Figure G-12.

10. **Save your work, preview the page in your browser, then close the browser**

FIGURE G-11: Image Description (Alt Text) dialog box

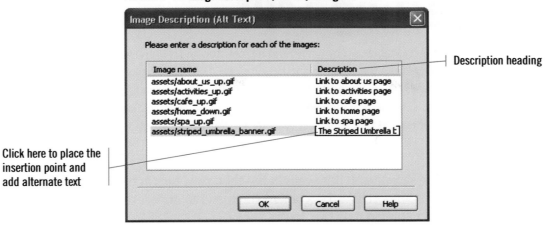

Description heading

Click here to place the insertion point and add alternate text

FIGURE G-12: Aligning images in cells

Centered images

Clues to Use

Vertically aligning cell contents

In addition to aligning cell contents horizontally, you can also align them vertically, in the top, middle, bottom, or on the baseline of the cell. To vertically align a graphic, select the graphic, click the cell tag icon `<td>` on the tag selector or place the insertion point in the cell, click the Vert list arrow on the Property inspector, then choose an alignment type. See Figure G-13.

FIGURE G-13: Vertically aligning cell contents

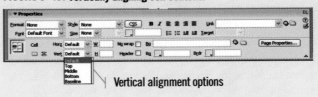

Vertical alignment options

Inserting Text

You can enter text in table cells by typing it in the cell, copying it from another source and pasting it into the cell, or importing it into the cell from another program. Then you can format the text for optimum readability and appearance. If you import text from another program, you should use the Clean Up HTML or Clean Up Word HTML command to remove unnecessary code. ▓▓▓▓ You import a Word file that describes the cafe, type two short text descriptions, then enter the three different dining area hours using a nested table.

STEPS

TROUBLE

If you receive an error message when you import the Word text, follow the instructions on the screen to correct the error.

1. **Merge the second and third cells in the third row, click in the newly merged cell, then use the File/Import/Word document command to import the Word document** cafe.doc **from the chapter_g data files folder**

   The text appears in the merged cell.

2. **Click in the cell under the cheesecake photo, type** Banana Chocolate, **press** [Shift] [Enter] **(Win) or** [Shift] [return] **(Mac), type** Cheesecake, **press** [Shift] [Enter] **(Win) or** [Shift] [return] **(Mac), then type** Our signature dessert

3. **Click in the next cell down and type** Reservations are recommended for The Dining Room during the peak summer season.

   You are ready to enter the cafe hours. You will use a nested table for this.

4. **Merge the two empty cells under the cafe photo, place the insertion point inside the newly merged cell, then click the** Table button ▦

5. **Type** 4 **in the Rows text box, type** 2 **in the Columns text box, type** 300 **in the Table width text box, click the** Table width list arrow, **click** pixels, **then type** 0 **in the Border thickness text box**

6. **Click the** Top row header icon **in the Header section, type** This table contains the cafe hours. **in the Summary text box, compare your Table dialog box to Figure G-14, then click** OK

   The Top header option will automatically center and bold the text that is typed into the top cells of the table. The header will be read by screen readers, providing more accessibility for the table.

7. **Merge the top row of cells in the nested table, then type** The Sand Crab Cafe Hours

8. **Enter the cafe dining area names and their hours, as shown in Figure G-15, then save your work**

Clues to Use

Using nested tables

Inserting another table inside a table is similar to adding a new row or column to a table. This is called a **nested table**. To create a nested table, click to place the insertion point inside the cell where you want the nested table to appear, click Insert on the menu bar, then click Table or click the Table icon on the Insert bar. The nested table is a separate table that you can format differently from the table in which it is placed. Nested tables can be used effectively if you want part of your table data to have visible borders and part to have invisible borders. For example, you can nest a table with red borders inside a table with invisible borders. Careful planning is important when you work with nested tables. It is easy to get carried away and have too many, which can make them difficult to select and edit. You may be able to achieve the same results by adding rows and columns or splitting cells instead of inserting a nested table.

FIGURE G-14: Table dialog box settings for nested table

Table

Table size

Rows: 4   Columns: 2

Table width: 300   pixels

Border thickness: 0   pixels

Cell padding: ▢

Cell spacing: ▦

Header

None   Left   Top   Both   ⊢ Top row header icon

Accessibility

Caption:

Align caption: default

Summary: This table contains the cafe hours.   ⊢ Summary text box

Help   OK   Cancel

FIGURE G-15: Adding a nested table

Banana Chocolate
Cheesecake
Our signature dessert

The Sand Crab Cafe Hours	
The Terrace	11:00 a.m. - 9:00 p.m.
The Dining Room	7:00 a.m. - 11:00 p.m.
The Cabana	10:00 a.m. - 6:00 p.m.

Reservations are recommended for The Dining Room during the peak summer season.

30% (218) ▼   30% (218) ▼   40% (347) ▼

Clues to Use

Importing and exporting tabular data

You can import and export tabular data into and out of Dreamweaver. **Tabular data** is data that is arranged in columns and rows and separated by a **delimiter**: a comma, tab, colon, semicolon, or similar character that tells Dreamweaver where to break the data into table cells. **Importing** means to bring data created in another software program into Dreamweaver, and **exporting** means to save data that was created in Dreamweaver in a special file format so that other programs can read it. Files containing tabular data that are imported into Dreamweaver must first be saved as delimited text files. Programs such as Microsoft Word and Excel offer many file formats for saving files, including saving as delimited text. To import a delimited file, click File on the menu bar, point to Import, then click Tabular Data. The Import Tabular Data dialog box opens, offering you choices for the resulting table that will appear on the Web page. To export a table that you created in Dreamweaver, click File on the menu bar, point to Export, then click Table. The Export Table dialog box opens, letting you choose the type of delimiter and line breaks you want for the delimited file when you save it.

Formatting and Modifying Cell Content

In addition to changing the height and width of cells, you can apply a background color or a background image to fill the entire table or individual cells. You can also change border colors and border widths. You can format cell text in Standard mode by changing the font, size, or color of the text, or by applying styles. You can also resize images placed in cells. It is easier to modify and format table contents in Standard mode than it is in Layout mode. You know that applying the styles from the Web site style sheet makes sense, so you attach the style sheet file to the cafe page and use those styles to format the text on the page. You also need to modify the navigation bar to change the down image state from the home button to the cafe button.

1. **Expand the CSS panel group (if necessary)**

2. **Click the Attach Style Sheet button 📟, then attach the su_styles.css file to the cafe page**
   The styles are now available to use on the cafe page.

3. **Select the paragraph under the navigation bar, then use the Property inspector to apply the body_text style.**
   The text changes to reflect the settings in the body_text style.

4. **Select the text Banana Chocolate Cheesecake, then apply the spa_names style.**

5. **Select the text Our signature dessert and the Reservations information, then apply the body_text style.**

6. **Repeat step 5 to apply the body_text style to the nested table text, as shown in Figure G-16.**
   All text on the page now has a style applied.

7. **Modify the navigation bar to show the home element in its up state and the cafe element in its down state.**

8. **Save your work, preview the cafe page in your browser window, then close your browser**
   Formatting the text in the table cells makes the cafe page look more professional.

Clues to Use

Formatting cells and cell content

You can format cell content using the Property inspector. Formatting cells is not the same as formatting the content inside them. You can format a cell by simply clicking the insertion point inside the cell that you want to format, then choosing options on the Property inspector. For example, you can click a cell, then choose a fill color for the cell by clicking the Bg Color list arrow on the Property inspector. (You must expand the Property inspector to see these options.) However, to format the cell content, you must select the content, not the cell itself. For instance, you can set a cell alignment to center align, but format individual cell contents to different alignments by selecting each one individually and formatting it. Thus, you can have left-aligned text and a centered graphic in a cell that has been formatted as center aligned.

FIGURE G-16: Table dialog box settings for nested table

body_text style applied

spa_names style applied

body_text style applied

Attach Style Sheet button

Formatting Cells

Formatting cells is different from formatting cell contents. Formatting a cell can include setting properties that visually enhance the cell appearance, such as setting a cell width, assigning a background color, or setting global alignment properties for the cell content. To format a cell, you need to either select the cell or place the insertion point inside the cell you want to format, then choose the cell formatting options you want to use in the Property inspector. You change the horizontal and vertical alignment settings for some of the table cells to improve the appearance of the cell contents on the page.

STEPS

1. **Click to place the insertion point in the cell with the reservations text.**

2. **Click the Vert list arrow on the Property inspector, then click Middle to force the cell contents to the middle of the cell.**
   Even if the cell is enlarged, the contents will stay aligned in the middle of the cell.

3. **With the insertion point in the cell with the reservations text, click the Horz list arrow, then click Center to center the cell contents.**
   This alignment command will center everything within this cell.

4. **Repeat step 3 to center the cell contents for the cell with cheesecake name and the cell with the nested table, then compare your screen to Figure G-17.**

5. **Save your work, preview the cafe page in your browser, then close your browser**

FIGURE G-17: Setting horizontal and vertical cell alignment

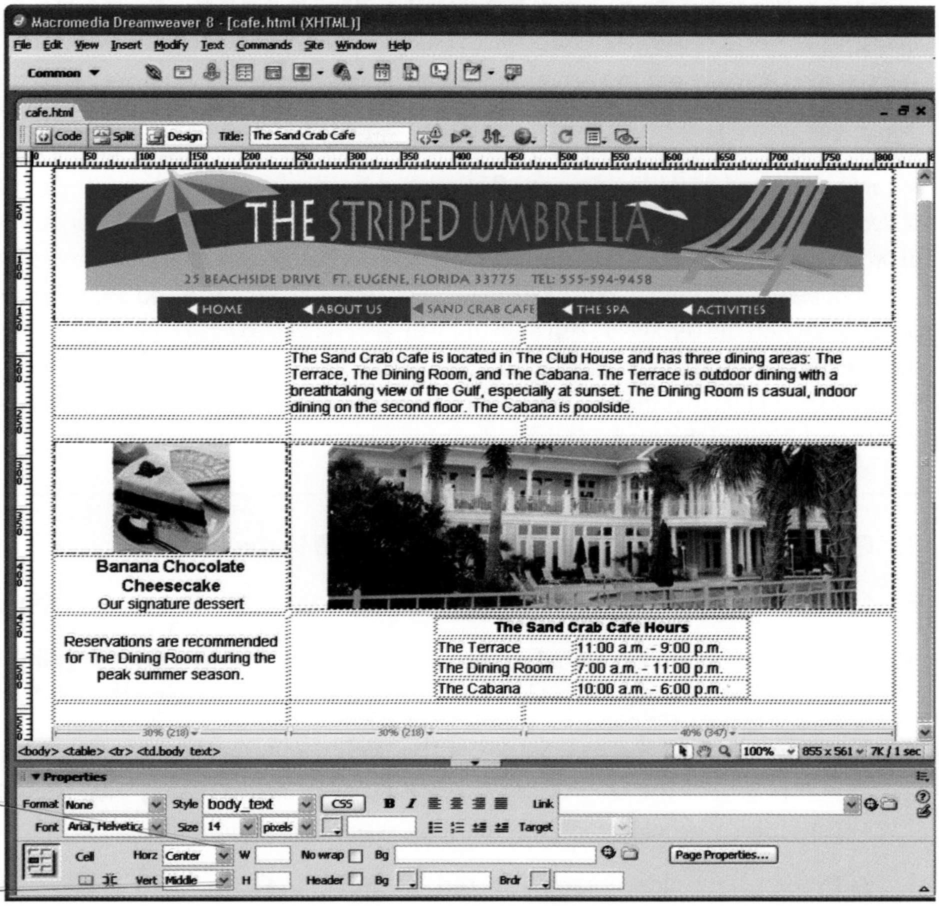

Horz list arrow

Vert list arrow

Adding Multimedia Content

You can use Dreamweaver to insert a wide variety of multimedia effects on your Web pages, including Flash buttons, movies, and text; Shockwave movies; and a series of built-in JavaScript behaviors, such as sounds, rollover images, popup messages, and menus. Macromedia Flash is a software program that allows you to create animations and interactive elements that can be placed on your Web pages. These animations use a series of vector-based graphics that load quickly and merge with other graphics and sounds to create short movies. In order to view Flash movies, you need the Macromedia Flash Player, a software program that is embedded in the latest versions of both Internet Explorer and Netscape Navigator. If you are using an older browser that does not support the version of Flash used to create your movie, you can download the latest Flash player from the Macromedia Web site, located at http://www.macromedia.com. ░░░░ You have been given a simple Flash animation that uses the cafe logo to incorporate animation and sound into the Web page. You place it in a cell near the top of the page.

STEPS

QUICK TIP

To play Flash movies in Dreamweaver and in your browser, you must have the Flash Player installed on your computer. If the Flash Player is not installed, you can download it at the Macromedia Web site (www. macromedia.com). To hear the sound, you must have your speakers turned on.

QUICK TIP

If you are using a different browser or a version of Internet Explorer that is earlier than 6.0, look for a similar setting.

1. **Click to place the insertion point in the left cell in the third row**

2. **Click the** Media list arrow **in the Common group on the Insert bar, then click** Flash

3. **Navigate to the unit_g Data Files folder, click** crab.swf, **then click** Yes **(Win) or** Choose **(Mac), then click** Yes **to close the dialog box asking if you want to copy the file to the Web site**

4. **Save the movie in the root folder of the Web site, type** Flash Movie of crab logo **in the Title text box of the Object Tag Accessibility Attributes dialog box, then click** OK

   A Flash movie placeholder appears on the page, as shown in Figure G-18.

5. **With the placeholder image selected, as shown in Figure G-18, click** Play **in the Property inspector to play the crab.swf movie, then click** Stop

6. **Save your work, preview the page in your browser**

   The crab movie plays in the browser one time, then stops.

7. **If the movie did not play in Internet Explorer, click** Tools **on the menu bar, click** Internet Options, **click the** Advanced tab, **then click the** Allow active content to run in files on my computer check box

8. **Close your browser, position the pointer so that it points to the left side of the second row, then when the pointer becomes an arrow →, click the pointer to select the row, click** Modify **on the menu bar, point to** Table, **then click** Delete Row

   The extra space under the navigation bar is not needed. Removing the empty row moved the rest of the page contents closer to the top of the page.

9. **Save your work, preview the page in the browser again, compare your screen to Figure G-19, then close the browser**

FIGURE G-18: Flash movie placeholder on the cafe page

Flash movie placeholder

Properties of selected Flash movie

Click to play movie

FIGURE G-19: Flash movie playing in Internet Explorer

Adding a Layer

While tables let you place elements in specific page locations, layers can provide even more flexibility. **Layers** are page elements in which you can place text or images, much as you would place them in a table cell. However, layers are more powerful in that they add another dimension to the Web page, similar to layers used in graphics programs, such as Adobe Photoshop. Layers can contain text, images, or any other HTML page content. You can place layers on top of each other, as well as hide, move, or animate them. A layer's position is determined by the top and left coordinates on the Property inspector when the layer is selected. Depending on the screen resolution and monitor size of the computer used to view the page in a browser, the layer may appear in a different location from the one you intended.  You decide to add The Striped Umbrella logo and copyright information to the home page and to use a layer for placement.

STEPS

1. **Close the cafe page and open the index page**
   You want to add the layer to the bottom of the index page.

2. **Click the Standard Mode button in the Layout group on the Insert bar if necessary, click the Draw Layer button ▦ in the Layout group on the Insert bar, position the pointer below the horizontal rule on the right side of the page, then drag to form a rectangle, as shown in Figure G-20**
   The layer will hold the The Striped Umbrella logo.

3. **Click to place the insertion point inside the layer if necessary, click the Image button ▦ in the Common group on the Insert bar, navigate to the drive and folder where your Unit G Data Files are stored if necessary, then double-click su_logo.jpg**

4. **Add The Striped Umbrella logo as the alternate text for the logo**
   The Striped Umbrella logo appears on the layer. You want to move the copyright information from its current position to the layer and place it under the logo.

5. **Select the copyright information, click Edit on the menu bar, click Cut, place the insertion point to the right of the logo in the layer, then press [Shift] [Enter] (Win) or [shift] [return] (Mac)**
   This gives you room for the copyright information to be placed under the logo.

6. **Click Edit on the menu, then click Paste, then remove any formatting applied to the text**
   The copyright information is placed under the logo.

7. **Click the border of the layer, then when the pointer changes to ✛ (Win) or the hand icon (Mac), drag the layer to place the bottom of the layer even with the last updated statement**
   The ability to position a layer precisely is one of the advantages of using layers.

8. **Select the default name in the Layer ID text box in the Property inspector, type logo, then press [Enter] (Win) or [return] (Mac)**
   The layer is now named logo. Notice the style for the layer that has been created in the CSS Styles panel, as shown in Figure G-21.

TROUBLE
You may have to reposition the layer several times before you are pleased with the placement.

9. **Save your work and preview the page in the browser**

10. **Close the browser and make any adjustments necessary**

FIGURE G-20: New layer added to the home page

Draw Layer button

Layout group

Layer icon

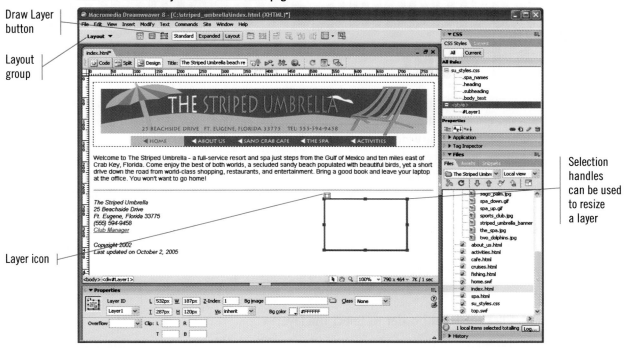

Selection handles can be used to resize a layer

FIGURE G-21: Property inspector showing properties of selected layer

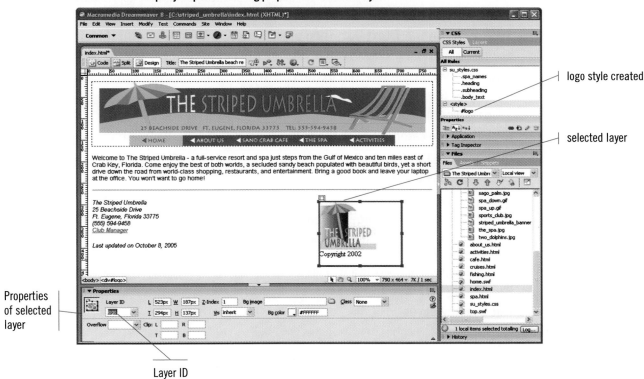

logo style created

selected layer

Properties of selected layer

Layer ID

Clues to Use

Converting layers to tables

Not all browsers can read layers correctly. In general, browsers older than Internet Explorer 4.0 and Netscape Navigator 4.0 cannot read layers. If you are concerned about your viewers not being able to view pages with layers, you can convert the layers to tables by selecting the layer, clicking Modify on the menu bar, pointing to Convert, then clicking Layers to Table. This command also works in reverse.

Positioning and Formatting a Layer

One of the greatest benefits of using layers to lay out a page is that you can position them precisely using a practice called **absolute positioning**. When you use absolute positioning for a layer, it holds its position in the browser when the window size changes. To position a layer absolutely, you specify the distance between the upper-left corner of the layer and the upper-left corner of the page or layer in which the layer is contained. You can control absolute positioning of layers by setting attributes, four of which are available on the Property inspector. These attributes work together to create a layer that will hold its position on a page. When a layer is created, a style is automatically generated that contains the layer properties. This type of style is called an **embedded style**, which means that the code for the style is part of the individual page, rather than part of the external style sheet. You use the Position property to lock the layer on the page so it will appear the same to all viewers.

STEPS

1. **Click the layer border to select the layer**

2. **Type 75% in the L text box, then press [Enter] (Win) or [return] (Mac), as shown in Figure G-22**

   The layer moves automatically to the position you specified. It will now appear on the right side of the browser window, regardless of the screen resolution or screen size.

3. **Type 295px in the T text box, then press [Enter] (Win) or [Return] (Mac)**

   The layer will remain at **295px** pixels below the top of the page in the browser window.

4. **With the #logo style selected in the CSS Styles panel, click the Edit Style... button in the CSS Styles panel**

   The CSS Rule definition for #logo dialog box opens.

5. **Click the Type category, click the Font list arrow, click Verdana, Arial, Helvetica, sans-serif**

6. **Click the Size list arrow, click 9, compare your screen to Figure G-22, then click OK**

   The copyright statement changes to reflect the settings in the style.

7. **Save your work, preview the page in your browser, compare your screen to Figure G-23, click each link in the navigation bar, then close your browser**

   If you are viewing the pages in a resolution higher than 800 × 600, notice how the page content spreads over the entire screen for every page except the page based on a table for layout. That page content is contained within the table. If one page in a Web site is based on a table for page layout, all pages should be designed in the same way to provide continuity.

8. **Exit Dreamweaver**

Clues to Use

Setting layer attributes

Besides positioning layers in reference to the top and sides of a Web page, you can also specify the dimensions of a layer through the Width (W) and Height (H) properties. You can also set other layer attributes, such as the Z-Index, which stacks layers vertically; you can name layers, add background images or color to layers, and adjust layer visibility. Layers, like tables, can be nested. The easiest way to format and edit layers is to use style sheets. The Layers panel keeps track of all the layers on a page, making it easy to review the settings for each one.

FIGURE G-22: Property inspector showing properties of selected layer

Font list arrow

Type Category

Size list arrow

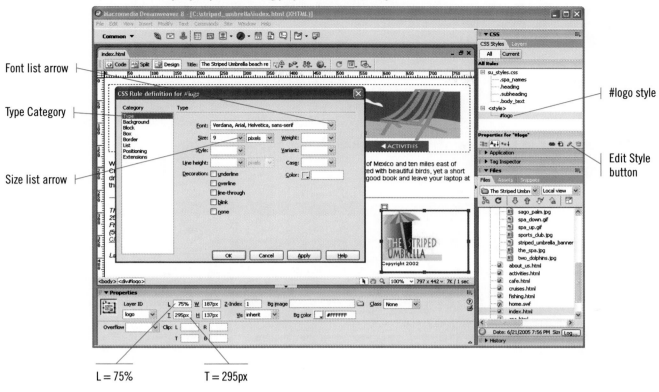

#logo style

Edit Style button

L = 75% T = 295px

FIGURE G-23: The finished project

Practice

▼ CONCEPTS REVIEW

Label each element in the Dreamweaver window shown in Figure G-24.

FIGURE G-24

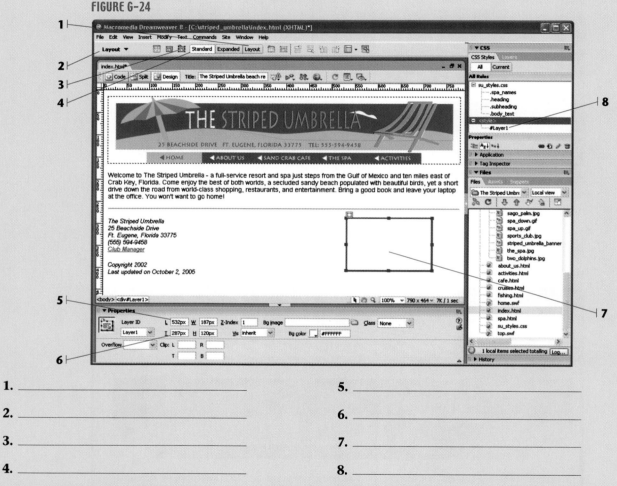

1. _____

2. _____

3. _____

4. _____

5. _____

6. _____

7. _____

8. _____

Match each of the following terms with the statement that best describes its function.

9. **Small boxes that make up columns and rows**

10. **Layout mode**

11. **Cell padding**

12. **Standard mode**

13. **Border**

14. **Import**

15. **Cell spacing**

16. **Export**

17. **Tag selector**

a. The mode that displays only the cells you draw

b. The space between cell content and cell walls

c. Displays HTML tags for the various page components, including tables and cells

d. Cells

e. The mode that you use to create a table with a specific number of rows and columns

f. Save data that was created in Dreamweaver in a special file format

g. The space between table cells

h. The outline of a table or an individual cell

i. To bring data into Dreamweaver from another program

Select the best answer from the following list of choices.

18. **Which of the following is true about nested tables?**
    a. Only one nested table can be inserted into a table.
    b. Nested tables are inserted using the Insert Nested Table button.
    c. Nested tables can have visible or invisible borders.
    d. Nested tables cannot be formatted like regular tables.

19. **Which of the following is used to select a row in a table?**
    a. `<div>`   c. `<tr>`
    b. `<td>`   d. `<table>`

20. **Which pointer is used to select a row?**
    a. →   c. ▐▖
    b. ✛   d. ▷

▼ SKILLS REVIEW

Important: *If you did not create this Web site in Unit B and maintain it during the preceding units, you will need to create a root folder for this Web site and define the Web site using files your instructor will provide. See the "Read This Before You Begin" section for more detailed instructions.*

1. **Understand table views.**
    a. Open the blooms & bulbs Web site.
    b. Open the classes.html page, which is blank.
    c. Use the Insert bar to change to the Layout group, then change to Layout mode.
    d. Change back to Standard mode.

2. **Create a table.**
    a. Type **Master Gardener classes begin soon!** in the Title text box on the toolbar, replacing Untitled Document.
    b. Use the Insert bar to insert a table on the page with the following settings:

       Rows = 5   Width = 750 pixels   Cell padding = 5
       Columns = 3   Border = 0   Cell spacing = 5
    c. Enter the text **This table is used for page layout** in the Summary text box.
    d. Center-align the table on the page.
    e. Save the file.

3. **Resize rows and columns.**
    a. Select the first cell in the first row and set the cell width to 25%.
    b. Select the second cell in the same row and set the cell width to 40%.
    c. Select the third cell in the same row and set the cell width to 35%.
    d. Save your work.

4. **Merge and split cells.**
    a. Merge the three cells in the top row.
    b. Merge the first two cells in the second row.
    c. Merge the third cell in the third row with the third cell in the fourth row.
    d. Split the first cell in the fourth row into two columns.
    e. Merge the three cells in the last row, then save your work.

5. **Insert and align graphics in table cells.**
    a. Copy the banner and the navigation bar together from the home page and paste them into the first row of the table.
    b. Center the banner and the navigation bar.

   c. Modify the navigation bar to show the classes element in the Down image state and the home element in the Up image state.

   d. Use the Insert bar to insert **flower_bed.jpg** in the last row. You can find the flower_bed.jpg file in the unit_g assets folder where your Data Files are stored. Add the alternate text **Flower bed in downtown Alvin** to the flower_bed.jpg image when prompted, then center the image.

   e. Use the tag selector to select the cell containing the flower_bed.jpg image, then set the vertical alignment to Top.

   f. Save your work.

6. Insert text.

   a. Type **Master Gardener Classes Beginning Soon!** in the first cell in the second row.

   b. Type **Who are Master Gardeners?** in the second cell in the second row.

   c. Type **Schedule** in the first cell in the third row.

   d. Type **Registration** in the second cell in the third row.

   e. Type the dates and times for the classes from Figure G-25 in the first and second cells in the fourth row.

   f. Use the Import Word Document command on the File menu to import the file **registration.doc** from the Unit G Data Files into the third cell in the fourth row, then use the Clean up Word HTML command on the Commands menu to remove any unnecessary code.

   g. Repeat Step f to place the text from the **gardeners.doc** file into the next empty cell.

   h. Save your changes to the page.

FIGURE G-25

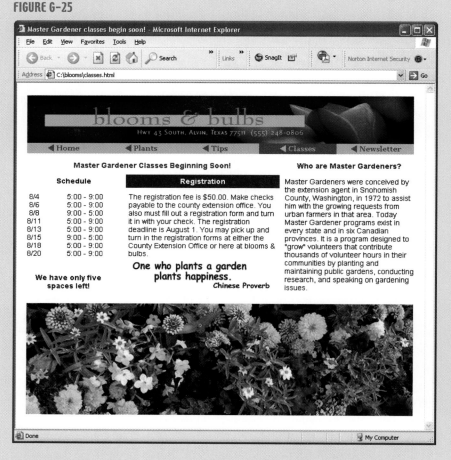

7. Format and modify cell content.

   a. Attach the **blooms_styles.css** file, then apply the body_text style to the dates, times, and two paragraphs of text describing the program.

   b. Create a new style in the blooms_styles.css style sheet named **subheadings** with the following settings: Font: Arial, Helvetica, sans-serif; Size: 14; Style: normal; Weight: bold; Color: #003366.

   c. Create another new style in the blooms_styles.css style sheet named **reverse_text** with the following settings: Font: Arial, Helvetica, sans-serif; Size: 14; Style: normal; Weight: bold; Color: #FFFFFF.

   d. Apply the reverse_text style to the word "Registration" and the subheadings style to the text "Who are Master Gardeners" and "Schedule."

   e. Apply the seasons style to the text "Master Gardener Classes Beginning Soon!"

   f. Center-align the four headings (Master Gardener Classes Beginning Soon!, Who are Master Gardeners?, Schedule, and Registration).

   g. Save the file.

8. Format cells.

   a. Set the horizontal alignment for the cells with the dates and times to Center.

   b. Set the horizontal alignment for the cells describing registration and Master Gardeners to Left.

   c. Select the cell with the word "Registration" in it, then change the cell background color to #000099.

   d. Select each cell that contains text and set the vertical alignment to Top.

   e. Save your work.

9. Add multimedia content.

   a. Insert the **garden_quote.swf** Flash movie located in the unit_g Data Files folder directly below the paragraph about registration, copy the file to the blooms root folder, then enter **Garden quote** in the Object Tag Accessibility Attributes dialog box. (*Hint*: Remember to refresh the Assets panel.)

   b. Play the garden_quote.swf movie in Dreamweaver using the Play button on the Property inspector.

   c. Save your work, then preview the page in your browser.

   d. Close the browser.

10. Add a layer.

   a. Draw a layer in the blank space below the schedule.

   b. Type **We have only five spaces left!** in the layer.

   c. Format the text using the subheadings style.

   d. Name the layer **alert**.

11. Position and format a layer.

   a. Select the layer if necessary.

   b. Set the L value to 30px.

   c. Set the T value to 375px.

   d. Set the W value to 140px.

   e. Set the H value to 30px.

   f. Save your work, view the page in the browser, and compare your screen to Figure G-25.

   g. Close the browser and exit Dreamweaver.

Important: If you did not create these Web sites in Unit B and maintain them during the preceding units, you will need to create a root folder for each Web site and define the Web site using files your instructor will provide. See the "Read This Before You Begin" section for more detailed instructions.

▼ INDEPENDENT CHALLENGE 1

You have been hired to create a Web site for a river expedition company named Rapids Transit, located on the Buffalo River in Arkansas. In addition to renting canoes, kayaks, and rafts, they provide overnight accommodations for those who want to spend more time on the river. River guides are available, if requested, to accompany clients on float trips. The clients range from high-school and college students to families to vacationing professionals. The owner's name is Mike Andrew. Mike has asked you to develop the page for the Web site that lists the equipment available for rental. Refer to Figure G-26 as you work on this page.

   a. Start Dreamweaver and open the Rapids Transit Web site.

   b. Open the rentals.html page, which is blank, then add the title **Rapids Transit rentals available** to the page.

   c. Create a table for page layout with three rows, two columns, 750 pixels wide, zero border, and type **Table used for page layout** in the Table Summary text box.

   d. Center-align the table and merge the cells in the top row.

   e. Use the Assets panel to insert rapids_banner.jpg into the top row, add the alternate text **Rapids Transit banner** when prompted, then center the banner.

FIGURE G-26

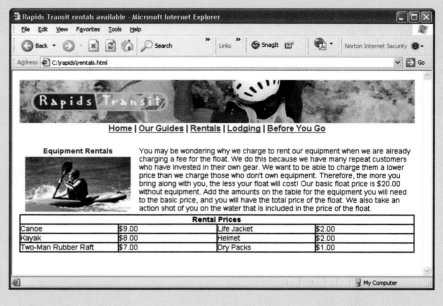

f. Copy the navigation bar from the index page, then close the index page.

g. Click to the right of the banner, enter a line break, then paste the navigation bar.

h. Attach the rapids_styles.css style sheet to the page.

i. Split the first cell in the third row into two rows.

j. Type **Equipment Rentals** in the first of the two split cells in the third row, then center it.

k. Format the Equipment Rentals text using the **lodging** style.

l. Insert the image kayak.jpg from the drive and folder where your Unit G Data Assets Files are stored into the second of the two split cells, adding **Kayaking is fun!** as the alternate text.

m. Center-align the image.

n. Use the tag selector to select the cell with the image and change the cell width to 30%.

o. Import the text from the Unit G Data File rentals.doc into the cell that is to the right of the kayak image.

p. Format the paragraph with the body_text style, and set the vertical alignment to Top.

q. Add a new row to the bottom of the table and merge the cells in it.

r. Insert a new nested table in the bottom row with 4 rows, 4 columns, 100% width, and a border of 1; select the Top header option; set the cell padding and cell spacing for the nested table to zero; type **This table contains rental prices.** for the table summary.

s. Format the nested table border to color #000066.

t. Set each cell width to 25%, then merge the cells in the top row to make room for the table header.

u. Enter the equipment data from Figure G-26 into your table and format the text with the body_text style.

v. Save your work and preview the page in your browser.

w. Close your browser, then exit Dreamweaver.

▼ INDEPENDENT CHALLENGE 2

Your company is designing a new Web site for TripSmart, a travel outfitter. TripSmart specializes in travel products and services. In addition to selling travel products, such as luggage and accessories, they sponsor trips and offer travel advice. Their clients range from college students to families to vacationing professionals. You are now ready to work on the catalog page. The catalog page will feature three items from their catalog.

a. Start Dreamweaver and open the TripSmart Web site.

b. Open the blank file catalog.html from the Web site, and enter the title **TripSmart featured catalog items.**

c. Insert a table with six rows, three columns, a width of 750 pixels, a border of zero, cell padding and spacing of zero, and an appropriate table summary, then set the cell widths to 33%, 33%, and 34%.

d. Center-align the table on the page.

e. Merge the cells in the top row, copy the TripSmart banner and navigation bar from the home page and paste them into the resulting merged cells.

f. Center-align the banner if necessary, enter a paragraph break after the navigation bar, then attach the tripsmart_styles.css file to the page.

g. Merge the three cells in the second row and type **Our products are backed by a 100% guarantee**, then center the text.

h. Type **Protection from harmful UV rays**; **Cool, light-weight, versatile**; and **Pockets for everything** in the three cells in the third row, then center each one.

i. Place the files hat.jpg, pants.jpg, and vest.jpg from the chapter_g assets folder in the three cells in the fourth row, add the following alternate text to the images: Safari hat, Kenya convertible pants, and Photographer's vest, then center the images.

j. Type **Safari Hat**, **Kenya Convertible Pants**, and **Photographer's Vest** in the three cells in the fifth row, then center each label.

k. Type **Item number 50501** and **$29.00** with a line break between them in the first cell in the sixth row, then center them in the cell.

l. Type **Item number 62495** and **$39.50** with a line break between them in the second cell in the sixth row, then center them in the cell.

m. Type **Item number 52301** and **$54.95** with a line break between them in the third cell in the sixth row, then center them in the cell.

n. Apply the body_text style to the three descriptions in the third row.

o. Create a new style in the tripsmart_styles.css style sheet named reverse_text with the following settings: Font: Verdana, Arial, Helvetica, sans-serif; Size: 14; Style: normal; Weight: bold; Color: #FFFFFF

p. Apply the reverse_text style to the text in the second row, then change the cell background color to #666666.

q. Apply the reverse_text style to the three item names under the images, then change the three cell background colors to #999999.

r. Create a style called item_numbers with the following settings: Font: Verdana, Arial, Helvetica, sans-serif; Size: x-small; Style: normal; Weight: bold.

s. Apply the item_numbers style to the three item numbers and prices.

t. Save your work, preview the page in the browser, and compare your page to Figure G-27.

u. Close your browser, then exit Dreamweaver.

FIGURE G-27

▼ INDEPENDENT CHALLENGE 3

Sondra Terrell asked you to design a Web site for her interior design shop that will incorporate the use of tables for both basic page layout and for detailed tabular merchandise and pricing data. She directed you to go to the Web site for the World Wide Web Consortium before you begin work to research accessibility issues regarding the use of tables in designing Web pages.

   a. Connect to the Internet and go to the World Wide Web Consortium at www.w3.org.
   b. Search the Web site for guidelines regarding the use of tables in Web content.
   c. Copy and paste any information you find into a document using your word processing software.
   d. Type a short paragraph summarizing your findings.
   e. Go to Dreamweaver's Help feature and search for information on how you can make tables more accessible with features available in Dreamweaver.
   f. Add another paragraph to your document summarizing your findings.
   g. Close the browser, then exit Dreamweaver.

▼ INDEPENDENT CHALLENGE 4

Dell Patterson has opened a new shop called Needles and Thread that carries needlepoint, cross-stitching, and smocking supplies. She would like to have a Web site and decided to gather some ideas before she hires a Web designer. She visited the L.L. Bean and Neiman Marcus Web sites to look for design ideas.

   a. Connect to the Internet and go to Neiman Marcus at www. neimanmarcus.com.
   b. Use the Source command on the view menu to view the source code and determine if the page layout is based on the use of tables.
   c. Go to L.L. Bean at www.llbean.com, as shown in Figure G-28.
   d. View the source code and determine if the page layout is based on the use of tables.
   e. Using your word processing software or paper, list five design ideas that you like from either of these pages and tell which page was the source of each idea.
   f. Exit the browser.
   g. Consider redesigning all existing pages based on tables using the same settings.

FIGURE G-28

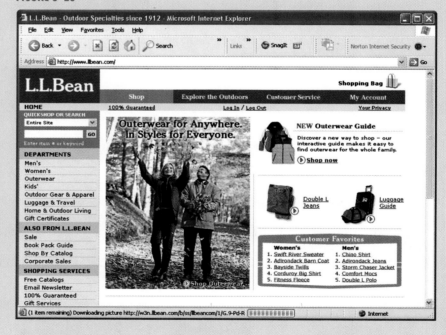

▼ INDEPENDENT CHALLENGE 5

This assignment will continue to build on the personal Web site that you created in Unit B. In Unit C you created and developed your index page. In Unit D you added a page with either an ordered or an unordered list, a CSS Style Sheet with a minimum of two styles, and Flash text. In Unit E you added a page that included at least two graphics. In Unit F you added a page that included several links and an image map. In this lesson, you will be working with one of the other pages in your Web site.

    a. Consult your storyboard and decide which page you would like to develop in this lesson.

    b. Sketch a layout for your page using a table for placement of the page elements.

    c. Experiment with splitting and merging cells and adding and deleting rows.

    d. Create content for this page and format the text attractively on the page using settings for Font, Size, Text Color, Style, and Alignment.

    e. Think about a creative use for a layer and add it to the page.

    f. Save the file and preview the page in the browser.

    g. Consider redesigning all existing pages based on tables using the same settings.

After you are satisfied with your work, verify the following:

    a. Each completed page has a page title.

    b. All links work correctly.

    c. The completed pages view well using a screen resolution of 800 × 600.

    d. All graphics are properly set showing a path to the assets folder of the Web site.

    e. All graphics have alternate text and are royalty-free.

    f. The link checker shows no broken links or orphaned files. If there are orphaned files, note your plan to link them.

    g. All main pages have a consistent navigation system.

You continue your work on the Emma's Book Bag Web site. You are now ready to begin work on a page that will showcase the small cafe in the bookstore. You decide to use a table to lay out the page. The image is muffins.jpg from the unit_g assets folder. The text about the book club can be imported from the book club.doc file in the unit_g data files folder. Use Figure G-29 as a guide to type the rest of the text on the page. (*Hint*: Be sure to attach the style sheet for the Web site. Consider adding new styles to use on this page.)

FIGURE G-29

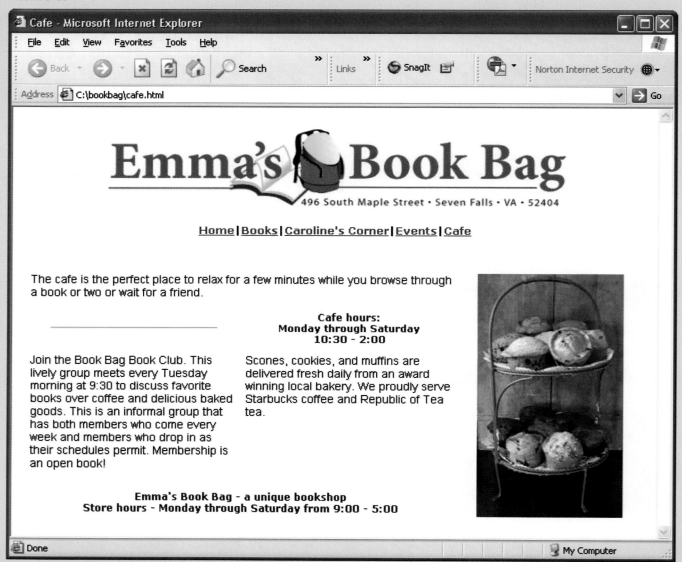

UNIT H
Dreamweaver 8

Collecting Data with HTML Forms

OBJECTIVES

Understand forms and form objects
Insert a form on a page
Add a text form field
Add a radio group
Add a check box
Insert a Submit and a Reset button
Format a form
Update files

HTML forms are a way to add interactivity to a Web page. Forms present users with a series of options for entering information. Dreamweaver lets you create HTML forms containing form objects, such as check boxes and option buttons. The form then sends information that users enter to the host Web server for you to collect. Forms are useful for tasks, such as ordering merchandise, responding to requests for customer feedback, and requesting information. ▞▞▞ The Striped Umbrella Marketing Department has asked you to design a form for the bottom of the activities page; the form will provide another way for interested clients to request additional information about fishing and dolphin cruises.

Understanding Forms and Form Objects

Forms are a convenient and efficient way to obtain information from Web site users. A form can either be a page by itself, collecting several pieces of information from a user with numerous form objects, or it can take up only a small part of a page. See Figures H-1 and H-2 for examples of long and short forms. **Form objects** are the individual form components that accept individual pieces of information. They include check boxes, radio buttons, text fields, and buttons. Many pages include a form with only one form object, such as a text box. You can insert tables in more complex forms to help organize the objects into rows and columns. It is possible for a page to have more than one form. However, you cannot place a form inside a form. In the HTML code, forms are surrounded by beginning and ending form tags.  You decide to place the form at the bottom of the activities page. Before you begin work, you review the various form objects you might use.

DETAILS

- **Form fields**

  A **field** is a form area into which users can insert a specific piece of data, such as their last name or address. Form fields include text fields, hidden fields, and file fields. **Text fields** can accept both numbers and letters, known as **alphanumeric** data. A text field can contain single or multiple lines of data. **Hidden fields** store information about the user and can be used by the company originating the form at a later time, such as the next time the user visits their Web site. **File fields** allow users to browse to a file on their computer and **upload**, or send, it to the form host Web server. In this unit, you will work with text fields.

- **Radio buttons**

  Radio buttons are small empty circles on a form that users click to select a choice. A selected radio button has a black fill. Radio buttons in a group are mutually exclusive, meaning that the user can select only one choice at a time.

- **Check boxes**

  Check boxes are small squares on a form. To select a choice, users click to place a check mark inside the box(es). In a series of check boxes, it is possible to select more than one check box.

- **List/menus**

  List/menus provide the user with a list or menu of choices to select. Lists display the choices in a scrolling format. Menus display the choices in a pop-up menu. List/menus provide a fast method of entering information that may be tedious for the user to type.

- **Buttons**

  Buttons (not to be confused with radio buttons) are usually small rectangular objects containing a text label. When a user clicks a button, a task is performed, such as submitting the form or clearing the form. To **submit** the form means to send the information on the form to the host Web server for processing. Clearing, or **resetting**, the form means to erase all form entries and set the values back to the default settings.

FIGURE H-1: Example of a Web page that is a form

Text box ⊢

Check box ⊢

Menu ⊢

Button

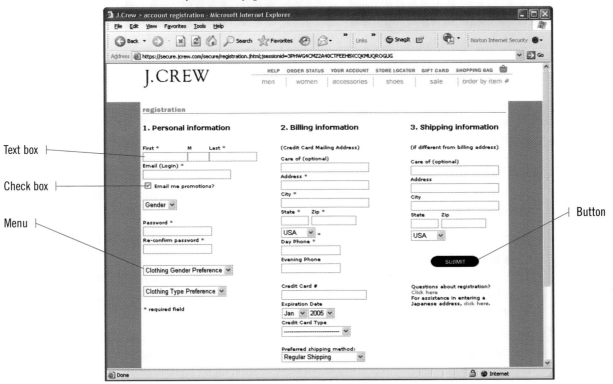

FIGURE H-2: Example of a small form on a Web page

Click list arrow to
see menu

Menu ⊢

Design Matters

Accessible forms

To ensure that your forms are accessible, use the Accessibility preference for Form Objects. To select it, click Edit (Win) or Dreamweaver (Mac) on the menu bar, click Preferences, then click the Accessibility category and select the Form Objects check box. With this option selected, each time you insert a new form, Dreamweaver will prompt you to enter a label tag that is then attached to the form. These labels are read by screen readers.

Inserting a Form on a Page

Before you can begin adding form objects to a page, you must create the form that will contain them. You can create a form by using the Form command on the Insert menu, or by using the Form button on the Insert bar. When you create a form, Dreamweaver adds beginning and ending form tags to the HTML code. You give the form a descriptive name that the program will use when it processes the data from the form. You decide to create a form on the activities page that will include form objects for the client name and address information.

STEPS

1. **Start Dreamweaver, open** The Striped Umbrella Web site, **then open the** activities.html **page**
   The form will go at the bottom of this page.

2. **Place the insertion point after the last sentence on the page, then insert a paragraph break**

3. **Click the** Form button ▢ **in the Forms group on the Insert bar**
   A red dotted outline appears on the page. It doesn't contain any form objects yet. The Property inspector displays the form properties. If you try to insert a form object before you create the form, Dreamweaver will ask if you want to add form tags before inserting the form object.

4. **Select the form name in the Property inspector if necessary, then type** feedback, **replacing the default form name in the Form Name text box, as shown in Figure H-3, then press** [Tab]
   The rest of the form properties relate to how the information users enter will be processed. They can be filled out with information provided by your instructor or left blank. (The programming involved in processing a form is beyond the scope of this book.) You can edit the form to add these properties at a later time. The form cannot be processed on a server without them.

5. **Click the** Show Code View button ⟨⟩ Code
   The form code appears, as shown in Figure H-4.

6. **Locate the tags for the form**
   You notice the tags for the form ID, form name, form method, and form action. The form method directs the way that the data will be sent to the server.

7. **Click the** Show Design View button ▣ Design **to return to Design View**

Design Matters

Creating user-friendly forms

When a form contains several required fields — fields that must be filled out before the form can be processed — it is a good idea to provide visual clues that label these fields as required fields. Often you see an asterisk next to a required field with a corresponding note at either the top or the bottom of the form explaining that all fields marked with asterisks are required. This encourages viewers to complete these fields initially, rather than submitting the form and then receiving an error message asking them to complete required fields that were left blank. Using a different font color for the asterisks and note is an easy way to call attention to them and make them more visible to users.

FIGURE H-3: Form on the activities page

Form

Form name

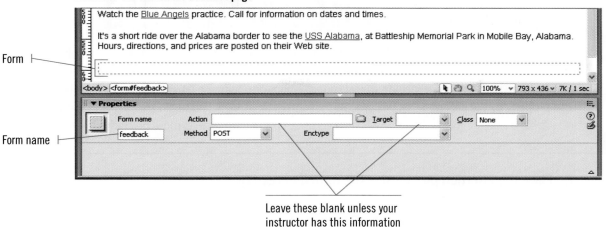

Leave these blank unless your
instructor has this information

FIGURE H-4: HTML code for the form on the activities page

Form tags

```
    "159" hspace="5" vspace="5" align="right" /><span class="body_text">We can also arrange dolphin
    cruises. We have a unique approach -- two boats go out side by side about 50 yards apart. The
    dolphins love it because it generates a huge wake! You'll see them jumping right between the
    boat</span>s. </p>
70  <p class="body_text">You can arrange for tickets for <a href="fishing.html">fishing excursions</
    a> or <a href="cruises.html">dolphin cruises</a> at The Club House desk.</p>
71  <p class="body_text">Check out these links for area attractions that are very kid-friendly: </p>
72  <p class="body_text">Watch the <a href="http://www.blueangels.navy.mil">Blue Angels</a>
    practice. Call for information on dates and times. </p>
73  <p class="body_text">It's a short ride over the Alabama border to see the <a href=
    "http://www.ussalabama.com">USS Alabama</a>, at Battleship Memorial Park in Mobile Bay, Alabama.
     Hours, directions, and prices are posted on their Web site. </p>
74  <form id="feedback" name="feedback" method="post" action="">
75  </form>
76  <p class="body_text"> </p>
77  </body>
78  </html>
79
```

Clues to Use

Processing HTML forms

Forms are processed according to the properties specified in the form action attribute. The **form action** attribute is the part of the form tag that specifies how the data in the form will be processed. If you do not need to save the data that a user enters on a form, it is better to use **client-side scripting**. This means that the form is processed on the user's computer. An example of this is a mortgage calculator that allows you to estimate mortgage payments. If you need to store and process the data, you must use **server-side scripting**. This means the form data is processed on the form's host Web server. An example of this is ordering books on a bookstore Web site. Client-side scripting is written with programs, such as JavaScript or VBScript. Server-side scripting is written with a program such as Common Gateway Interface (CGI) script.

Adding a Text Form Field

One of the most common form fields is a text field. You can create a Single-line text field or a Multi-line text field. Each field should have a descriptive label so users have a visual clue as to what to enter in the field. Form field names should not include spaces, punctuation, or uppercase letters, to ensure that they can be read properly by the program that will process the form data. ▓▓▓▓▓ You begin creating your form by placing a table inside the form. The table will help you line up the form objects more precisely.

STEPS

1. **Place the insertion point inside the form if necessary**
   The table must be placed inside the form to work properly.

2. **Click the Table button ▦ in the Common group on the Insert bar**

3. **Set the table rows to 7, the table columns to 3, the table width to 700 pixels, the border to 0 if necessary, leave the cell padding text box blank, the cell spacing to 3, the Top header option, type This table is used for form layout. for the Summary, then click OK**

4. **Using Figure H-5 as a guide, enter the labels for your text fields into the table, select and format the labels as the subheading style, then drag the column border closer to the edge of the text labels**
   You want the corresponding form fields to appear next to each label.

5. **Place the insertion point in the cell next to the First Name label, then click the Text Field button ▭ in the Forms group on the Insert bar**

QUICK TIP
The default
Char Width is 20
characters.

6. **Click the No Label tag style option in the Input Tag Accessibility Attributes dialog box, click OK, type first_name in the TextField text box on the Property inspector, replacing the default name, then type 30 in both the Char Width and the Max Chars fields**
   You have named the text field first_name. The character width and max characters settings set the size of the text field and the number of characters, respectively, that can be input in the field. If more characters are entered in the field than the character width setting allows, they will not all be visible. They will, however, be submitted with the form data. A user will not be able to enter more characters in the field than the max characters setting allows.

QUICK TIP
If you have to create
many fields of the
same size, you can
copy the first field,
paste it in the new
locations, then
change the name for
each one.

7. **Repeat steps 5 and 6 to enter Single-line text fields for each text label, using the information in Table H-1**
   All text form fields now have labels, names, and settings for the character width on the screen, and the maximum characters the user can enter in each field.

8. **Drag the column border closer to the edge of the form fields, click the first_name field to select it, then save your work**
   Compare your screen to Figure H-6.

TABLE H-1: Form field attributes for the tours form

label	form field name	char width	max chars
First Name	first_name	30	30
Last Name	last_name	30	30
Street	street	30	30
City	city	30	30
State	state	2	2
Zip Code	zip_code	10	10

FIGURE H-5: Adding and formatting form labels

Drag column border closer to labels

Text labels

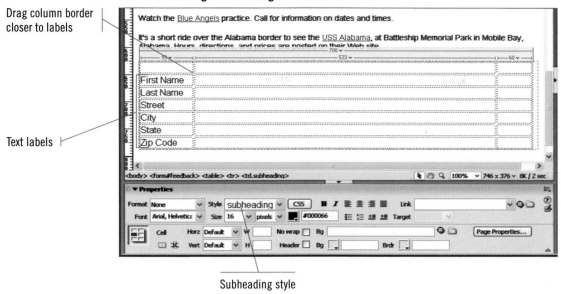

Subheading style

FIGURE H-6: Text form fields added to the feedback form

Selected field

Text form fields

Field name

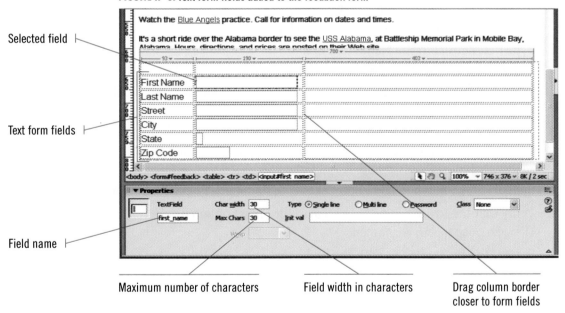

Maximum number of characters

Field width in characters

Drag column border closer to form fields

Clues to Use

Understanding text fields

Dreamweaver has three types of text fields: Single-line text fields, Multi-line text fields, and password fields. **Single-line text fields** are useful for small pieces of data, such as a name or telephone number. **Multi-line text fields**, also called Textarea fields, are useful for entering comments that may take several sentences to complete. **Password fields** are unique fields that display asterisks or bullets when the data is entered to prevent others from viewing the data as it is entered. There are three ways to create a Multi-line text field.

You can click the Text Field button in the Forms group on the Insert bar, select the field, then click the Multi-line option on the Property inspector. Or you can create a Textarea field by clicking the Textarea button in the Forms group on the Insert bar. You can also use the Input Tag Accessibility Attributes dialog box if you have set your preferences to provide accessibility for form objects. To create a password field, create a text field, select the field, then select the Password option on the Property inspector.

Adding a Radio Group

Radio buttons let users select options. When used as a group, they are mutually exclusive: If a user tries to select two radio buttons in the same group, the first one becomes deselected when the second one is selected. Radio buttons are useful in situations where you want users to select only one choice from a group of possible choices. For example, on a shoe order form, radio buttons could represent the different shoe sizes. To order one pair of shoes, users would select only one size. You continue designing your form for the activities page by adding a group of two radio buttons for users to indicate whether they would like to receive newsletters in the mail.

STEPS

1. **Select the third cells in the second, third, and fourth rows, expand the Property inspector if necessary, then click the** Merges selected cells using spans button 🔲 **on the Property inspector**
   The radio group will go in the space you created.

2. **Place the insertion point in the newly merged cell in the third column, then type** Would you like to receive our quarterly newsletters?
   It is important to include instructions so users will know how to fill in the form.

3. **Press** [Shift][Enter] **(Win) or** [shift][return] **(Mac), then click the** Radio Group button 🔳 **in the Forms group on the Insert bar**
   The Radio Group dialog box opens, as shown in Figure H-7.

4. **Type** newsletters **in the Name text box**
   Newsletters is the name of the radio group. Next you configure the two buttons you will use for the group.

   > **TROUBLE**
   > If your table has extra space in the rows, click the table tag **<table>** on the tag selector.

5. **Using Figure H-8 as a guide, select** the first instance of Radio **in the Label column of the Radio Group dialog box to select it, then type** Yes

6. **Press** [Tab] **to select the first instance of radio in the Value column, then type** positive
   You specified that the first radio button will be named Yes and set positive as the value that will be sent to your script or program when the form is processed.

7. **Repeat steps 5 and 6 to add another radio button named** No **with a value of** negative

8. **Verify that the** Lay out using Line breaks (
 tags) **option is selected, then click** OK
   The radio group appears on the form.

9. **Format the button labels with the** body_text style **and the sentence above them using the** subheading style, **save your work, then compare your screen to Figure H-9**

FIGURE H-7: Radio Group dialog box

Enter Radio
Group name

Add Radio button

Delete radio button

Select to change label
for Radio buttons

Click to change
the button order

Select which
Layout to use

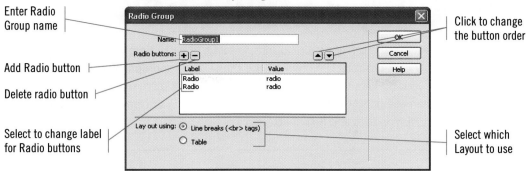

FIGURE H-8: Radio Group properties for newsletters radio group

Name of
Radio Group

Labels for the
two buttons

Button values

Lay Out Using
Line Breaks

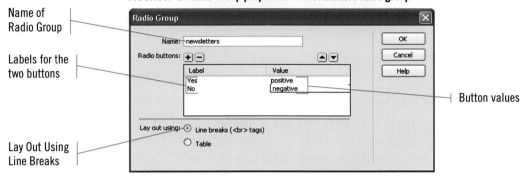

FIGURE H-9: Formatting the Radio Group

Sentence in
subheading
style

Labels in
body_text
style

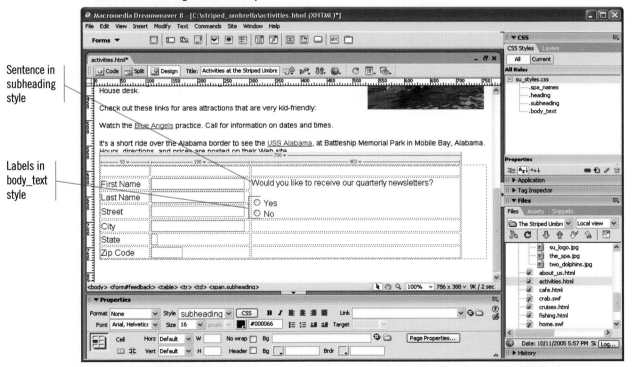

Design Matters

Using List/menus

Often a form will include a field where the user is asked to select only one item, but there are so many items from which to choose that radio buttons would take too much space on the form. In those cases, List/menus are the more appropriate choice for a form object. This object can either take the form of a scrolling list or a shortcut menu. Lists differ from menus in that they allow multiple selections to be made. Menus only allow one selection. Both make efficient use of space on a form.

Adding a Check Box

Check boxes are very much like radio buttons, in that a user can simply click one to select it. However, with check boxes, the user can select more than one choice when appropriate. For example, a form with options for checking your hobbies from a group allows you to check more than one hobby because many people have more than one hobby.  You insert check boxes in the form so users can request more information about the fishing trips and dolphin cruises.

STEPS

1. **Place the insertion point in the third row of the third column, drag to select that cell and the cell beneath it, then click the** Merges selected cells using spans button 🔲 **on the Property inspector**
   These newly merged cells will contain the check boxes.

2. **Place the insertion point in the newly merged cell and type** Please select the materials you would like to receive:, **then press** [Shift][Enter] **(Win) or** [shift][return] **(Mac)**

3. **Click the** Checkbox button 🗹 **in the Forms group on the Insert bar**

> **TROUBLE**
> If you need to edit one of the check boxes, click the check box to select it and edit the properties on the Property inspector.

4. **Type** Fishing **in the Label text box in the Input Tag Accessibilities Attributes dialog box, click the** Wrap with label tag option button **in the Style section, click the** After form item option button **in the Position section, as shown in Figure H-10, then click** OK
   A check box appears in the cell, and the Property inspector displays its default properties.

5. **Select the checkbox, then type** fishing **as the CheckBox name in the Property inspector, replacing the default name, and** fish **as the Checked value**
   You have assigned the check box a name and a value, as shown in Figure H-11. You leave the initial state as unchecked, since you don't want the check box to be selected when the form is first opened.

6. **Click to place the insertion point after the word "Fishing" on the form, press** [spacebar] **once, then repeat Steps 3 through 5 to place one more check box on the form using Figure H-12 as a guide for the check box properties**

> **TROUBLE**
> You may need to resize your cell widths to match Figure H-13.

7. **Format the labels with the** body_text **style and the text line above it as the** subheading **style and compare your screen to Figure H-13**

8. **Save your work**

Design Matters

Creating accessible HTML form objects

The Input Tag Accessibility Attributes dialog box allows you to set the tab order for form objects by entering values in the Tab Index text box. The default for tab orders is from left to right across the page. Screen readers read from left to right. Setting the tab order allows you to override where the insertion point moves each time the user presses the tab key. This forces the insertion point to travel in a designated, logical order. For example, regardless of where the fields for First Name and Last Name are placed on the form, the insertion point can be directed to the Last Name field after a user enters a first name and presses the tab key.

FIGURE H-10: Input Tag Accessibility Attributes dialog box for Fishing label

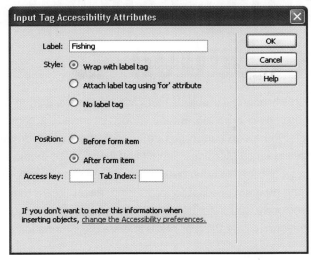

FIGURE H-11: Properties for first check box

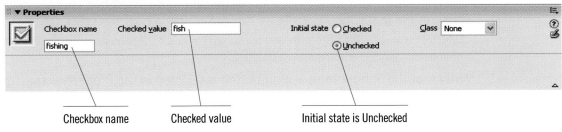

Checkbox name   Checked value   Initial state is Unchecked

FIGURE H-12: Properties for second check box

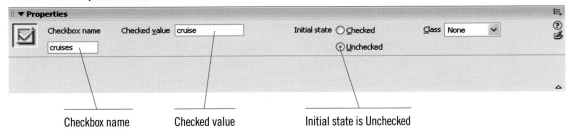

Checkbox name   Checked value   Initial state is Unchecked

FIGURE H-13: Check boxes on form

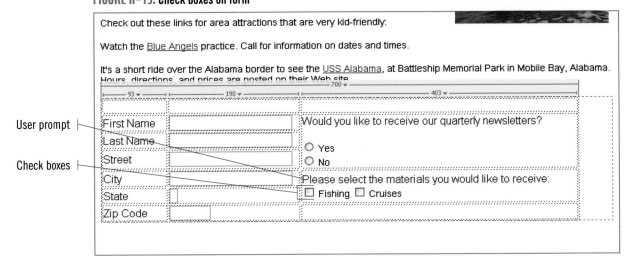

Dreamweaver 8

Inserting a Submit and a Reset Button

Buttons are small rectangular objects that have actions assigned to them. **Actions** are activities that take place after a user clicks a button. Button properties include a name, a label, and an action. As with all selected objects, you assign button properties using the Property inspector. There are two reserved button names that have assigned meanings: Submit and Reset. These should only be used for buttons that are used to submit or reset a form. No other buttons should use these names. **Submit** means to send the form data to the processing program or script for processing. **Reset** means to clear the form fields to the original values. You add a button to the bottom of the form that will submit the form for processing and a button to clear the form in case the user needs to erase the information and start over.

STEPS

1. **Place the insertion point in the third column of the last row**

2. **Click the Button button 🔲 in the forms group on the Insert bar, click the No label tag option in the Input Tag Accessibility Attributes dialog box, then click OK**

   A Submit button appears on the form, and the Property inspector displays its properties. Note that the default button name "Submit" is automatically assigned.

3. **Verify that the Submit form option button is selected in the Property inspector, as shown in Figure H-14**

   When a viewer clicks this Submit button, the information in the form will be sent to the processing script.

4. **Verify that "Submit" is entered in the Button name text box and in the Value text box in the Property inspector**

   The name Submit is automatically set when you select the Submit form option in the Property inspector.

5. **Click the Button button 🔲 on the Insert bar, click the No label tag option in the Input Tag Accessibility Attributes dialog box, click OK, click the Reset form option in the Property inspector, verify that Reset is entered in the Button name text box and the Value text box, then compare your screen to Figure H-15**

   When a viewer clicks this Reset button, the form will clear any information typed by the viewer.

6. **Save your work**

FIGURE H-14: Inserting a Submit button

Button button

Submit button

Button action

Button value

Button name

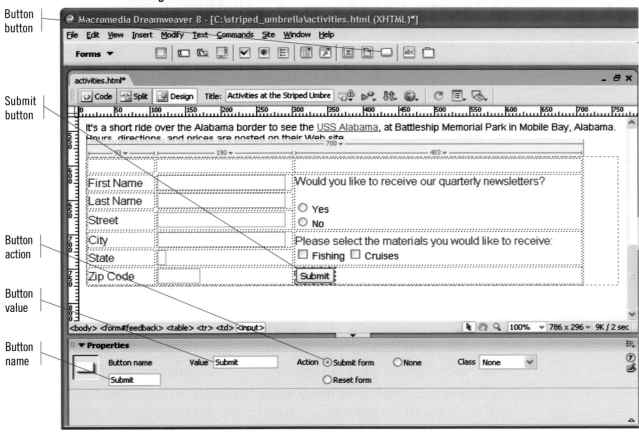

FIGURE H-15: Inserting a Reset button

Reset button

Button action

Button value

Button name

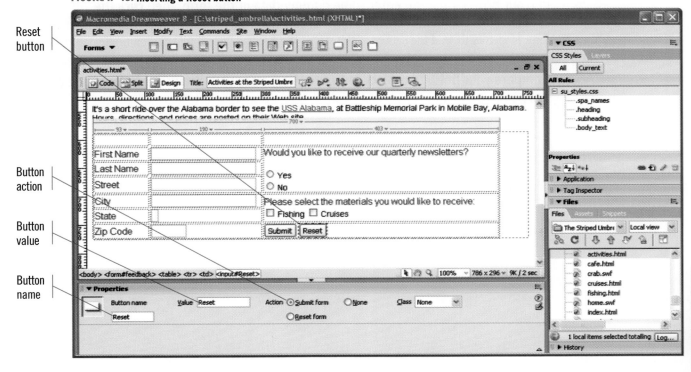

Dreamweaver 8

Formatting a Form

In addition to adding descriptive labels to each form object, there are several ways you can format a form to make it easier to use. You can add brief instructions to the top of the form that will guide the user in filling it out. Simple formatting such as adding a horizontal rule above and below the form can set it off from the rest of the page content. Only the data the user enters using the form objects will be processed; any additional form text and formatting will not be processed. ▰▰▰ You add a short instructional sentence to serve as the form header at the top of the form, right-align some of the labels, then set off the form with a horizontal rule.

STEPS

1. **Merge the top three cells in the table, then type** To request further information please complete this form.

2. **Apply the** spa_names **style to the sentence**
   Notice that the sentence is automatically centered across the table and appears bold because it is a table header.

3. **Select the labels in the first column and right-align them, as shown in Figure H-16**
   The labels are now closer to the text boxes.

4. **Place the insertion point in the last cell of the table, press** [Tab] **to create a new row, select all the cells in the new row, then merge them**
   The new row is merged. You will insert a horizontal line here to end the form.

5. **Place the insertion point in the newly merged cell, click the** Horizontal Rule button ▦ **in the HTML group on the Insert bar, then set the width to** 95% **and the alignment to** Center

6. **Select the table, then center the table in the form**

7. **Save your work, click the** Preview/Debug in Browser button ◉ **, then select** Preview in [your browser name], **enter some dummy data in the form, then click the** Reset **button**
   The Reset button works correctly, but the Submit button will not work correctly because you have not set the form properties to send the data to a Web server. You need additional information from your instructor to do this.

8. **Compare your finished project to Figure H-17, close your browser window, then close the page**

FIGURE H-16: Formatting button labels

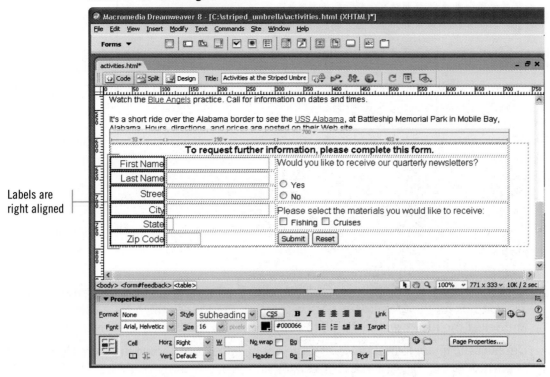

Labels are right aligned

FIGURE H-17: The finished project

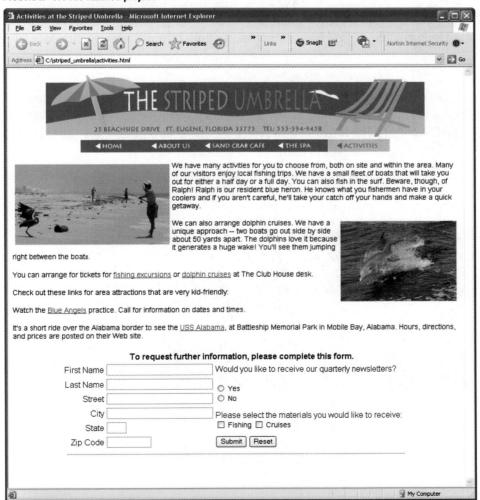

Updating Files

As your Web sites grow, it is easy to forget to take the time to keep your files in good order. Good "housekeeping" habits will save you lots of time later when you have many folders and files. In Unit F, you learned to run reports to identify broken links and orphaned files. When you are using incomplete pages for placeholder pages, they will not show up as orphaned files if they have links to them from other pages. Before they can be published to a Web server, however, they must be completed. Publishing files with "Under Construction" notations are irritating to most viewers. Deleting files that are no longer needed and keeping your other files updated are important to insure quality Web sites. ⬛⬛⬛ You are ready to add content to the fishing and cruises pages so they will be ready for publication.

STEPS

1. **Open the file** dwh_1.html **from the unit_h folder where your Data Files are stored, then save it as** fishing.html **in the striped_umbrella root folder, overwriting the existing fishing page, but not updating links**

2. **Click the** broken link graphic placeholder, **click the** Browse for File **icon ⬛ next to the Src text box on the Property inspector, then browse to the unit_h Data Files assets folder and select the file** heron_small.jpg **to copy the file to the striped_umbrella assets folder**

3. **Deselect the image placeholder, and the image appears as shown in Figure H-18**
   Notice that the text is automatically updated with the body_text style. The code was already in place on the page linking the su_styles.css to the file.

4. **Close the page**

5. **Open the file** dwh_2.html **from the the unit_h folder where your Data Files are stored, then save it as** cruises.html **in the striped_umbrella root folder, overwriting the existing cruises page, but not updating links**

6. **Click the** broken link graphic placeholder, **click the** Browse for File icon **⬛ next to the Src text box on the Property inspector, then browse to the unit_h Data Files assets folder in your Data File location and select the file** boats.jpg **to copy the file to the striped_umbrella assets folder**

7. **Deselect the image placeholder, and the image will appear as shown in Figure H-19**
   Notice that the text is automatically updated with the body_text style. The code was already in place on the page linking the su_styles.css to the file.

8. **Close the page, then exit Dreamweaver**

FIGURE H-18: Fishing page updated

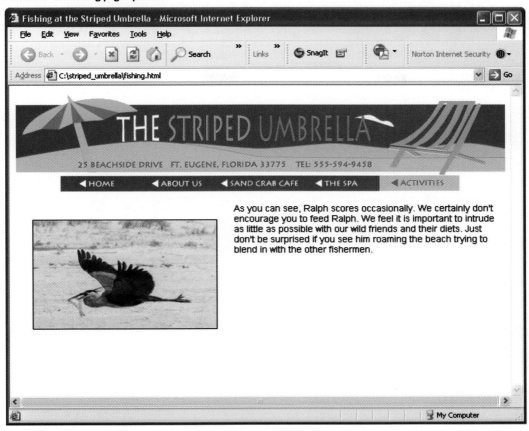

FIGURE H-19: Cruises page updated

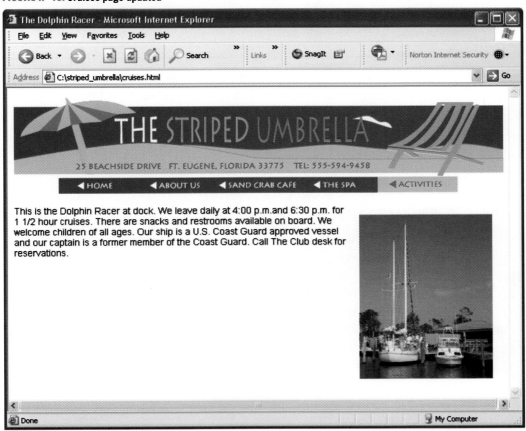

Practice

▼ CONCEPTS REVIEW

Label each element in the Dreamweaver window shown in Figure H-20.

FIGURE H-20

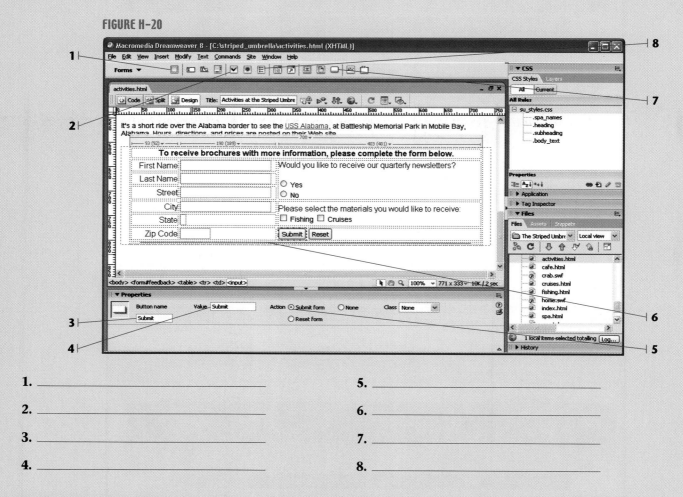

1. _____
2. _____
3. _____
4. _____
5. _____
6. _____
7. _____
8. _____

Match each of the following terms with the statement that best describes its function.

9. **Check boxes**
10. **Radio buttons**
11. **Submit button**
12. **Reset button**
13. **Action**
14. **Password fields**
15. **Multi-line text fields**

a. Sets the form object values to the default settings
b. When in a group, are mutually exclusive; only one can be selected
c. What happens after a button is clicked
d. Display data as asterisks or bullets
e. Send(s) the data to be processed
f. Contain space for more than one line of data
g. More than one can be selected

Select the best answer from the following list of choices.

16. Which of the following is not classified as a form field:

  a. text field.

  b. hidden field.

  c. default field.

  d. file field.

17. Button properties include:

  a. A name, a field, and an action.

  b. A name, a label, and an action.

  c. A name, a label, and a value.

  d. A name, a value, and an action.

18. Server-side scripting means that:

  a. The form is processed on the user's computer.

  b. The form is processed by a JavaScript program.

  c. The form is processed on the form's host server.

  d. b and c.

▼ SKILLS REVIEW

Important: If you did not create this Web site in Unit B and maintain it during the preceding units, you will need to create a root folder for this Web site and define the Web site using files your instructor will provide. See the "Read This Before You Begin" section for more detailed instructions.

1. Understand forms and form objects.

  a. Refer to Figure H-21 to locate a text field, a check box, a radio button, and a Submit button.

2. Insert a form on a page.

  a. Start Dreamweaver and open the tips.html page in the blooms & bulbs Web site.

  b. Place the insertion point after the last sentence on the page and create two paragraph breaks to end the unordered list.

  c. Insert a form.

  d. Name the form **tips**.

  e. View the HTML code for the form.

  f. Return to Design View.

  g. Save your work.

3. Add a text form field.

  a. Place the insertion point inside the form and insert a table with 8 rows and 3 columns, a width of 750 pixels, a border of zero, the cell padding blank, the Top header option, and a table summary "This table is used for form layout."

  b. Center the table in the form.

  c. Using Figure H-21 as a guide, enter labels that will be used for Single line text fields in the first column, beginning in row 2.

  d. Format the labels with the body_text style.

  e. Drag the column border close to the text labels.

  f. Use the information in Table H-2 to add text fields with no label tags in the column next to the labels, beginning in row 2.

  g. Drag the column border close to the text fields.

  h. Save your work.

  i. Merge the second through fifth rows in the third column.

  j. Type **My favorite gardening tip:** in the resulting merged cell.

TABLE H-2: Form field attributes for the tips form

label	form field name	char width	max chars
First Name	first_name	40	40
Last Name	last_name	40	40
Street	street	40	40
City	city	40	40
State	state	2	2
Zip Code	zip_code	10	10
E-mail Address	e_mail	40	40

k. Top-align the text.

l. Create a line break after the text and insert a Multi-line text field (or a Textarea field).

m. Name the new textarea field **my_tips** and set the Char Width to 40 and the Num Lines to 4.

n. Click the table tag to tighten up the table, then save your work.

4. Add a radio group.

a. In the third column in the last row, insert a radio group.

b. Name the radio group **contact**.

c. Enter the label **Please contact me with special offers** for the first radio button and a value of **yes**.

d. Enter the label **Don't contact me** for the second radio button and a value of **no**.

5. Add a check box.

a. In the cell below the text area type **I would be interested in reading Gardening Tips:**.

b. In the same cell, below the text, insert a check box with the label **On the Web** wrapped with the label tag after the form item. Name it **on_web** and assign it a Checked Value of **web**.

FIGURE H-21

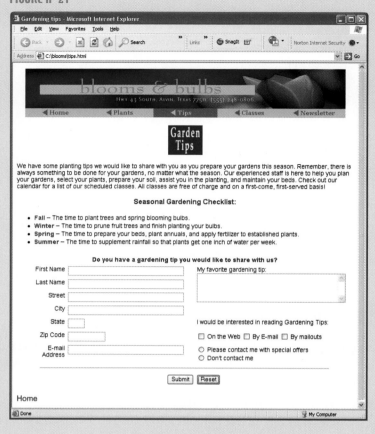

c. Enter a space and insert a check box with the label **By E-mail** wrapped with the label tag after the form item, enter **e_mail** as the name and **e_mail** as the Checked value.

d. Enter a space and insert a check box with the label **By mailouts** wrapped with the label tag after the form item, enter **mailout** as the name and **mail** as the Checked value.

e. Save your work.

6. Insert a Submit and a Reset button.

a. Add a new row to the table.

b. Insert a Submit button with no button label in the second column of the new row.

c. Right-align the Submit button in the cell.

d. Insert a Reset button in the third column of the new row.

e. Verify that **Reset** is the button name, **Reset** is the value, and the action is set to Reset form.

f. Save your work.

7. Format a form.

a. Merge the cells in the top row of the table, then type **Do you have a gardening tip you would like to share with us?** and format the text with the subheadings style.

b. Right-align the labels in the first column of the form.

c. Add a new row between the last two rows in the table and merge all cells in the row.

d. Place a horizontal rule in the new row and format it as 90%, centered.

e. Format all text that is not formatted in the form with the body_text style.

f. Select the table, then set the cell spacing to 5.

g. Save your work, then preview the page in the browser, test all fields, then test the Reset button.

h. Close the browser, then exit Dreamweaver.

Important: If you did not create these Web sites in Unit B and maintain them during the preceding units, you will need to create a root folder for these Web sites and define the Web sites using files your instructor will provide. See the "Read This Before You Begin" section for more detailed instructions.

▼ INDEPENDENT CHALLENGE 1

You have been hired to create a Web site for a river expedition company named Rapids Transit, located on the Buffalo River in Northwest Arkansas. In addition to renting canoes, kayaks, and rafts, they also have a lodge, cabins, and tents for overnight stays. River guides are available, if requested, to accompany clients on float trips. The clients range from high school and college students to families to vacationing professionals. Mike Andrew, the owner of Rapids Transit, has asked you to add a form to the page that describes the three categories of lodging available. The purpose of this form will be to allow users to request brochures for each lodging category.

a. Open the Rapids Transit Web site.

b. Open the page lodging.html.

c. Place a paragraph break after the last sentence on the page and insert a form called lodging.

d. Insert a table inside the form with 7 rows and 3 columns, 750 pixels wide, no border, a Top header, an appropriate table summary, and center aligned.

e. Enter text labels in the first column beginning with the second row, using Figure H-22 as a guide.

f. Format the labels with the body_text style.

g. Adjust the column border adjacent to the text labels.

h. Add Single line text fields in the column next to the text labels using 30 characters for all text fields except the zip code and state. Use a width of 2 for the state. Use a width of 10 for the zip code. Name the fields appropriately.

i. Adjust the column border.

j. In the third column of the second row type **Please check the brochures you would like to receive.**, then format it with the body_text style.

k. Place a check box in the third column of the third row named **option_1** with a value of **lodge** and a text label of **The Lodge**.

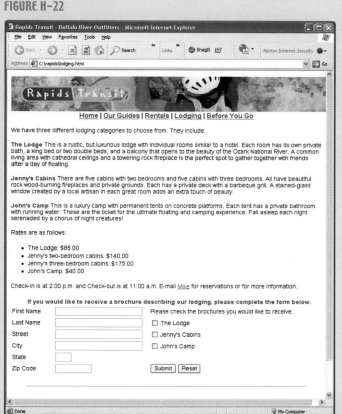

FIGURE H-22

l. Place a check box in the third column of the fourth row named **option_2** with a value of **jenny** and a text label of **Jenny's Cabins**.

m. Place a check box in the third column of the fifth row named **option_3** with a value of **john** and a text label of **John's Camp**.

n. Format the three labels next to the check boxes with the body_text style.

o. Insert a Submit button in the third column of the last row.

p. Insert a Reset button to the right of the Submit button in the same cell, and change the Action to **Reset form**, the button value to **Reset**, and the Action to **Reset form**.

q. Merge the cells in the top row, then type **If you would like to receive a brochure describing our lodging, please complete the form below.**

r. Format the sentence with the **lodging** style.

s. Insert a new row at the end of the table and merge the cells in the new row.

t. Insert a horizontal rule with a 90% width and centered in the new row.

u. Preview the page in the browser, compare it to Figure H-22, and test the text fields and the Reset button.

v. Make any adjustments to improve the page, save your work, then exit Dreamweaver.

▼ INDEPENDENT CHALLENGE 2

In this exercise you will continue your work on the TripSmart Web site. The owner, Thomas Howard, wants you to create a form to collect information from viewers who are interested in receiving more information on one or more of the featured trips.

a. Open the TripSmart Web site, then open the destinations page.

b. Insert a paragraph break after the last sentence on the page, then insert a form named **information**.

c. Insert a table in the form that contains 11 rows, 2 columns, a Table width of 700 pixels, a Border thickness of 0, Cell padding of 1, Cell spacing of 1, and add an appropriate table summary. Center the table.

d. Merge the cells in the top row, type **Please complete this form for additional information on these tours.**, apply the reverse_text style, then change the cell background color to #666666.

e. Beginning in the second row, type the following labels in the cells in the first column: **First Name**, **Last Name**, **Street**, **City**, **State**, **Zip Code**, **Phone**, **E-mail**, and **I am interested in:**, adjust the column border to a position of your choice, then right-align the labels and apply the body_text style to each one.

f. Insert single-line text fields in the eight cells in the second column and assign the following names: **first_name**, **last_name**, **street**, **city**, **state**, **zip**, **phone**, and **email**, setting the Char width to **30** and the Max Chars to **100** for each of these text fields. (*Hint*: To save time create the first_name field, then use copy and paste to create the other fields, changing the name of each pasted field in the Property inspector.)

g. In the second cell of the tenth row, insert a checkbox with the label **The Amazon**, the name **amazon**, and a Checked value of **yes**.

h. Repeat Step g to add another checkbox next to the Amazon checkbox with the label **Kenya**, the name **kenya**, and a Checked value of **yes**.

i. Apply the body_text style to the Amazon and Kenya labels.

j. Left-align the cells with the text boxes and checkboxes, then set each cell's vertical alignment to Top.

k. Insert a Submit button and a Reset button in the second cell of the eleventh row.

l. Insert a horizontal rule that is 550 pixels wide below the form.

m. Save your work, preview the page in your browser, test the form, compare your screen to Figure H-23, close your browser, then close the destinations page.

FIGURE H-23

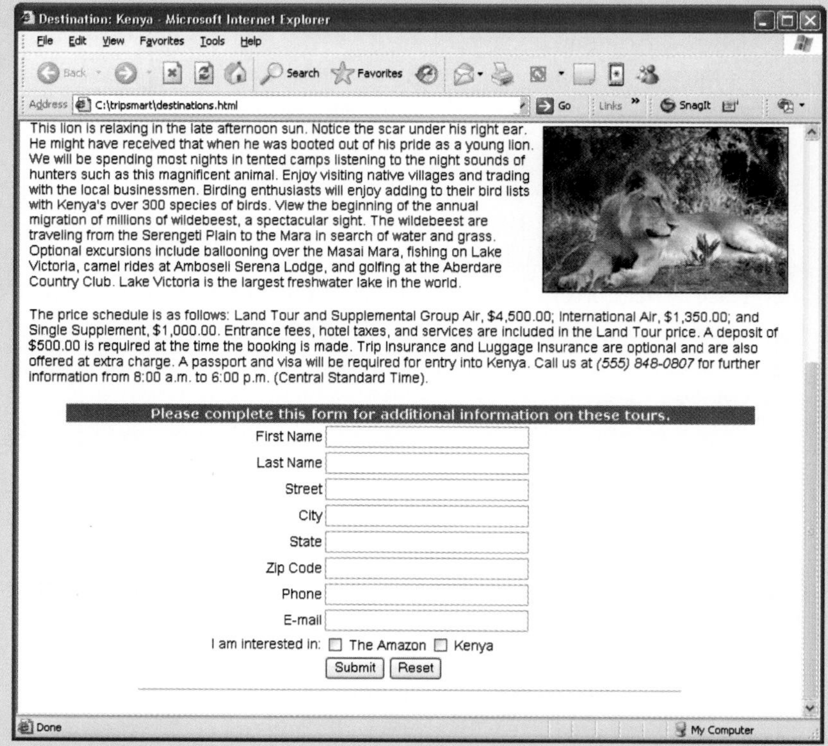

▼ INDEPENDENT CHALLENGE 3

Dr. Glen McGraw teaches a class in folklore at the University of Toronto. On his Web page at the university, he would like to insert a form that would encourage people to send him folk sayings that they heard as children. He knows that he could construct an appropriate form for his page, but he doesn't know how to tell it to process the data. He knows that there are some free CGI scripts available on the Internet.

a. Connect to the Internet and go to www.google.com, as shown in Figure H-24.
b. Type **free CGI scripts** in the Search text box, then click **Google Search**.
c. Browse several articles to gather information about CGI scripts.
d. Print the article that you find most informative.

FIGURE H-24

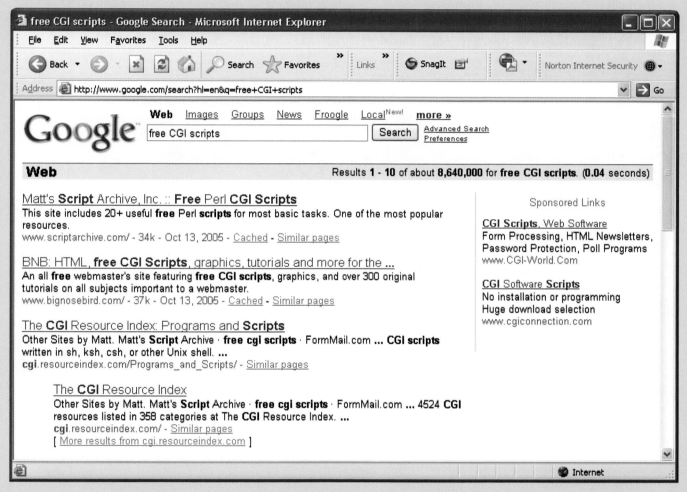

▼ INDEPENDENT CHALLENGE 4

Paul Patrick and his partner Donnie Honeycutt have a construction business in Southern California. They have recently published a Web site for their business and would like to add a search form to their Web site to help their customers quickly find the data they are looking for. They first do some research on the Internet to critique other Web site search pages.

    a. Connect to the Internet and go to the Smithsonian Institute site at www.si.edu.

    b. Click the Search link to search the Smithsonian Web site, as shown in Figure H-25.

    c. How is the search form organized?

    d. What form objects were used?

    e. Try the Tips link. What information did you find to help viewers search the Web site?

    f. Find one more example of a Web site that uses a search page and explain which of the two sites you prefer and why.

FIGURE H-25

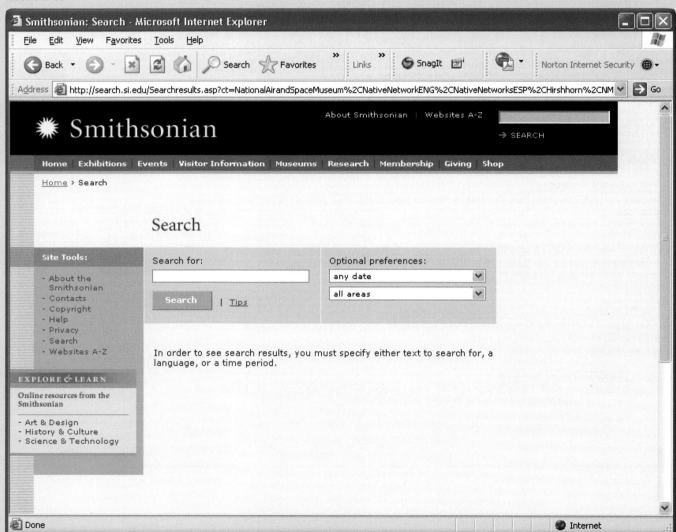

▼ INDEPENDENT CHALLENGE 5

This assignment will continue to build on the personal Web site that you created in Unit B. In Unit C you created and developed your index page. In Unit D you added a page with either an ordered or an unordered list, a CSS Style Sheet with a minimum of two styles, and Flash text. In Unit E you added a page that included at least two graphics. In Unit F you added a page that included several links and an image map. In Unit G you created a page layout using tables and a layer. In this lesson, you will add a form to one of the pages in your Web site.

    a. Consult your storyboard and decide which page you would like to develop in this lesson.

    b. Sketch a layout for your page to place the form objects you would like to use.

    c. Create the form using at least three different form objects. Include clear instructions that will help users fill out the form correctly.

    d. Add text labels to each form object.

    e. Add a Submit and Reset button and format them appropriately.

    f. Format the form attractively to help it stand out on the page.

    g. Save the file and preview the page in the browser, testing the Reset button to make sure it works correctly.

    h. Make any adjustments that are necessary to improve the appearance of your form.

After you are satisfied with your work, verify the following:

    a. Each completed page has a page title.

    b. All links work correctly.

    c. The completed pages view well using a screen resolution of 800 × 600.

    d. All graphics are properly linked to the assets folder of the Web site.

    e. All graphics have alternate text and are royalty-free.

    f. The link checker shows no broken links or orphaned files. If there are orphaned files, note your plan to link them.

    g. All main pages have a consistent navigation system.

    h. The form is attractive and easy to understand and use.

Use Figure H-26 as a guide to continue your work on the Emma's Book Bag Web site. You are adding a form to the events page that will allow customers to add their names to the e-mail list for future events. Insert the form at the bottom of the events page, using a table for form layout.

FIGURE H-26

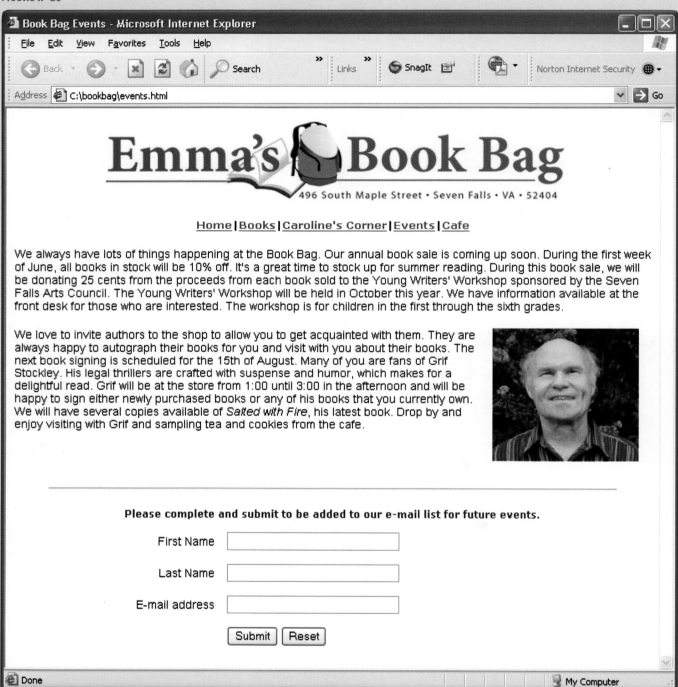

APPENDIX A
Dreamweaver 8

Updating, Maintaining, and Publishing Your Web Site

OBJECTIVES

Update a growing site using templates
Manage your site with Macromedia Contribute
Maintain your site
Test your Web pages
Publish your site

As you prepare to publish your site, it is important to develop an effective site-maintenance routine that you will continue to follow after it is published. If you have used template-based pages, you can update information quickly and easily. For instance, rather than having to change each item on several template-based pages, you can make one change to an item on a template page. All pages based on that template then update automatically. Several relatively easy maintenance tasks can help you keep your Web site clean and vibrant. These include checking, testing, and organizing site components. You should tackle these tasks at regular intervals to prevent Web site errors. After you have run your initial maintenance checks and you are assured that your Web site works correctly, the Web site is ready to publish. Before you can publish your site, you must select the settings to transfer the files to the Web server. You begin by looking at the advantages that templates offer for creating and updating Web sites.

Update a Growing Site Using Templates

When you create a Web site, it's important to make sure that each page has a unified look so that viewers know they are in your site no matter what page they are viewing. Common elements, such as the navigation bar and company banner, should appear in the same place on every page, and every page should have the same background color. If you are the only site developer, you can easily copy elements from one page to another. As your organization grows and your Web site becomes more complex, one way to update your site and maintain a consistent appearance on every page is through the use of templates. **Templates** are Web pages that contain the basic layout for other related pages in a Web site. ▰▰▰ Your organization is growing. You consider the advantages of incorporating templates in your increasingly complex Web site.

DETAILS

- **Templates save development time, especially when different people will be creating pages in your site.** The ideal process for using templates is for one person (the template author) to create a page and save it as a template with a .dwt file extension. Other team members use the template to create pages for the same site. The template author creates **locked regions**, which are areas of the page that other page designers cannot modify, and **editable regions**, in which other designers can add or change content. Locked regions usually contain design elements common to every page in the site. Figure AP-1 shows a template with an editable region.

- **Templates ensure both continuity and flexibility throughout a Web site.** Each page a team creates from a template is connected to the original template file, so if the template author changes the template, all pages to which the template is attached can be automatically updated. **Nested templates** are templates that are based on other templates. Templates also allow for design flexibility: an **optional region** is an area in the template that other contributors can choose to show or hide.

- **Templates simplify the updating process.** A Web site needs to change with the times: When changes occur in your company, on a small or large scale, you will need to change your Web site's appearance and functionality. If your Web site pages are based on a template or a group of nested templates, you will be able to make those changes quickly and easily.

  Once the author develops the template (using one of the template page options shown in Figure AP-2) and distributes it to other team members (usually graphic artists and writers), they can apply the template to their site pages, adding appropriate content to the editable regions of each page.

To create a new template:

1. **Click File on the menu bar, click New, click Template page, then double-click HTML template**
   As the Web page author, you would usually select the HTML template option.

2. **Click Insert on the menu bar, point to Template objects, click the region type you want to add, then add content for the region if necessary**
   See Table AP-1 for a description of the available regions. By default, all template content is locked except for editable regions, which allow designers to add their own content.

3. **Click File on the menu bar, click Save As, type a template name, noting that the Template folder is the save location, and .dwt is the file extension for the template page, then click Save**

To create a page based on a template:

1. **Click File on the menu bar, click New, then click the Templates tab**

2. **Click the site name, then double-click the template name**
   A new Dreamweaver document opens, based on the template.

3. **Add text to the template regions, then save the page**

FIGURE AP-1: Template with editable regions

Locked region

Editable region label

Editable region marked by blue outline

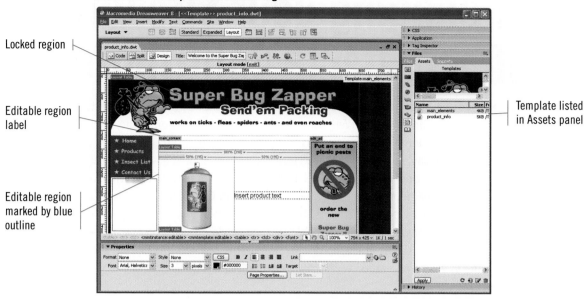

Template listed in Assets panel

FIGURE AP-2: Template page options

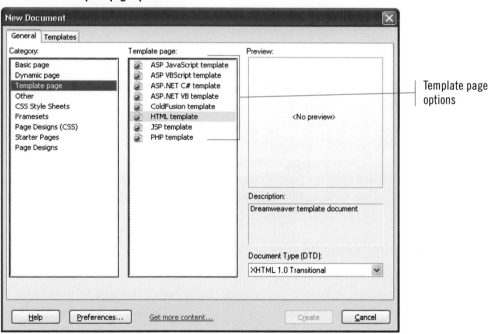

Template page options

TABLE AP-1 Template regions

region type	meaning to users
Editable	A region that allows users to edit the content.
Optional	A region that allows users to choose to either show or hide content.
Repeating	A region that contains content that is used multiple times.
Editable Optional	A region that allows users to both edit the content and choose to show or hide the content.
Repeating Table	A table that has a predefined structure and allows users to add content.

Managing your Site with Macromedia Contribute

Macromedia Contribute is a Web development tool that can be invaluable to both professional Web developers and non-technical Web content contributors. With Contribute, Web developers can design pages similar to templates that others can then use to insert content specific to their area. For example, a university might decide that all faculty members should have a Web page on the school Web site with their photo, a brief biography, and a list of the classes that they teach. This would be a difficult task for faculty members without a technology background. With Contribute, the school's webmaster can design a page to be used by all faculty members. The faculty members would then open the page in Contribute and simply insert their own photo, bio, and classes. They would not need a copy of Dreamweaver on their computer. Figure AP-3 shows the Contribute Start page. ██████ You explore the advantages of using Contribute in your organization to develop Web content.

DETAILS

The advantages for Web professionals include the following:

- **Consistency across the Web site**

  By designing pages that can be used as the template for many similar pages, developers can create a Web site with a consistent, professional look without the webmaster's direct involvement in developing each page.

- **Time savings**

  Contribute is a huge timesaver for the Web professional. The ability to create templates for others to use gives the developer control over the pages, but frees up the time that would have been spent working on each page individually. The developer has a choice of several levels of permissions that can be attached to the pages that will allow contributors to add their own content without changing the basic layout.

- **Support for basic features**

  Contribute supports basic features, such as Cascading Style Sheets and Dreamweaver templates, that promote continuity across a Web site. Contribute also includes Flash paper. **Flash paper** converts existing documents into Flash (.swf) files so they may be distributed as printable documents for Web distribution.

The advantages for content contributors include the following:

- **Ease of use**

  Content contributors can open, edit, and publish a Web page with only basic computer skills. For example, they can easily drag and drop content from applications that they may be more familiar with, such as Microsoft Word or Microsoft Excel. In Contribute, they can correct errors using a feature that allows them to revert back to a previously-saved version of each page. The Contribute interface is simple and includes a Breeze tour of the product, as well as a tutorial that includes a practice Web site, as shown in Figure AP-4. **Breeze** is a Macromedia program that produces multimedia presentations for Web communications.

- **More freedom for advanced users**

  With the different levels of permissions possible, a person with more Web experience can be given more freedom than one who is not comfortable with Web editing. Less experienced users can be required to have their pages reviewed before publishing, while more experienced users can publish their pages without review.

FIGURE AP-3: **Contribute Start page**

Help files

Breeze tour

Interactive tutorial

FIGURE AP-4: **Editing a Web page using the tutorial**

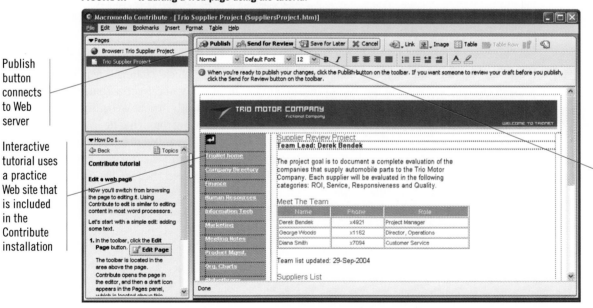

Publish button connects to Web server

Interactive tutorial uses a practice Web site that is included in the Contribute installation

Send for Review sends the page to be reviewed before publishing

Maintaining Your Site

At fairly frequent intervals, you should perform routine Web site maintenance tasks. As you have probably learned from working on the projects for this book, Web sites can quickly become complex and difficult to manage. Checking links and organizing the Assets panel will help you keep a Web site "clean." You review the routine maintenance tasks to make sure your Web sites are always in great shape.

DETAILS

Follow these guidelines to maintain your Web site:

- **Check links**

  Use the Link Checker to check all links in the Web site, both external and internal. The Link Checker, in the Results panel, alerts you to any broken internal links and helps you repair them. It also lists the external links but does not verify their validity. In addition, the Link Checker alerts you to orphaned files. **Orphaned files** are files that are not linked to any other pages in the Web site. Often, orphaned files are simply files that you have not completed so are not yet ready to be linked to the Web site. If you find orphaned files, evaluate each file, then either delete it or develop it further. Even if you are not ready to link these files, routinely running a list of orphaned files will remind you of the work you must complete in preparation for linking them to the Web site. Figure AP-5 shows the options for using the Link Checker. You can either check the links on a single page, the entire Web site, or selected files or folders. You can open the Link Checker as a panel, or access it by right-clicking a file in the Files panel, then clicking Check Links, or by clicking Window in the menu bar, pointing to Results, and then clicking the tab Link Checker (Win), or by clicking Site in the menu bar and clicking Check Links Sitewide (Mac). Once you have located broken links or orphaned files, you must fix them. You can fix a broken link in the Link Checker panel, or by using the Property inspector. To correct a broken link, use the Browse for File icon to browse to the file that is the correct destination.

- **Organize the Assets panel**

  Use the Assets panel to check the list of images and colors used in your Web site. If there are images listed that are not in use, consider moving them to a storage folder outside the Web site until you need them. Also, check the Colors list to make sure that all colors listed are Websafe. If you find non-Websafe colors in the list, locate the elements to which the non-Websafe colors are applied and apply Websafe colors to them. Figure AP-6 shows a list of colors in a Web site. One of the colors shown is non-Websafe, and must be replaced with a Websafe color.

TROUBLE

Note that you can only designate assets as favorites, not .htm files.

If your list of images or multimedia files has grown to the point that much scrolling is required to find one, consider creating subfolders in the Assets panel to organize them. You can categorize some files as favorites. **Favorites** are files you designate as those that you expect to use frequently in your Web site. They then appear in a separate window in the Assets panel to provide fast access. Scrolling through long lists of assets to find them is not necessary. Figure AP-7 shows files that have been designated as favorites. Favorites still appear in the list of Site files. To designate a file as a favorite, right-click (Win) or [ctrl]-click (Mac) it in the Assets panel, then click Add to Favorites or Add to Image Favorites. Then when you select the Favorites option at the top of the Files panel, only your Favorites appear.

FIGURE AP-5: Link Checker options

Click list arrow to access options

Options

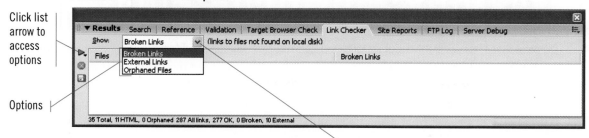

Click Show list arrow, then choose the type of report to run

FIGURE AP-6: Locating Non-Websafe colors

Non-Websafe color

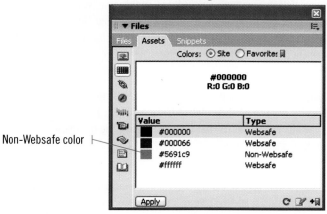

FIGURE AP-7: Favorites category on Assets panel

Graphic files listed in the Favorites list, in addition to the Site list

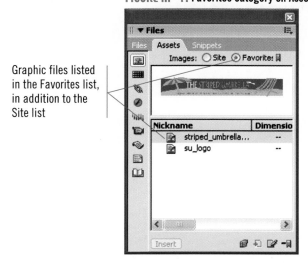

Testing Your Web Pages

Dreamweaver has several helpful reports you can run that identify problems in your Web site. You should run these reports on a regular schedule. The more frequently you run them, the easier it will be to correct any problems. If you allow errors to build up, it will be more difficult to find and correct them. Besides taking advantage of the Dreamweaver report features, nothing takes the place of actually viewing your pages in a browser so you can see what editing and formatting changes are necessary. ▰▰▰▰ You review the site report features available in Dreamweaver and consider how you can use them in your Web sites.

DETAILS

- **Site reports**

  The Reports option, found on the Site menu, provides a checklist of reports that you can generate for your Web site. Figure AP-8 shows the Reports dialog box. You can create reports for the current document, the entire local site, selected files in the site, or a selected folder by clicking the Report On list arrow and choosing an option. You can create a Workflow report to see files that other designers are using or create a report to view Design Notes, which are notes you can add to a file for other designers who are working on different parts of your site. You can also create a Workflow report that will list all files that have been modified recently. There are six HTML reports that you can generate, including Combinable Nested Font Tags, Accessibility, Missing Alt Text, Redundant Nested Tags, Removable Empty Tags, and Untitled Documents. The Missing Alt Text and the Untitled Documents are especially important for Web site accessibility. After you run a report, you can save it as an XML file. You can then import it into a database, spreadsheet, or template to view.

- **Site map**

  View the site map in the expanded Files panel, and ask yourself the following questions: Does the navigation structure reflect a logically organized flow chart? Is each page a maximum of three or four clicks from the home page? If not, make any adjustments that would improve the navigation structure. Figure AP-9 shows an example of a site map displaying external and internal links.

- **Test pages**

  Test each page again for design layout, using several types and versions of browsers. Test each page using many different screen resolutions, and test your site on different platforms. Test all external links to make sure they connect to valid, active Web sites. Notice how long it takes each page to download, and consider trimming pages that download slowly. Considering the volatility of the Web, testing external links should be done at regular intervals, such as once a week. Nothing is more frustrating to a user than to click on a link that no longer works.

- **Enjoy positive feedback and respond to negative feedback**

  Everyone enjoys hearing positive feedback. When you receive positive feedback, record the comments so that you can refer to them in the future as you edit the site. Note the negative feedback and use it to your advantage to improve the Web site.

FIGURE AP-8: Reports dialog box

Report On options

Workflow reports

HTML reports

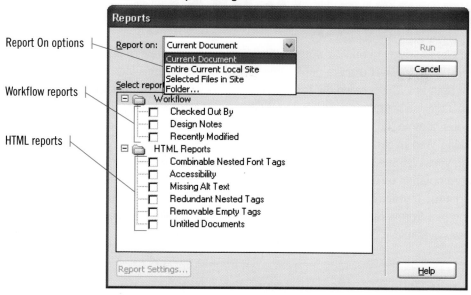

FIGURE AP-9: Site map

Child pages to home page

Internal links

External links

E-mail link

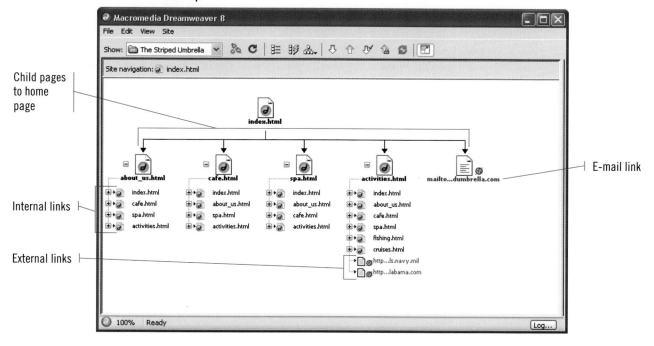

Publishing Your Site

Once your files are ready to publish, you must tell Dreamweaver where to place your files. The process follwed by most Dreamweaver users to publish their sites is first to create a local root folder to house all of the files for the Web site. This is called the **local site**. Next, they gain access to a remote site. A **remote site** is a folder on a Web server that is connected to the Internet, hosts Web sites, and is not directly connected to the computer housing the local site. Often the **ISP**, or Internet Service Provider, will furnish users with space for publishing Web pages. This space then becomes the remote site. After setting up remote access and completing your Web site, you transfer your files to the remote server through the Files panel. The transfer is easily accomplished by using the Put button on the Files panel. This is similar to the process used by FTP client programs. Transferring your files from your computer to a remote computer is called **uploading**. Transferring files from a remote computer to your computer is called **downloading**. ⬛⬛⬛ You review the processes available in Dreamweaver for publishing a Web site.

DETAILS

- **Using the Define Sites Remote Access dialog box**

  When your pages are ready to publish, the files must be transferred from the local site to the remote site. In Dreamweaver, you use the Define Sites Remote Access dialog box to enter the information about the remote site, such as the FTP host, host directory, the login, and the password. **FTP (File Transfer Protocol)** is the process of uploading and downloading files to and from a remote site. After the remote site information is entered, the files are transferred using the Put button in the Files panel. Figure AP-10 shows the Site Definition dialog box. You open this window by using the Site/New Site, or Site/Manage Sites command to open the Site Definition dialog box, clicking Edit, clicking the Advanced tab, then clicking Remote Info. The choices for remote access appear when you click the Access list arrow.

- **Setting up FTP**

  The method most people use to transfer files is FTP. If you choose the FTP option, you then see several text boxes you need to complete, as shown in Figure AP-11. This information will come from your ISP. The FTP Host is the address on the Web where you will send your files. The Host Directory is your folder on the remote server where you will place your files. The Login and Password will be provided by your ISP. There are also some security options that you can check when transferring your files.

- **Using Put**

  Click the Put File(s) button on the Files panel (Win), shown on Figure AP-12, to transfer the files from the Local site to the Remote site. Click the Get File(s) button to transfer the files from the Remote site to the Local site. (There is also a Connects to Remote Host button that connects to the remote host, but the Put File(s) button also connects automatically.) After selecting the files you want to transfer, click the Put File(s) button. Answer YES when asked if you want to transfer dependent files; this transfers associated files, such as graphic files, in the Web site.

- **Synchronizing files**

  You can choose to **synchronize** your site. The Synchronize command allows you to transfer only the latest versions of files, rather than all the Web site files. To synchronize your site, click Site on the menu bar with the Files panel expanded (Win), or click Site on the menu bar (Mac), then click Synchronize. If no files have changed since the last transfer, Dreamweaver notifies you that you do not need to synchronize.

Clues to Use

Choosing remote access options

Remote access choices include FTP, Local/Network, RDS, SourceSafe Database, and WebDAV. Local/Network refers to publishing a Web site on either the local drive (that is, your own hard drive) or a local network drive. RDS stands for Remote Development Services and is used with a remote folder running ColdFusion. SourceSafe Database is available under the Windows platform using Microsoft Visual SourceSafe Client. WebDAV stands for Web-based Distributed Authoring and Versioning. WebDAV is used with servers such as the Microsoft Internet Information Server (IIS) and Apache Web server.

FIGURE AP-10: Site Definition dialog box

Advanced tab

Remote Info category

Access options

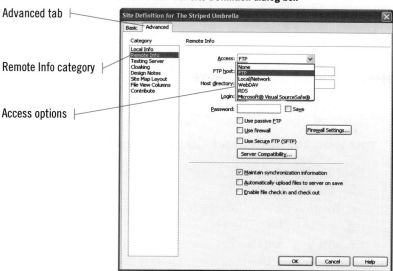

FIGURE AP-11: Remote Info for FTP

FTP Access

FTP Host

Host Directory

Login

Password

Security options

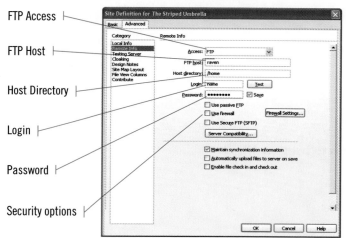

FIGURE AP-12: Files panel

Get File(s)

Put File(s)

Connects to Remote Host

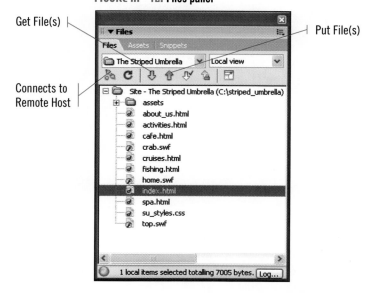

Practice

▼ CONCEPTS REVIEW

Match each of the following terms with the statement that best describes its function.

1. **Put File(s) button**
2. **Get File(s) button**
3. **Orphaned files**
4. **Favorites file list**
5. **Missing Alt Text**
6. **Link Checker**
7. **Checked Out By**
8. **Template**

a. Files that are not linked to any other pages in a Web site
b. An HTML report
c. Transfers the files from the remote site to the local site
d. Checks for broken links
e. Files that have been designated to use frequently in your Web site
f. Transfers the files from the local site to the remote site
g. Pages that can be used as a basis for creating other pages
h. A Workflow report

Select the best answer from the following list of choices.

9. **FTP is the acronym for:**
   a. File Transfer Protocol.
   b. File Transfer Process.
   c. File Transfer Pending.
   d. File Transferring Process.

10. **The most commonly used process to transfer files is:**
    a. Local/Network.
    b. RDS.
    c. FTP.
    d. SourceSafe Database.

11. **The list of Websafe colors is viewed in the:**
    a. Files panel file list.
    b. Assets panel.
    c. Site map.
    d. Site report.

12. **The Link Checker can check for broken links on:**
    a. One Web page.
    b. The entire Web site.
    c. Selected files and folders.
    d. All of the above.

13. **An area in a template where users can add or change content is called:**
    a. A locked region.
    b. An editable region.
    c. An optional region.
    d. A hidden region.

Managing Your Files

OBJECTIVES

Understand your computer's file structure
Organize and name files and folders
Find and manage files

One of the major stumbling blocks people encounter when learning new software is how to organize, save, and find their files and folders, a skill known as **file management**. Often, students learn only enough to "get by" in the programs, yet they "lose" files or don't remember where they've saved them. With a good overview of files, folders, and how to organize them, students can use their computers more effectively. This appendix provides the vocabulary and concepts you need for a basic understanding of file management.

Understanding Your Computer's File Structure

To manage your computer files effectively, you must understand how your computer stores and organizes files. Then you can navigate from one computer location to another to save and find the files you need. If you were planning a cross-country road trip, you wouldn't leave without looking at a map. You would want to visualize the "path" (route) you will take and be able to use signs along the way so you can find your destination. Computers also use paths to lead us to the files stored in various locations. **▄▄▄** You examine the structure of files on your computer so you can better manage your files.

DETAILS

- **What is in my computer's file structure?**

  Your computer stores files on physical objects called **drives** (also called **disks**). Each storage drive is designated with a **drive letter** (A, B, C, etc.) and a **drive name** (local disk, floppy disk, etc.) See Figure FM-1. If your computer is part of a network, you may see **network drives**, called **remote drives**. Network drive folders are often **mapped**, which means they have a shortcut created for each of them, with separate assigned letters such as "J" or "K."

  The main storage location is the **hard drive**, sometimes called the **local disk**, which can store program and data files. **Program files**, such as Microsoft Word or Macromedia Dreamweaver, let you perform specific tasks, such as writing letters or creating Web pages. Each program lets you create **data files**, such as letters, reports, or Web pages, that you save on a drive so you can open and use them again later.

  When you store data files on a computer drive, it's best to organize them using electronic **folders**, similar to paper folders in a file cabinet that let you group related files together. You store paper folders in file cabinet drawers; in your computer's electronic drives, folders and files are organized in a **file hierarchy**, a tree-like structure that connects all the drives, folders, and files on your computer. *To successfully save and open files on your computer, you must understand this structure.* Then you can navigate among the various storage locations to the location you want and not have to worry about "losing" files.

- **How is the file hierarchy organized?**

  Although every computer has its own unique structure, Figure FM-2 shows typical file hierarchies. On a Windows computer, the Desktop is always at the top, and My Computer is always on the Desktop. The Desktop, My Network Places, the Recycle bin, and My Computer are electronic locations that are part of the Windows operating system. The Drive icons (such as A: and C:) appear below My Computer because they are physical drives connected to your computer. The My Documents folder, where the user stores folders and files, is below the appropriate drive icon. On a Macintosh computer, each computer user has a folder on the Hard Drive, in which to store documents. Within this folder, the user stores folders and files. On a Macintosh computer, the drives are usually on the Desktop. On any drive, you can create and modify the folder and file structure. Folders can contain files or more folders. As you create folders inside folders, you add to the file hierarchy.

- **How do you get around in the file hierarchy?**

  Windows Explorer shows this hierarchy as different indented levels, rather than a tree, as shown in Figure FM-3. To move down through the hierarchy, you click folders until you find the file you want. To move up, you open higher-level folders or click the Up icon on the Explorer toolbar. As you work your way up or down the hierarchy, you are following a **path** from the beginning to the end. To describe a path, Windows uses a series of folder names and filenames separated by backslashes (\). Figure FM-4 shows the path to the Word file "Arts in Schools Grant.doc", which is **C:\data\Docs\Arts Council\Arts in Schools Grant.doc**. *Knowing how to follow a path is the key to understanding file management.*

FIGURE FM-1: Windows Explorer displaying the local drives

The title bar and the address box show the drive letter and name of the selected drive

Floppy drive

Hard drive (selected drive)

DVD drive

CD-writeable drive

Mapped network drives

The left pane displays drives and folders, but not files

The right pane displays both folders and files in the drive selected in the left pane

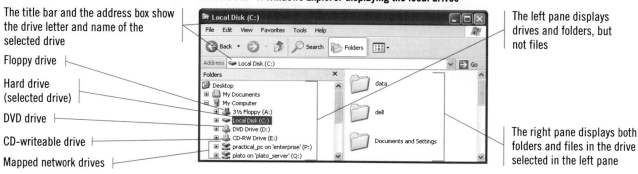

FIGURE FM-2: Typical file hierarchies (Windows and Macintosh)

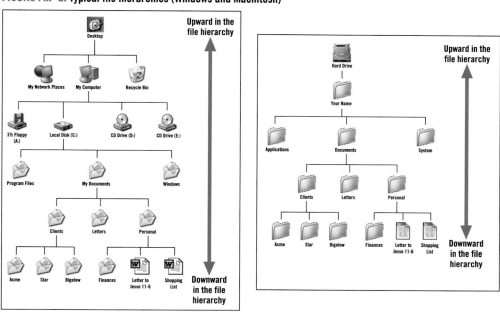

FIGURE FM-3: Folder hierarchy in Windows Explorer

The Address text box tells you which drive or folder is selected

The minus sign shows that a disk or folder is open; you can see the folders on the next level below it

Click the plus sign to open a folder to see lower levels in hierarchy

Selected folder

Alphabetical listing of folders in selected drive or folder

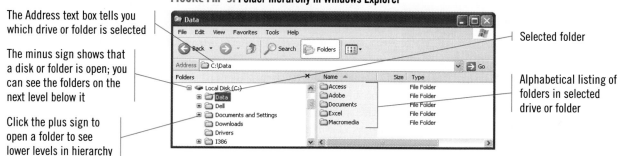

FIGURE FM-4: Path for file "Arts in Schools Grant.doc"

1. Expand the Local Disk drive

2. Expand the data folder

3. Expand the Docs folder

4. Click to select the Arts Council folder to display the files it contains in the right pane

Path to file "Arts in Schools Grant.doc"; each slash denotes a change in folder level

Click the Up arrow to move up the hierarchy

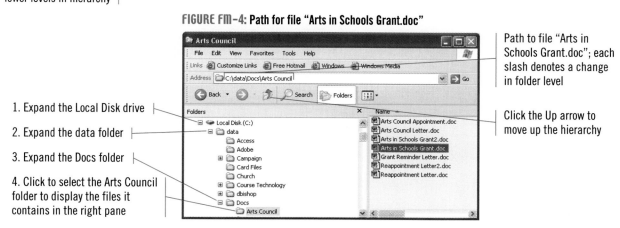

Organizing and Naming Files and Folders

In your household, if you leave your correspondence and bills haphazardly around the house, you spend wasted hours looking for a particular piece of paper when you really need it. It is much easier and more efficient to organize your papers using paper folders in a file cabinet, arranged logically, so you can find them when you need them. Similarly, you should organize your files on your computer by creating folders to store them. ▓▓▓▓ You examine the files and folders on your computer and consider how you can better organize them for easier retrieval.

DETAILS

Before you can organize your computer files, however, you must understand good file management practices.

- **Use subfolders**

  With computer folders, you can create levels of folders inside other folders, often called **subfolders**, to help categorize and group your files. For example, you might store your tax calculation spreadsheet using a structure like Data\Taxes\2005 taxes\Calculations.xls. The 2005 Taxes subfolder is inside the Taxes subfolder.

- **Use a logical folder structure**

  Say you need to find the telephone number for a person in Houston, Texas. You are in a library with telephone books from all over the United States. If the books are randomly stacked on top of each other on shelves, it would take you a long time to find the number. If, however, the phone books were organized on shelves by states, then by cities, you could go quickly to the correct place to find the telephone number. This is the theory of file management. If you compare the shelves holding the telephone books to folders, the "path" to find the phone number would look like the illustration in Figure FM-5.

QUICK TIP

If you plan to use a file on a Web page, it is a good idea not to use spaces, capital letters, or special characters in your file or folder names.

- **Assign intuitive folder names and filenames**

  A file or folder name should immediately communicate what is inside. *The more logically you name your folders, subfolders, and files, the easier they will be to find.* A well-named file or folder should make sense to you, even if you see it years later.

- **Don't store all your files or folders on your desktop or "loose" in the My Documents folder**

  You may be tempted to store files on your desktop because that's what you see when you start your computer, or in the My Documents folder because that is the default location in the Save in text box. Rather than accept the default location, click the Save in list arrow to navigate to a logical folder. You can create new folders inside the My Documents folder by clicking the Create New Folder button in the Save As dialog box. See Figure FM-6.

- **Rearrange your folders and subfolders as necessary**

  You can easily change your file structure as your needs change. To move a file or folder, drag it into the folder where you want to place it. See Figure FM-7. If you want to be more cautious, you can right-click and drag the file or folder instead. When you release the right mouse button, you see a shortcut menu asking you whether you want to move or copy the file. This gives you a chance to verify that what you're doing is what you really mean to do.

FIGURE FM-5: **Thought process used to find a telephone number**

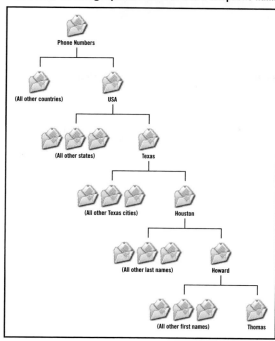

FIGURE FM-6: **Save in default location for files**

"My Documents" subfolder in the Desktop folder usually defaults as the Save in location when you save a file

Create new folder button

Rather than accept this default location, click the list arrow to navigate to the desired folder

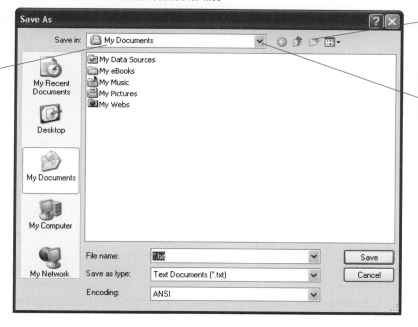

FIGURE FM-7: **Select and drag a folder or file to move it**

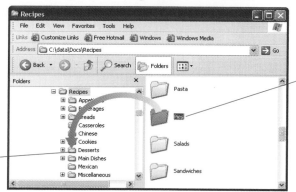

1. Select the folder you want to move, then hold down the left mouse button and drag to the destination folder

2. When the destination folder is selected, drop the folder by releasing the mouse button

Finding and Managing Your Files

Even if you have created folders with logical names, in a logical sequence, and carefully saved the files you created in them, you might occasionally forget where they are. This is a common problem, especially when you have downloaded a file from either the Internet or as an attachment from an e-mail message. Fortunately, it is simple to find missing files. You use Windows Explorer or Macintosh Finder to quickly locate missing files. ▒▒▒▒ You are having trouble locating a particular file and decide to review the options for locating it.

DETAILS

- **Browse through the folder names**

    When you select a folder on the left side of the Explorer or Finder pane, the contents of that folder appear in the right pane. The folders and files in the right pane are sorted in alphabetical order by filename. You have a choice of Views, or ways to look at the files, as shown in Figure FM-8. Each view has advantages, but the Details view is often your best choice when you are searching for a file. Click the View list arrow and select a view option.

    In Details view, the right pane is divided into columns. The first four columns are Name, Size, Type, and Date Modified. You can click each column heading to sort the files by that category. For instance, if you know the approximate date you saved a file, you can click the Date Modified column heading and the files are resorted by the date and time they were last modified. If you click the column heading again, they sort by date and time in the reverse order. This allows you to sort with the most current time on top or the oldest time on top. To sort the files again by Name, click the Name column heading.

- **Use the Search feature**

    If you want to search through files more quickly, you can use the Search button in Windows Explorer. After you click the Search button, you see prompts that ask you questions about how you want to conduct the search. See Figure FM-9. If you choose All Files and Folders, you can then choose the level in the hierarchy that you want to use to begin the search. The higher in the hierarchy you choose (the closer to the Desktop folder), the more extensive the search will be. However, if you know in which folder the file may be, use that folder to begin the search. You then enter keywords that you think may be in the filename. Figure FM-10 shows a search with the keyword "biscuits" used to find files with "biscuits" in the filename. Figure FM-11 shows the results of that search.

- **Keep your drive contents current**

    Because most computers have a vast amount of storage capacity, it is tempting to keep everything on your hard drives, particularly digital pictures, which can be very large files. As you add more and more to your drives, it becomes harder to manage your files. To keep your file management task as simple as possible, move old files and folders to removable disks, such as CDs or USB storage devices.

FIGURE FM-8: View choices for Windows Explorer

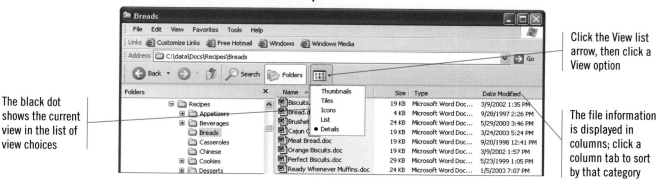

Click the View list arrow, then click a View option

The black dot shows the current view in the list of view choices

The file information is displayed in columns; click a column tab to sort by that category

FIGURE FM-9: Search feature in Windows Explorer

Click the Search button to start the search

Answer the prompts to direct the search

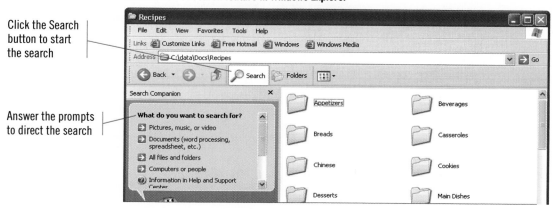

FIGURE FM-10: Keyword search for files

The selected folder is where the computer begins the search; to search the Recipes folder, you select it before you begin the search

Enter a keyword or keywords to use for the search

FIGURE FM-11: Search results for "biscuits"

The search found three files with the word "biscuits" in the Breads folder

In the future you can use this path to find each file in the file hierarchy

Practice

▼ CONCEPTS REVIEW

FIGURE FM-12

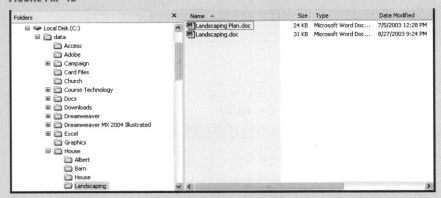

1. Based on the hierarchy shown in Figure FM-12, write the path for the file Landscaping Plan.doc.

_____

Label the elements of the Save as dialog box shown in Figure FM-13.

FIGURE FM-13

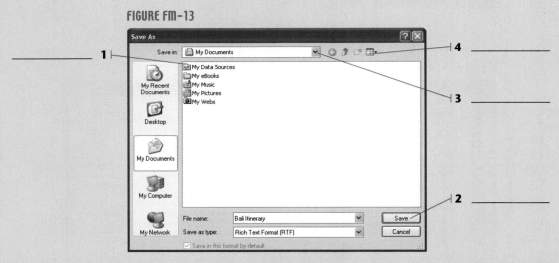

2. You have just created a file in WordPad and are ready to save the file. Which item in Figure FM-13 would you click first to save the file in a folder called "Docs" on your local disk drive?
   a. 1
   b. 2
   c. 3
   d. 4
3. Which of the following is the most logical file structure for organizing recipes?
   a. Cookies\Desserts\Recipes\Bar Cookies
   b. Cookies\Bar Cookies\Recipes\Desserts
   c. Recipes\Desserts\Bar Cookies\Cookies
   d. Recipes\Desserts\Cookies\Bar Cookies
4. If you want to sort files in Windows Explorer to quickly find a file you created yesterday, which column heading would you click?
   a. Type
   b. Size
   c. Name
   d. Date Modified

Data Files List

To complete the lessons and practice exercises in this book, students need to use Data Files that are supplied by Course Technology. Once they obtain the files, students select where to store the Web site files they create using the Data Files, such as to the hard disk drive, network server, or USB storage device.

Below is a list of the Data Files that are supplied and the unit or practice exercise to which the files correspond. For information on how to obtain Data Files, please refer to the last page of this book. The following list includes only Data Files that are supplied; it does not include the Web site files students create from scratch or the files students create by revising supplied files.

Unit	File supplied on Data Disk	Location file is used in unit
Unit A	**Unit A folder** about_us.swf accommodations.swf activities.swf cafe.swf dwa_1.html index.swf shop.swf spa.swf **Unit A Assets folder:** pool.jpg striped_u_background.jpg striped_umbrella_banner.gif	**Lessons** (The Striped Umbrella site)
	Unit A folder: dwa_2.html **Unit A Assets folder:** blooms_banner.jpg blooms_logo.jpg	**Skills Review** (Blooms & Bulbs site)
	Unit A folder: dwa_3.html **Unit A Assets folder:** tripsmart_banner.jpg	**Independent Challenge 1** (TripSmart site)
Unit B	**Unit B folder:** dwb_1.html **Unit B Assets folder:** striped_umbrella_banner.gif	**Lessons** (The Striped Umbrella site)
	Unit B folder: dwb_2.html **Unit B Assets folder:** blooms_banner.jpg	**Skills Review** (Blooms & Bulbs site)
	Unit B folder: dwb_3.html **Unit B Assets folder:** rapids_banner.jpg	**Independent Challenge 1** (Rapids Transit site)

Unit	File supplied on Data Disk	Location file is used in unit
	Unit B folder: dwb_4.html **Unit B Assets folder:** tripsmart_banner.jpg	**Independent Challenge 2** (TripSmart site)
	Unit B folder: dwb_5.html **Unit B Assets folder:** book_bag_banner.jpg	**Visual Workshop** (Emma's Book Bag site)
Unit C	**No Data Files supplied**	
Unit D	**Unit D folder:** dwd_1.html spa.doc **Unit D Assets folder:** striped_umbrella_banner.gif the_spa.jpg	**Lessons** (The Striped Umbrella site)
	Unit D folder: dwd_2.html gardening_tips.doc **Unit D Assets folder:** blooms_banner.jpg garden_tips.jpg	**Skills Review** (Blooms & Bulbs site)
	Unit D folder: dwd_3.html **Unit D Assets folder:** rapids_banner.jpg	**Independent Challenge 1** (Rapids Transit site)
	Unit D folder: dwd_4.html **Unit D Assets folder:** tripsmart_banner.jpg	**Independent Challenge 2** (TripSmart site)
	Unit D folder: dwd_5.html **Unit D Assets folder:** book_bag_banner.jpg	**Visual Workshop** (Emma's Book Bag site)
Unit E	**Unit E folder:** dwe_1.html **Unit E Assets folder:** boardwalk.jpg club_house.jpg pool.jpg sago_palm.jpg sports_club.jpg striped_umbrella_banner.gif stripes_back.gif umbrella_back.gif	**Lessons** (The Striped Umbrella site)
	Unit E folder: dwe_2.html	**Skills Review** (Blooms & Bulbs site)

Unit	File supplied on Data Disk	Location file is used in unit
	Unit E Assets folder: blooms_banner.jpg daisies.jpg lantana.jpg petunias.jpg verbena.jpg	
	Unit E folder: dwe_3.html **Unit E Assets folder:** buster_tricks.jpg rapids_banner.jpg	**Independent Challenge 1** (Rapids Transit site)
	Unit E folder: dwe_4.html **Unit E Assets folder:** lion.jpg tripsmart_banner.jpg zebra_mothers.jpg	**Independent Challenge 2** (TripSmart site)
	Unit E folder: dwe_5.html **Unit E Assets folder:** book_bag_banner.jpg reading.jpg	**Visual Workshop** (Emma's Book Bag site)
Unit F	**Unit F folder:** dwf_1.html **Unit F Assets folder:** about_us_down.gif about_us_up.gif activities_down.gif activities_up.gif cafe_down.gif cafe_up.gif heron_waiting.jpg home_down.gif home_up.gif spa_down.gif spa_up.gif striped_umbrella_banner.gif two_dolphins.jpg	**Lessons** (The Striped Umbrella site)
	Unit F folder: dwf_2.html **Unit F Assets folder:** b_classes_down.jpg b_classes_up.jpg b_home_down.jpg b_home_up.jpg b_newsletter_down.jpg b_newsletter_up.jpg b_plants_down.jpg b_plants_up.jpg b_tips_down.jpg b_tips_up.jpg blooms_banner.jpg	**Skills Review** (Blooms & Bulbs site)

Unit	File supplied on Data Disk	Location file is used in unit
	Unit F folder: dwf_3.html **Unit F Assets folder:** buffalo_fall.gif rapids_banner.jpg	**Independent Challenge 1** (Rapids Transit site)
	Unit F folder: dwf_4.html **Unit F Assets folder:** tripsmart_banner.jpg	**Independent Challenge 2** (TripSmart site)
	Unit F folder: dwf_5.html **Unit F Assets folder:** book_bag_banner.jpg grif_stockley.jpg	**Visual Workshop** (Emma's Book Bag site)
Unit G	**Unit G folder:** cafe.doc crab.swf **Unit G Assets folder:** cafe_photo.jpg cheesecake.jpg su_logo.jpg	**Lessons** (The Striped Umbrella site)
	Unit G folder: garden_quote.swf gardeners.doc registration.doc **Unit G Assets folder:** flower_bed.jpg	**Skills Review** (Blooms & Bulbs site)
	Unit G folder: rentals.doc **Unit G Assets folder:** kayak.jpg	**Independent Challenge 1** (Rapids Transit site)
	Unit G Assets folder: hat.jpg pants.jpg vest.jpg	**Independent Challenge 2** (TripSmart site)
	Unit G folder: book club.doc **Unit G Assets folder:** muffins.jpg	**Visual Workshop** (Emma's Book Bag site)

Unit	File supplied on Data Disk	Location file is used in unit
Unit H	**Unit H folder:** dwh_1.html dwh_2.html **Unit H Assets folder:** boats.jpg heron_small.jpg striped_umbrella_banner.gif	**Lessons** (The Striped Umbrella site)

Glossary

Absolute path A path containing an external link that references a link on a Web page outside the current Web site, and includes the protocol "http" and the URL, or address, of the Web page.

Absolute positioning Positioning a layer so it will hold its position in the browser window when the window size changes.

Action The event that happens after a button on a form is clicked.

Alias (Mac) An icon that represents a program, folder, or file stored on your computer.

Align an image Position an image on a Web page in relation to other elements on the page.

Alphanumeric A type of form field that will accept both numbers and letters or a combination of the two.

Alternate text Descriptive text that can be set to display in place of an image, while the image is downloading or when users place a mouse pointer over an image.

Assets In Dreamweaver, most files that are not Web pages, such as images, audio files, and video clips.

Assets folder A subfolder in which you store most of the files that are not Web pages, such as images, audio files, and video clips.

Assets panel A panel that contains nine categories of assets, such as images, used in a Web site. Clicking a category button will display a list of those assets.

Background color A color that fills the entire Web page, a table, or a cell.

Background image An image used in place of a background color.

Banners Images that appear across the top of the screen that can incorporate the company's logo, contact information, and navigation bars.

Baseline The bottom of a line of text, not including letter descenders such as in "y" or "g."

Body The parts of a Web page, such as text, images, and links, that are visible when the page is viewed in a browser window.

Borders Outlines that surround images, cells, or tables.

Broken links Links that cannot find the intended destination file.

Browser *See* Web browser.

Bullet A small image used to call attention to items in an unordered list.

Bulleted list A list of items that do not need to be placed in a specific order; also called an unordered list.

Buttons On a form, small rectangular objects with a text label that usually have an action attached to them.

Cascading Style Sheets A file used to assign sets of common formatting characteristics to page elements such as text, objects, and tables.

Cell padding In a table, the distance between the cell content and the cell walls.

Cell spacing In a table, the distance between cells.

Cell walls In a table, the edges surrounding a cell.

Cells Small boxes within a table that are used to hold text or images. Cells are arranged horizontally in rows and vertically in columns.

Check boxes A classification of a form object that appear as boxes that, when clicked by the user, have a check mark placed in the box to indicate that it is selected.

Client-side scripting A script that processes on the user's computer.

Clip art collections Groups of image files collected on CDs and sold with an index, or directory, of the files.

Code and Design Views The view that is a combination of Code View and Design View.

Code View The view that shows a full screen with the HTML code for the page. Use this view to read or directly edit the code.

Coder layout A layout in the Dreamweaver workspace in which the panels are docked on the left side of the screen and Code view is the default view.

Coding Toolbar A toolbar used when you are working with the code and can only be accessed in Code View.

Columns Table cells arranged vertically.

Comments Helpful text describing portions of the HTML code, such as a JavaScript function.

Contents The Dreamweaver Help feature that lists Dreamweaver topics by category.

Cropping Removing part of an image, both visually (on the page) and physically (the file size).

Data file File created using a software program; for example: a letter, report, or Web page, that you save on a drive so you can open and use it again later.

Debug To correct errors in HTML code.

Declaration Part of a Cascading Style Sheet; contains a property and a value.

Default alignment For images, the automatic alignment with the text baseline.

Default base font Size 3 text without any formatting applied to it.

Default font colors The colors the browser uses to display text, links, and visited links if no other colors are assigned.

Default link color The color the browser uses to display links if no other color is assigned. The default link color is blue.

Define a Web site Specify the site's local root folder location to help Dreamweaver keep track of the links among Web pages and supporting files and set other Web site preferences.

Definition lists Lists composed of terms with indented descriptions or definitions.

Delimiter A comma, tab, colon, semicolon, or similar character that separates tabular data in a text file.

Deprecated Features that are being phased out and will soon be invalid or obsolete, such as Directory or menu lists, which are deprecated in HTML 4.

Description A short summary of Web site content that resides in the Head section.

Design View The view that shows a full-screen layout and is primarily used when designing and creating a Web page.

Designer layout A layout in the Dreamweaver workspace, in which panels are docked on the right side of the screen and Design view is the default view.

Document toolbar A toolbar that contains buttons for changing the current Web page view, previewing and debugging Web pages, and managing files.

Document window The large area to the left of the Dreamweaver panels; displays open documents, each one represented by a tab.

Document-relative path A path referenced in relation to the Web page that is currently displayed.

Domain name An IP address expressed in letters instead of numbers, usually reflecting the name of the business represented by the Web site, such as tripsmart.com.

Down Image state The state of a page element when the element has been clicked with the mouse pointer.

Download To transfer files from a remote computer to your computer.

Download time The time it takes to transfer a file to another computer.

Drive A computer storage device designated by a drive letter (such as C:) and a drive name (such as Local Disk).

Drive letter *See* Drive.

Drive name *See* Drive.

DSL Digital Subscriber Line; a type of Internet connection.

Dynamic images Web page images that change frequently. *See also* recordset.

Edit To insert, delete, or change page content, such as inserting a new image, adding a link, or correcting spelling errors.

Editable regions In a template, an area the template author creates that allows other design team members to inset text or images.

Element In the Insert Navigation Bar dialog box, an image link.

Embedded style A style whose code is part of a Web page, rather than in a separate external file.

Enable Cache A setting to direct the computer system to use space on the hard drive as temporary memory, or cache, while you are working in Dreamweaver.

Expanded tables mode An environment for creating tables that features expanded borders and expanded white space between cells.

Export data To save data that was created in Dreamweaver in a special file format to bring into another software program.

External links Links that connect to Web pages in other Web sites.

External style sheet A file that contains formatting code and can be attached to multiple Web pages to quickly apply formatting to their content.

Favorites Assets that you expect to use repeatedly while you work on a site and are categorized separately in the Assets panel; also, the Dreamweaver Help feature that allows you to add topics to the Favorites window that you might want to view later without having to search again.

Field A form area into which users can insert a specific piece of data, such as their last name or address.

File fields In forms, fields that let users browse to and send files.

File hierarchy A tree-like structure that connects all the drives, folders, and files on your computer.

File management Organizing, saving, and finding files and folders on a computer.

File server *See* Server.

File Transfer Protocol *See* FTP.

Files panel A Dreamweaver panel similar to Windows Explorer or Finder, which contains a listing of all the folders and files in your Web site.

Flash Button Objects Image and text objects created in the Macromedia Flash program that you can insert onto a Web page without having the Macromedia Flash program installed. *See also* Macromedia Flash.

Flash Player *See* Macromedia Flash Player.

Folders A named location on a disk that helps you group related files together, similar to the way you might group papers in file folders in a file cabinet.

Font combinations Groups of similar fonts such as Arial, Helvetica, sans-serif.

Forms A collection of input fields that allow one to obtain information from Web site users.

Form action Part of a form tag that specifies how the form will be processed.

Form fields A classification of form objects that includes text fields, hidden fields, and file fields.

Form objects The individual components of a form that accept individual pieces of information.

Format To adjust the appearance of page elements, such as resizing an image or changing the color of text.

FTP Stands for File Transfer Protocol, the process of uploading and downloading files to and from a remote site.

GIF file A Graphics Interchange Format file; a type of file format used for images placed on Web pages.

Hard drive The main storage disk on a computer.

Head content Items such as the page title, keywords, and description that are contained in the Head section. *See also* Head section.

Head section A part of a Web page that is not visible in the browser window. It includes meta tags, which are HTML codes that include information about the page, such as keywords and descriptions.

Headings Six different text styles that can be applied to paragraphs: Heading 1 (the largest size) through Heading 6 (the smallest size).

Hexadecimal value A value that represents the amount of red, green, and blue in a color.

Hidden fields On a form, invisible fields that store user information.

History panel A Dreamweaver panel that lists the steps that have been performed while editing and formatting a document.

Home page The first Web page that appears when users go to a Web site.

Horizontal and vertical space Blank space above, below, and on the sides of an image that separates the image from the text or other elements on the page.

Hotspot A clickable area on an image that, when clicked, links to a different location on the page or to another Web page.

HTML The acronym for Hypertext Markup Language, the language Web developers use to create Web pages.

HTML forms A Web page or a portion of a Web page that includes one or more form objects that allow a user to enter information and send it to a host Web server.

http Hypertext transfer protocol; the hypertext protocol that precedes absolute paths to external links.

Hyperlinks *See* Links.

Hypertext Markup Language *See* HTML.

Image map An image that has clickable areas defined on it that, when clicked, serve as a link that will take the viewer to another location.

Import data To bring data created in another software program into Dreamweaver.

Index The Dreamweaver Help feature that displays topics in alphabetical order; also, a directory of files on a CD containing image files.

Insert bar A toolbar containing icons that allow you to insert objects, such as images, tables, and horizontal rules.

Inspectors Panels that display the properties of the currently selected object; allow you to make formatting changes quickly and easily, without having to open menus.

Interlaced graphic A characteristic of JPEG files that allows an image to appear on a Web page before the browser has fully downloaded it, giving the viewer something to look at while they are waiting for the image to finish downloading.

Internal links Links to Web pages within the same Web site.

Internet Protocol *See* IP address.

Internet Service Provider *See* ISP.

Intranet An internal Web site without public access; companies often have intranets that only their employees can access.

IP address Also called an Internet Protocol address, an assigned series of numbers, separated by periods, that designates an address on the Internet.

ISP Stands for Internet Service Provider, a company that supplies accounts that allow Internet access.

JavaScript Code that adds dynamic content, such as rollovers or interactive forms, to a Web page.

JPEG file A file format that stands for Joint Photographic Experts Group file; used for images that appear on Web pages. Many photographs are saved in the JPEG file format.

Keywords Words that relate to the content of the Web site and reside in the Head section. Keywords are used by many search engines to match viewer queries with Web pages.

Layer An HTML page element you can "draw" on a page; can contain any other type of page elements, such as text or images and can be positioned on top of other page elements.

Layout Mode A Dreamweaver mode that is used when you draw your own table.

Line break Code that places text on a separate line without creating a new paragraph. You create a line break by pressing [Shift] [Enter] (Win) or [Shift] [return] (Mac).

Links Images or text elements on a Web page that users click to display another location on the page, another Web page on the same Web site, or a Web page on a different Web site. Links are also known as hyperlinks.

List/Menus A classification of a form object that provides the user with a list or menu of choices to select. Lists display the choices in a scrolling menu. Menus display the choices in a shortcut menu.

Local disk *See* Drive.

Local root folder A folder on your hard drive, Zip disk, or USB device that will hold all the files and folders for a Web site.

Local site The folder location that contains all the files for a Web site.

Locked regions Areas in a page that are controlled by the template author. Other design team members cannot change them.

Macromedia Contribute
A Web site development tool that enables both Web developers and non-professionals to contribute Web site content.

Macromedia Flash A Macromedia software program used to create animations for Web pages. See also Flash button objects.

Macromedia Flash Player Software added to a Web browser to display animation, video, or sound.

Mapped drive An icon representing a network drive, identified by a letter such as "J" or "K" and a name.

mailto: link An e-mail address on a Web page that is formatted as a link that will open the default mail program with a blank, addressed message.

Menu bar A bar across the top of the Dreamweaver window that is located under the title bar and lists the names of the menus that contain Dreamweaver commands.

Menus Lists of commands that you can display by clicking a menu name on the menu bar, just under the title bar.

Merge cells To combine multiple cells into one cell.

Meta tags HTML codes that include information about the page, such as keywords and descriptions, and reside in the head section.

Multi-line text fields In forms, data entry areas that are useful for entering text that may take several sentences to complete. Also called Textarea fields.

Multiple Document Interface (MDI) All the document windows and panels are positioned within one large application window.

Named anchor
A specific location on a Web page that is used to link to that portion of the Web page.

Navigation bar A set of text or image links that viewers can use to navigate among the pages of a Web site.

Nested table A table that is placed inside the cell of another table.

Nested templates Templates that are based on other templates.

Network drive A remote drive connected to another computer, not directly connected to your computer, as is a local drive.

Nonbreaking space A space that will be left on the page by a browser; holds the cell until content is placed in it.

Non-Web-safe colors Colors that may not appear uniformly across platforms.

Objects
Web page content such as tables, images, forms, and layers.

Optional regions In a template, areas that a development team member can choose to show or hide.

Ordered lists Lists of items that need to be placed in a specific order and are preceded by numbers or letters.

Orphaned files Files that are not linked to any pages in the Web site.

Over Image state The state of a page element when the mouse pointer is over the element.

Over While Down Image state The state of a page element when the mouse pointer is being held over the element.

Panel group title bar
The bar at the top of each panel group; contains the expander arrow that opens the panel group, and the Panel options list arrow, which you click to select commands that affect that panel group.

Panel groups Collections of panels such as Design, Code, Application, and Files, that are displayed through the Window menu. Sets of related panels are grouped together.

Panels Individual windows that display information on a particular program area, such as Answers or History.

Password fields In forms, fields that display asterisks or bullets when a user types in a password.

Path A series of folder and filenames separated by backslashes (\) that describes the exact location of a file on a computer, starting with the highest level in the file hierarchy; Microsoft Windows uses paths to store and locate files on a computer.

Path The location of an open file in relation to any folders in the Web site.

PNG file A file format that stands for Portable Network Graphics file; used for Web page images and is capable of showing millions of colors, but is small in file size.

Point Refer to, such as an image that points to its source file by displaying its path on the Property inspector.

Point of contact A place on a Web page that provides viewers a means of contacting a company, usually an e-mail link. *See also* mailto: link.

Program file Software such as Microsoft Word or Macromedia Dreamweaver that allows you to perform specific tasks, such as writing letters or creating Web pages.

Property inspector A Dreamweaver panel that displays the characteristics of the currently selected object on the page.

Public Domain Images or text that is free to use without restrictions.

Publish a Web site To make a Web site available for viewing on the Internet or on an intranet.

Quick Tag Editor A Dreamweaver panel that is used to insert or edit HTML code.

Radio buttons A classification of a form object that appear as hollow circles on a form that, when clicked by the user, are then filled in to indicate that they are selected.

Recordset A database stored on a server which can contain image files for a dynamic image. *See also* Dynamic images.

Reference panel A panel that is used to find answers to coding questions, covering topics such as HTML, JavaScript, and Accessibility.

Refresh Local File List Automatically option A setting that directs Dreamweaver to automatically reflect changes made in your file listings.

Relative path A path used with an internal link to reference a Web page or image file within the Web site.

Remote drive *See* Network drive.

Remote site The folder location on a Web server that contains all the files for a Web site.

Reset a form To erase the entries that have been previously entered in a form and set the values back to the default settings.

Rollovers Screen elements that change in appearance as the user places the mouse over them.

Root-relative path A path referenced from a Web site's root folder.

Roundtrip HTML The Dreamweaver feature that allows HTML files created in other programs, such as Microsoft FrontPage, to be opened in Dreamweaver without adding additional coding, such as meta tags or spaces.

Rows Table cells arranged horizontally.

Royalty-free graphics Images that you can purchase and use in your published Web pages without having to pay a royalty fee to the company that created them.

Sans-serif fonts Block style characters used frequently for headings, sub-headings, and Web pages. In this Glossary, all the blue terms are in a sans-serif font; they do not contain small strokes at the tops and bottoms of letters.

Screen reader A device used by the visually impaired to convert written text on a computer monitor to spoken words.

Seamless image A tiled image that is blurred at the edges so that it appears to be all one image.

Search The Dreamweaver Help feature that allows you to enter a keyword to begin a search for a topic.

Selector In Cascading Style Sheets, the name or the tag to which the style declarations have been assigned.

Serif fonts Fonts with small extra strokes at the top and bottom of the characters; used frequently for paragraph text in printed materials. All the definitions in the Glossary are set in a serif font. The blue terms are in a sans-serif font.

Server A computer that is connected to other computers to provide file storage and processing services.

Server-side scripting A script that processes a form on the form's host Web server.

Shortcuts (Win) Icons that represent a software program, folder, or file stored elsewhere on your computer system.

Single-line text fields In forms, data entry areas that are useful for small pieces of data such as a name or telephone number.

Site map A graphical representation of how Web pages relate to each other within a Web site.

Snippets panel A panel that lets you create, insert, and store pieces of code, called snippets, for reuse.

Split cells To divide cells into multiple rows or columns.

Standard toolbar A toolbar that contains buttons for some frequently used commands on the File and Edit menus.

Standard Mode A Dreamweaver mode that is used when you insert a table using the Insert Table icon.

State On a graphical navigation bar, the appearance of an image, such as Up, Down, Over, and Over While Down.

Status bar A bar that appears at the bottom of the Dreamweaver window; the left end displays the tag selector, which shows the HTML tags being used at the insertion point location, and the right end displays the window size and estimated download time for the page displayed.

Storyboard A small sketch that represents each page in a Web site; like a flowchart, shows the relationship of each page to the other pages in the site.

Style A named group of formatting characteristics; also called a rule.

Style Rendering Toolbar A toolbar that contains buttons that can be used to render different media types.

Subfolder A folder inside another folders on a computer; you can have many subfolder levels on your computer.

Submit a form To send the information on a form to a host Web server for processing.

Synchronize To transfer the latest version of Web files to a server.

Tables Grids of rows and columns that can either be used to hold tabular data on a Web page or as a basic design tool for page layout.

Tabular data Data arranged in columns and rows and separated by a delimiter.

Tag Chooser A Dreamweaver feature that lets you insert tags from the Dreamweaver tag libraries such as ColdFusion or ASP.NET tags.

Tag selector A location on the status bar that displays HTML tags for the various page elements, including tables and cells.

Target The location on a Web page that the browser will display in full view when the user clicks an internal link.

Templates Web pages that contain the basic layout for similar pages in a Web site.

Text fields On a form, a box in which a user can enter text.

Tiled image A small graphic that repeats across and down a Web page, appearing as individual squares or rectangles.

Title bar A bar across the top of the Dreamweaver window that displays the name of the program, the name of the file, and the title of the open page enclosed in parentheses; also includes buttons for minimizing, resizing, and closing the window in the upper-left or upper-right corner, depending on which type of computer you are using.

Transparent background A background composed of transparent pixels, rather than pixels of a color, resulting in images that blend easily on a Web page background.

Unordered lists Lists of items that do not need to be placed in a specific order and are usually preceded by bullets.

Up Image state The state of a page element when the user's mouse pointer is not on the element.

Upload To send a form or files to a host Web server.

URL The acronym for Uniform Resource Locator. A URL is the "address" for a Web page that can be typed in the address box in a browser to open a Web page.

Vector-based graphics Graphics based on mathematical formulas rather than pixels.

Visited links Links that the user has previously clicked, or visited; the default color for visited links is purple.

Web browser Software used to display pages in a Web site. The two most common Web browsers are Internet Explorer and Netscape Navigator. Also called a "browser."

Web design program A program for creating interactive Web pages containing text, images, hyperlinks, animation, sounds, and video.

Web pages Collections of text and images in HTML format.

Web server A computer that is connected to the Internet with a static IP (Internet Protocol) address.

Web site A set of related Web pages stored on a server that users can display using a Web browser.

Web-safe colors Colors that will display consistently in all browsers, and on Macintosh, Windows, and Unix computers.

White space An area on a Web page that is not filled with text or graphics.

Workspace The Dreamweaver interface made up of the document window, the menu bar, toolbars, inspectors, and panels.

WYSIWYG An acronym for What You See Is What You Get, which means that as you design a Web page in Dreamweaver, you are seeing the page exactly as it will appear in a browser window.

XTHML The acronym for eXtensible HyperText Markup Language, the most recent standard for developing Web pages.

Index